Europe's Century of Crises Under Dollar Hegemony

Brendan Brown • Philippe Simonnot

Europe's Century of Crises Under Dollar Hegemony

A Dialogue on the Global Tyranny of Unsound Money

palgrave
macmillan

Brendan Brown
Hudson Institute
Washington, DC, USA

Philippe Simonnot
Paris, France

ISBN 978-3-030-46652-7   ISBN 978-3-030-46653-4 (eBook)
https://doi.org/10.1007/978-3-030-46653-4

© The Editor(s) (if applicable) and The Author(s), under exclusive licence to Springer Nature Switzerland AG 2020
This work is subject to copyright. All rights are solely and exclusively licensed by the Publisher, whether the whole or part of the material is concerned, specifically the rights of translation, reprinting, reuse of illustrations, recitation, broadcasting, reproduction on microfilms or in any other physical way, and transmission or information storage and retrieval, electronic adaptation, computer software, or by similar or dissimilar methodology now known or hereafter developed.
The use of general descriptive names, registered names, trademarks, service marks, etc. in this publication does not imply, even in the absence of a specific statement, that such names are exempt from the relevant protective laws and regulations and therefore free for general use.
The publisher, the authors and the editors are safe to assume that the advice and information in this book are believed to be true and accurate at the date of publication. Neither the publisher nor the authors or the editors give a warranty, expressed or implied, with respect to the material contained herein or for any errors or omissions that may have been made. The publisher remains neutral with regard to jurisdictional claims in published maps and institutional affiliations.

Cover illustration: © Andrii Vodolazhskyi, shutterstock.com

This Palgrave Macmillan imprint is published by the registered company Springer Nature Switzerland AG.
The registered company address is: Gewerbestrasse 11, 6330 Cham, Switzerland

In memory of Irene Brown
Brendan Brown
To Marie Solies
Philippe Simonnot

Invitation to Our French-Speaking Readers

How to Access the Original French Content of This Book

If you would like to read the questions and conclusion by Philippe Simonnot in his original French, these can be found in the Appendices at the end of the book. These are also available to download on SpringerLink.

Brendan Brown
Philippe Simonnot

Acknowledgments

The inspirator and creator of this dialogue is Philippe Simonnot.

Little did I know when he wrote to me two years ago saying that he would like to work on introducing my ideas to the French-speaking public that we would progress to a multi-year dialogue which then was to take the form of the present book. Throughout this process, his questions to me have been a continuous source of thinking and rethinking about sound money and how to get there from the present highly unsound monetary regime. We have a mutual passion for understanding financial history and its political or geo-political links. Philippe has been the catalyst to my re-focusing on the dilemmas of the present European monetary situation, more than a decade on from the collapse of any hard money possibility for the euro in its present form. The proposals in our dialogue for a new euro are truly a joint creation.

Along the way I have gained tremendously from my continuous dialogue with Robert Pringle and acknowledge his work in reading and editing the introductory essay. Key ideas on how to anchor sound money only developed here in consequence of our work together over many years.

PJ Johnson, who has immersed himself for so long with such enthusiasm in promoting and navigating my work around its core ideas whilst treading so gently on the idealism behind it, has read and made painstaking recommendations.

Alex Pollock has provided invaluable insights which I use (hopefully with due attribution) in my thinking and writing about this subject and I acknowledge his great contribution to drawing up our project at the start.

Joseph Salerno at Mises Institute has been hugely important to my work in providing encouragement and feedback at crucial points. I acknowledge the continuous support there of Ryan McMaken who edits my regular contributions to Mises Wire.

I graciously acknowledge the cooperation of Hudson Institute and their making introductions around the Hill so that I could pursue and develop some of the key themes in this dialogue.

Tula Weis, my editor, has given me huge encouragement from the day I first communicated with her about my dialogue with Philippe, whilst keeping us within the path of journeying as far as possible into the reading public.

Brendan Brown

Contents

Part I	**Introduction**	1
1	**The Tyranny of Unsound Money**	3
	How to Judge Monetary Soundness	4
	Sound and Unsound Exits from the False Dawn of Monetarism	5
	US Hegemon Leads World Down Unsound Path	7
	Prices Are Not Stable Under Sound Money	8
	Crucial Evidence from the 1920s	10
	The Fallacies of Interest Rate Policy	11
	Asset Inflation: Ignored by Monetarists and Keynesians	13
	Two Percent Inflation Standard, Monetary Repression Tax and Monopoly	14
	Malinvestment and Over-Rapid Digitalization	16
	Could Europe Turn Against the Unsound Dollar Hegemon?	17
	References	19
Part II	**Dialogue**	21
2	**Phobia of Deflation**	23
	Question 1	23
	Question 2	24
	References	25

3	**The Great War and the End of the Gold Standard**	27
	Question 3	27
	Observation	30
	References	30
4	**From Birth of Dollar Hegemony Towards the 1929 Crisis**	33
	Question 4	33
	Question 4, Part 2	34
	Question 4, Part 3	35
	Question 4, Part 4	36
	Question 4, Part 5	41
	Question 4, Part 6	45
	References	48
5	**Explaining 1929**	51
	Question 5	51
	Question 5, Part 1	54
	Question 5, Part 2	55
	References	57
6	**How Gold Financed Nazi Germany**	59
	Question 6	59
	Comment	60
	References	60
7	**Bretton Woods: The False Gold Standard**	61
	Question 7	61
	Question 8	63
	Reference	64
8	**The Strategic Choice for Germany**	65
	Question 9	65
	Reference	67
9	**For or Against Friedman**	69
	Question 10	69
	Question 11	70
	Question 11, Part 2	71
	Question 11, Part 3	71
	Question 11, Part 4	73
	Question 11, Part 5	74
	References	75

10	**How the Euro Was Born**	77
	Question 12	77
	Question 13a	78
	Question 13b	79
	Question 13c	80
	References	81
11	**Trichet in Front of Trichet**	83
	Question 14	83
	Question 14, Part 2	85
	References	86
12	**The Great Crisis of 2008**	87
	Question 15	87
	Question 16	88
	Question 17	90
	Question 18	92
	Question 19	92
	Reference	94
13	**American Capitalism Versus European Capitalism**	95
	Question 20	95
	Question 20, Part 2	97
	Question 20, Part 3	97
	Question 20, Part 4	98
	Reference	102
14	**The Submission of the Euro to the 2% Inflation Standard**	103
	Question 21	103
	Question 22	105
	Question 23	106
15	**Draghi: "Whatever It Takes"**	109
	Question 24	109
	Question 24, Part 2	110
	Question 25	113
	Question 25, Part 2	114
	References	116

16	**The Greek Crisis**	117
	Question 26	117
	Question 26, Part 2	119
	Question 26, Part 3	120
17	**Banking Union**	123
	Question 27	123
	Question 28	125
	Question 29	125
	Question 29, Part 2	126
	Question 29, Part 3	127
	Question 29, Part 4	127
	Question 30	128
18	**The Underperformance of Europe**	131
	Question 31	131
	Question 32	132
19	**The Balance Sheet of Draghi**	135
	Question 33	135
	Question 34	137
	Question 35	140
	Question 36	141
20	**The Principles of the New Euro**	145
	Question 37	145
	Question 37, Part 2	147
	Question 37, Part 3	150
	Question 38	151
	Question 39	152
	Question 40	155
	Question 40, Part 2	158
	Question 40, Part 3	159
	Question 40, Part 3	160
	Question 40, Part 4	161
	Question 41	162
	Question 41, Part 2	164
	Reference	165

21	The Launch of the New Euro	167
	Question 42	167
	Question 42, Part 2	169
	Question 43	170
	Question 44	173
	Annex: A Little Note on Gold	174

Part III	Conclusion	177
22	At the Heart of the World	179
	References	184
23	Epilogue: From Pandemic to High Inflation	185
	Question 1	185
	Question 2	189
	Question 3	191
	Question 4	196
	Question 5	199

Appendixes	203
Index	231

Part I

Introduction

1

The Tyranny of Unsound Money

In a sentence which Milton Friedman made famous, J.S. Mill wrote: "most of the time the machinery of money does not matter but when it gets out of control it becomes the monkey wrench in all the machinery of the economy" (Friedman 2006). In the century of US dollar hegemony, since the breakdown of the international gold standard during the First World War, money has mattered most of the time because it has been almost continuously out of control. Money has been profoundly unsound.

Unsound money has spawned and enabled tyranny in multiple ways. Sometimes the link runs from the generating of bubbles and busts to devastating geopolitical consequences. The extreme example here was the role of a massive bubble in stocks and global credit fuelled by the Federal Reserve and its subsequent burst in the Weimar Republic's collapse. Other times political malaise forms due to unsound money's destruction of opportunities for general sustained advances in economic prosperity over long periods.

Always, under unsound money regimes, the state gains tremendous power to obtain revenue without explicitly levying new taxes or hiking old taxes. Monopolists and would-be monopolists use bubble finance as generated by monetary inflation—including fantastically priced equity issues to investors mesmerized by speculative narratives of vast eventual profit margins—to crush free market competition. Historical examples extend from the Dutch East India Company in seventeenth-century Holland to the notorious list of suspects under anti-trust investigation in the US at the start of the 2020s. Monopoly power is inimical to free society.

Individuals constrained by laws and practice to use fiat monies whose issuers pursue monetary inflation are exposed to the huge risks of sudden evaporation of their financial well-being, whether from asset inflation turning to asset crash, or from the outbreak of goods and services inflation. Widespread economic and financial suffering imperils always fragile liberty. The propaganda machine of the tyranny (including the central banks and their "transparent communications") grinds on relentlessly. In sum, the severe ways in which "the machinery of money" has acted as monkey wrench go well beyond anything that J.S. Mill imagined or Milton Friedman described.

How to Judge Monetary Soundness

The essence of sound money is its high quality services (store of value and medium of exchange) produced by "machinery" (as in J.S. Mill quote) under the continuous control of automatic mechanisms. These are well protected from governments or other authorities (including central banks) who would tamper with them in pursuit of wider objectives including general economic policy and taxation. Beyond that general statement, what are the criteria by which we should judge the soundness of an actual monetary regime?

There should be a clear and well-understood pivot or anchor to the monetary system. This takes the form of monetary base for which a broad and stable demand exists over the long run, and whose supply is strictly limited. Automatic mechanisms determine and enforce those limits. The mechanisms operate within the context of constitutional rules sometimes including a pledge of convertibility into gold, other metals, or real assets.

Short- as well as long-term interest rates are set wholly by market forces, without official fixing or manipulation. Prices of goods and services are observed to fluctuate widely, sometimes over sustained periods, downwards and upwards, but show a tendency to revert to the mean over the very long run, as determined by the pivot or anchor. There can be no assurance that this mean is constant. There should be widespread conviction, though, that any drift upwards or downwards in this mean will be well-bounded and at any point in time the prospects of an upward drift over the long run should be equal to those of a downward drift.

As illustration under the pre-1914 gold standard it was possible that big new gold discoveries could bring an upward drift in the long-run mean to prices; but it was equally possible that a secular growth in demand for money and trends in the gold mining industry (lack of new discoveries or new technologies) could bring a downward drift.

By contrast, the essential aspects of unsound money include manipulation of interest rates by the government or its central bank (there exists a wide spectrum of possible manipulation practices), the absence of an anchor to the monetary system, and a fixation of the monetary policy makers on stabilizing prices (the so-called price level or the inflation rate) whilst moderating the fluctuations of the business cycle (in the process, lengthening economic expansions).

The ways in which the monkey wrench jams up the economic machinery go far beyond the traditional (and sometimes misplaced) concerns of consumer price inflation (or deflation) or violent business cycle fluctuations. The starting point (for the monkey wrench) is the haywire signalling of prices, particularly in asset markets. This leads on to a general malfunctioning of the invisible hands, together with misallocation of resources—especially capital.

The false signalling guides capital into a whole range of projects far more intensely than what would have occurred otherwise (with correct signalling). The resulting opportunity losses in prosperity from such malinvestment are potentially huge and long-lasting, even though there might be for a considerable periods of time some apparent benefits to consumers. Extraordinarily low-cost capital to some firms, reflecting wild speculative narratives about future monopoly profits, allows these to gain market share by predatory action, including extended periods of cheap pricing and also systematic elimination of any new entrant challenger by pre-emptive buyouts.

Sound and Unsound Exits from the False Dawn of Monetarism

Sound money requires skilful architecture and construction. By contrast, the monetarism as pioneered by Milton Friedman rested on a firm belief in positive economics (see Friedman 1966). There it is for the economic scientist to find out whether a stable demand function could be reliably estimated for a money supply aggregate, having once selected this in the given monetary and banking system. If successful, then the task of the monetary authorities would be to keep the growth of that aggregate in line with demand (the product of real demand and the targeted price level) over the medium and the long run.

That task could be fulfilled via the control of monetary base, so long as a stable relationship could be demonstrated between this and the chosen wider monetary aggregate (another test for the scientist). With no big gap between the growth in supply and demand for that aggregate, money should not get out of control and the feared monkey wrench would remain locked up. The monetarists in general did not contemplate what damage the monkey wrench might do (if not locked up) in terms of malinvestment and asset price inflation. Their focus was on goods and services inflation and its potential ill effects.

In practice, monetarism has long since withered away. The US experiment in applying this doctrine was particularly short (1979–82). Under actual institutional arrangements, the authorities had considerable difficulty in determining exogenously the supply of a broad or semi-broad money aggregate with any precision at all (the Bundesbank came closest by utilising high reserve requirements on banks). In any case, earlier empirically determined stable demand functions for the chosen monetary aggregate often proved to be erroneous.

Yes, the supply of monetary base (the narrowest aggregate) is completely under the control of the authorities in a fiat money regime. But the demand for monetary base, under post-1914 monetary regimes in the US and abroad, even before considering the radical changes (in particular, QE and payment of market interest on reserves) of the past two decades, has been far from broad or stable or easily estimated, even over long-run periods. The problem here has been that the components of the monetary base under modern fiat money regimes—deposits of the banks at the central bank and cash—have many close substitutes (for example Treasury bills, instant non-penal credit facilities at the central bank, payment and credit cards which the holder can use to transact at the same retail prices as users of cash). They are not in effect high-powered money except in name. Small changes in interest rates, rate spreads and fees can induce big shifts in demand for monetary base. By contrast, under a regime where the monetary base includes mainly instruments with a distinctive high "moneyness", as would be the case for gold coin, gold bars and banks' holdings of reserves as aggregated across countries on a gold standard, demand for monetary base is firmly related to income and wealth.

In principle, there are two exits from the disillusions of monetarism.

The first is to move forward along the road to sound money, learning where appropriate from past errors including those of the monetarists.

Progress would consist of eliminating the government (and central bank) manipulators of interest rates and constructing a monetary system based around a strong anchor. Price level and inflation targets would be scrapped in favour of automatic monetary mechanisms (operating in effect to set upper and lower bounds to monetary base expansion), which should mean a very long-run tendency for prices of goods and services on average to revert to the mean (moving down or up for sustained periods in the medium term). This mean is not absolutely fixed nor totally pre-determined.

The biggest challenge for the sound monetary system architects would be the designing of a monetary base. It is important that there should be a broad and stable demand for this aggregate. That requires structural reforms in the sense of curtailing radically "too big to fail" (whereby systemically important banks in effect have access to government bail outs), deposit insurance, credit and payment card oligopolies (which try to prevent retailers passing on interchange and other fees to card users), and other barriers to cash circulation (e.g. small upper limits to size of banknote denomination). All these reforms together would powerfully bolster and broaden the demand for monetary base.

The second exit from the failure of monetarism is to abandon the quest for sound money and instead install top macro-economic managers in the monetary administration (via the central bank) whose stated aims would be high employment and stable prices.

The tools at the disposal of these managers would be designed to manipulate interest rates along a path mapped out by powerful econometric models. They do not use the monetary base as a control mechanism, though in principle they determine its size. They would not return to the practice of the Federal Reserve at times between 1920 and the mid-1980s in cross-checking that their chosen path for short-term money market rates results in the monetary base cumulatively staying within a target or quasi-target range. (The cross-check in the 1920s and 1960s occurred in the context of whole and then partial convertibility of the dollar into gold; growth in the fiat component of monetary base as consistent with the Fed's chosen rate path could bring into question whether gold reserves were sufficient and trigger a tightening of policy.)

The managers would also have "emergency access" to a bag of unconventional tools to be deployed towards reaching their aims. The monetary administration, headed by political appointees, is a part of government, albeit with some weak outward semblance of independence. A key unstated part of the monetary administration's purpose is the levying of monetary repression tax and inflation tax; their success in this is very important in terms of their relationship with government.

US Hegemon Leads World Down Unsound Path

The US as monetary hegemon led the world along a deeply flawed path out of monetarism.

Stanley Fischer (1977) amongst others was at the forefront of the academic assault on monetarism and advocated enlightened central bank economic management based on the power of modern econometrics. Later, these economists demonstrated great skills in the corridors of monetary power, scaling the ladder to become top monetary bureaucrats and advisors to Presidents, who saw the potential for neo-Keynesian engineering to win a second term at the next election (and after that le déluge, possibly, but who cares).

Before this ascent of the neo-Keynesians, dollar devaluation policy had resumed in the second Reagan Administration. In early autumn 1985, Fed Chief Volcker joined with Treasury Secretary James Baker in implementing the Plaza Accord. The turbulence this produced on the European currency scene—including a new revaluation of the Deutsche mark—played a big role in powering the train towards European Monetary Union (see James 2012).

Through the 1990s, after the global asset price deflations and recessions of 1989–92, the Federal Reserve having totally abandoned the last vestiges of monetary rules with respect to monetary aggregates (broad or narrow) and focusing under Alan Greenspan on masterly piloting of short-term interest rates, gained acclaim for the so-called Great Moderation. The NASDAQ crash and apparent mini recession of 2001/2 blemished that record, such that in 2002/3 President George W. Bush, facing difficult elections in 2004, resolved to use the power of appointment to guide the Fed on to a "pro-growth course".

Accordingly, President Bush appointed renowned "inflationist" and neo Keynesian Professor Ben Bernanke (a disciple of Stanley Fischer) as a Fed Governor (then fast-tracking him into the "Economic Cabinet" in preparation for the top Fed post), and meanwhile extended Greenspan's tenure for a half-term—all in the implicit expectation (no evidence of any direct negotiation on this) that policy would be "stimulatory" in the run-up to the 2004 elections. The "breathing in of inflation" on the basis that this was too low at around 1% became a milestone in the development of the 2% inflation standard and in Europe similarly we had the famous press conference of the ECB's eminence grise, ex-Bundesbanker Otmar Issing, in early 2003.

The payment of market interest rates on monetary base (authorized by Congress in autumn 2008) and successive bouts of quantitative easing (QE) dealt the final coup de grace to any residual ailing anchor to the US monetary system. The demand for monetary base became so unstable and indeed unknowable that it could not possibly function as anchor. All of this was a far cry from the norm of Fed practice through most of its prior existence, at least until the early 1990s, where in setting the interest rate path, it accepted that the growth of monetary base in some loose fashion constrained its freedom of action.

Counterfactually, what would have been the sound money way out of the flaws of monetarism? Short answer: to reconstruct the monetary regime in a way which would ensure a strong and resilient anchor to the monetary system such that the principles of sound money could triumph.

A longer answer starts with a look at what we should learn from the flaws of monetarism.

Prices Are Not Stable Under Sound Money

We have already considered the problems in applying monetarism due to no stable demand and exogenously determined supply for wide or semi-wide money aggregates. But there is a deeper issue. Even if the holy grail of such an aggregate and its supply conditions could have been found, would all have ended happily under monetarism?

Most likely not: for prices do not follow a smooth monotonic path under a sound money regime. Yet that is the implicit standard of success for the monetarists, albeit that Friedman cautioned against making the price level the target of monetary policy. He argued that the central bank should be judged by what it can control, the money supply, not prices. The latter, over the short term at least, are influenced by factors outside the central bank's control. Even so, Friedman embraced the idea that the authorities, in setting the money supply target, should acknowledge the aim of stable prices over the medium and long run. The sound money critic would say that "medium and long run" should have been replaced by "very long run" and in the sense of a tendency for prices to revert to the mean (which could shift through time).

We should mention here a key insight of Austrian School economics—the existence of a natural rhythm to prices (upwards, downwards, and sideways) for goods and services. Multi-year bouts in productivity growth or in the momentum of globalization—or acceleration of technological change or a sudden abundance of key natural resources—can go along with a sustained natural rhythm downward of prices and conversely.

Big changes in the structure of the labour market, even if not accompanied by a bout of positive or negative productivity growth, can set wages and prices in a downward or upward direction for some considerable time. For example, if the bargaining power of labour is declining (as may be the case where technological change is favouring monopoly creation and reducing simultaneously the scope of restrictive practices or unions to influence pay rates in some sectors), then wages could drift down on average until a lower level is reached consistent with the new balance of forces in the labour market. An additional factor here (to bargaining power) can be the waxing or waning of scope for types of labour to earn rental income with respect to specific qualities, perhaps because these become obsolete and new employment growth is in highly standardized jobs.

The business cycle itself is a source of natural rhythm—downward pressure on prices to a low level during the weak phase and upward pressure to a higher level during the expansion phase. This pro-cyclical move of prices is a key mechanism in economic recoveries as the expectation of higher prices eventually incentivizes some businesses and households to bring forward spending into the weak phase (see Brown 2017).

A sound money regime should not interfere with this natural rhythm except in the sense that in the very long run movement or prices up or down is bounded (by the operation of the regime) with some tendency for a regression towards the mean. Any monetary regime—including monetarist—which tended to fight the natural rhythm, producing a smooth outcome for nominal economic variables, whether "price level" or "incomes", would inflict much damage.

The pre-1914 gold standard regime, where in effect the monetary base for the total gold area (all countries with gold monies) was made up primarily of above-the-ground gold, fully allowed such price fluctuations to occur upwards and downwards. Fighting the natural rhythm of prices did not occur under gold; instead velocity of base money fluctuated considerably in the short and the medium term. The struggle under fiat money regimes to stabilize the "price level" or "low inflation" has induced serious problems under the heading of asset inflation and malinvestment.

No one estimated a demand function for monetary base under the classical gold standard, where this function would have included principally real income and prices and interest rates, fitted against say monthly or quarterly observations. The success of gold and gold monetary base as the anchor depended on a long-run stability in demand for gold. That should be the model for ersatz gold monetary systems.

The extent to which monetarism set out to be an ersatz gold system, at least in one country, is debatable. Sceptics on that hypothesis can point out that the natural rhythm of prices, intrinsic to sound money regimes including the gold standard, is not a concept found in monetarism.

Crucial Evidence from the 1920s

As a historical example, Milton Friedman and Anna Schwartz describe the years 1922–8 as the high tide of the Federal Reserve (see Friedman and Schwartz 1963). The narrow money supply was growing at a steady low rate in line with their estimated demand for real money balances. Prices were stable.

Yet, for the Austrian school economists this was a period of huge monetary inflation.

Rapid productivity growth was putting serious downward pressure on prices (and simultaneously there was a growing glut of commodities). Under a classical gold standard, monetary forces would not have resisted price declines in the short run even though empirical estimates might have shown supply of narrow money in excess of demand (given the boost to this aggregate in real terms from the fall in prices which could outweigh the fillip to demand from a trend rise in real incomes).

Nothing to worry about here: individuals' holdings of narrow money are not being continuously re-balanced. There is quite a lot of slack over short and medium-term periods around whether they are holding the "right amount of money" given the value of the variables assumed to determine their optimal holdings. Over the long run, slack in both directions tends to diminish

Over the longer term, monetary forces would put some upward pressure on prices from their low level (relative to historic mean). These would emanate from an increased supply of newly mined gold (spurred by fall in cost of production). But that could work itself out over many years. So initially the observed velocity of narrow money would fall below the long-run average and empirical estimates, but then it would rise back again. The stability of monetary velocity and prices which Friedman observed reflected direct stimulus from activist interest rate policy. The Fed's tampering with the supply path of monetary base, boosting this in various key episodes (most famously in 1927 when Governor Strong came to the help of the Bank of England and simultaneously gave a boost to Wall Street) made that activism possible over a sustained period of time.

Missing from the monetarist analysis of the 1920s amidst the acclaim of the Fed for having successfully steered money supply in line with real demand is this new key element of "interest rate policy" which the Fed introduced into policy making.

Under the pre-1914 international gold standard, interest rate policy did not exist (unless we interpret this to include crisis rate adjustments to stem flows of gold). Short-term rates there were determined by supply and demand for monetary base (in gold); local shortages or gluts of monetary base could occur, symptomized by sometimes wide spreads between local and foreign money rates (albeit all monies on gold) related to a whole range of factors, but these would be relieved by gold shipments (but whilst they lasted there could be spreads sometimes wide between different centres). Under a deeply corrupted and no longer global gold standard, the newly created Fed from 1919 onwards explicitly set interest rates in short-term markets with a view to influencing overall economic conditions in some way. It deliberately on occasion administered boosts to the supply of monetary base on a totally discretionary basis, flaunting the automatic control system central to sound money, specifically towards helping the UK authorities stabilize the pound or towards accelerating economic recovery or overcoming stock market weakness. These injections of monetary base prevented the path of this aggregate from getting in the way of the Fed's interest rate policy (even though the time of the injection did not coincide with an actual clash).

The Fallacies of Interest Rate Policy

For any given path of monetary base there is a corresponding path of money market rates. But once the Fed (or any other central bank) gives prime place to interest rate policy, the monetary base path becomes the dependent variable (albeit still under the control of the central bank but via the indirect route of setting the money market interest rate path). Dependence is constrained (equivalently the freedom to set the path for short-term interest rates is limited) if nonetheless the Fed is explicitly aiming to keep the monetary base growth as averaged over say half-year periods within an implicit or explicit target range; and if there is still gold convertibility, either full (as from 1919–32) or partial (as from 1934–71), this sets limits to the monetary base growth path, in turn limiting the degrees of freedom for interest rate policy.

This power of short-term rates to influence economic outcomes depended on prevailing expectations that these would follow a path as talked about by the monetary officials, and long-term rates took their cue from short-term rates.

Yes, there were occasions when the Fed directly stimulated monetary conditions by embarking on open market operations designed to boost the monetary base; but this was accompanied by a well-recognized shift in interest rate policy. Long-term interest rates took their cue from the Fed's policy as regards short-term interest rates not just on the basis of rational expectations; some irrationality may have crept into the process of long-term rate determination around what behavioural finance theorists described as an "anchoring process". This was not relevant in the gold standard world where short-term rates were highly volatile and had no signalling function.

Bottom line: The Fed's policy of holding down short-term rates in the years 1922–7 was driven by a political dynamic where Congress had strongly rebuked Benjamin Strong for having aggravated the 1919/20 recession. At that time prices fell sharply. Congress now expected (not formally) the Fed to stabilize prices. In doing so, the Fed surely contributed to the strength of the US economic boom, which in turn worked against the natural downward rhythm of prices manifesting itself. It is also possible that broad knowledge in the economy that the Fed was working to stabilize prices could have directly affected price-setting behaviour (dissuading businesses from say cutting prices in response to micro-economic circumstances). In reality, prices in general did remain stable, there was no observed fall in velocity of narrow money (as would have occurred if the natural rhythm downwards of prices had been allowed to occur, rather than meeting resistance from the Fed's low interest rate policy pursued consistent with the dollar on its gold standard), and Friedman/Schwartz congratulated the Federal Reserve of Benjamin Strong on this outcome.

By contrast, the Austrians lament the powerful asset inflation which all this gave rise to—symptoms including not just the high speculative temperature on Wall Street but the huge carry trade flows into the Weimar Republic, culminating eventually in that country's bankruptcy with cataclysmic political consequences (see Rothbard 1963).

Asset Inflation: Ignored by Monetarists and Keynesians

Neither the monetarists nor the neo-Keynesians really broach the issue of asset inflation.

For Milton Friedman, this may seem strange given that he walked the same campus as Hayek; but it is likely that the notion jarred in some respects with his mission to establish economics as a positive science (based on empiricism). Prime of place here is measurement. It is no easy matter, however, to measure asset inflation.

For the neo-Keynesians asset inflation does not exist. If the central bank is successful in divining the ideal path for interest rates such as to achieve the optimal combination of inflation (in goods and services markets) and unemployment, then that is game won. Yes, there can be bouts of irrationality and bubbles in asset markets, but best to just let these come and go; bursting them or pre-empting them is no job of monetary policy; rather the monetary bureaucrats should focus on their contingency stimulus plans should asset prices suddenly crash for whatever reason.

The refusal of the monetary policy makers to recognize asset inflation as a strictly monetary phenomenon coupled with their refusal to acknowledge a natural rhythm of prices has had highly damaging consequences in the quarter century from the mid-1990s to the present day. For, during this period there have been persistent (changing in composition) strong non-monetary forces downwards on prices.

The second half of the 1990s witnessed a surge of productivity growth stemming from the internet revolution. That was a global phenomenon. Then the forces of globalization (including the emergence of China) brought downward pressure to bear on prices—perhaps most of all in the case of Japan, but also in different ways for Southern Europe (e.g. in Italy, much of the small enterprise economy was in direct competition with emerging markets). Into the second decade of the twenty-first century, these same forces applied together with two new factors—the super-abundance of fossil fuels (including the production boom of shale oil and gas), and the rapid spread of digitalization with its proclivity for generating star firms in each sector with considerable market power which had the effect of forcing competitors into cutting wages and prices. The spread of the "gig economy" (e.g. with its power to erode quasi monopoly rents stemming from restrictive practices or unionization) has likely been an additional source of some downward rhythm in wages and prices.

Also bearing down on prices was a factor of monetary origin (and thereby not included in the natural rhythm)—fantastic speculative narratives which bestowed such cheap cost of capital on some firms that they could offer great deals to their customers (and at the same time destroy potential competition). Furthermore, malinvestment in the form of over-expansion of global supply chains may well have intensified downward pressure on prices.

Two Percent Inflation Standard, Monetary Repression Tax and Monopoly

The pursuit by central banks led by the Fed of 2% inflation just when the natural rhythm of prices was powerfully downwards stimulated directly asset inflation. They responded to inflation below target by holding rates of interest at extremely low levels—generating irrational forces including a desperate hunt for yield and positive feedback loops from capital gains. As we have seen, the patterns of malinvestment stimulated by asset inflation added further downward pressure on prices in some ways, though the drag on productivity could have offset this in some degree. Fantastic speculation in companies which boasted of future monopoly power, such as Amazon, meant that in the present they could slash prices to ruin the competition; no simple tale of creative capitalism here, but a stark sub-plot about old-fashioned predatory power under a new guise. Overinvestment in shale oil and gas contributed to the price collapse of 2014/16. Speculative fervour for the star firms in each non-oil sector gave these more power to retain their competitive lead and prevent this seeping out, meaning that other firms in the same industrial sector to survive had to slash costs.

Moreover, central bankers in holding down rates to achieve their 2% inflation targets at a time when the natural rhythm of prices was downwards, could deliver something which governments were hungry for given the ailing condition of public finances—revenues. The revenue comes in the form of monetary repression tax (the amount by which interest rates are below the hypothetical level they would be at under sound money conditions). Yes, some (generally elderly) households may resent the MRT, but even they could feel good meanwhile about the capital gains accruing to them from asset inflation.

Indeed, there has been a pervasive illusion that individuals can escape the MRT by investing in assets not subject to this—for example, real estate and equities. These, however, sell at a premium, which reflects the fact that they are not subject to MRT. For some considerable time this premium may be invisible, camouflaged by a stream of capital gains. But it shows up eventually most likely in the form of a stream of low or negative returns.

Reported low inflation has been soothing and we should not ignore the general tonic of apparently free services from the tech giants (in exchange for private data) and "give away" prices from firms favoured by speculatively low capital costs. This situation was ideal for the politicians: collect a huge tax (MRT) against which there is not much resentment because the citizens are fooled by present speculative gains and transitorily or falsely low prices. In brief, the monetary policies described directly encouraged government to spend and spend or cut taxes for their crony friends—in the belief that there would be no political price to pay for a largely so far hidden tax.

Many households believe they have escaped the monetary repression tax (MRT) by moving into risk assets which are not directly subject to the tax. The frothy (some would say sky-high) prices of such assets, however, reflect the fact that they are free of MRT; prospective rates of return calculated in sober-rational fashion to take account of this premium paid upfront for freedom from tax (and which can suddenly rode in any subsequent asset deflation) are in fact no better than on the heavily tax money and debts. But as long as asset inflation continues, most individuals (and managers of their wealth) in their chasing of yield ignore this fact. True there is much written about one such MRT haven—residential real estate, which gains also from the fact that indebted homeowners can in fact obtain an MRT credit (monetary repression tax credit). The related growing shortage of land in metropolitan cities in turn impoverishes people who pay rents or who did not buy ahead of the monetary inflation; but this may be outweighed politically by the happiness of those who have in fact scored big capital gains.

The neo-Keynesian response to all this is to ask blandly, if the so-called Phillips curve has broken down, meaning that unemployment falls to record lows and yet inflation does not accelerate, why not meet this situation by keeping interest rates subdued? These economists implicitly reject all analyses which point to the costs of malinvestment and the growing burden of government, as a consequence of their monetary policies. Nor do they concede that the huge monetary uncertainty created, especially the possibilities of massive asset deflation shock further down the road, have held back business investment in aggregate, so contributing to the sluggishness of productivity and real income growth. Certainly, the new era of outsized monopoly profits in aggregate is a threat to the future of free market competitive capitalism.

Malinvestment and Over-Rapid Digitalization

The forms of malinvestment described in our dialogue go far beyond what we have in the classical Austrian texts, though the economists who wrote those in many cases would not be surprised by them. Also transcending the original texts is the nature of the irrational forces and their links to modern research in psychology.

"Classical" Austrian school economics describes a process where entrepreneurs are fooled by an apparently low cost of capital held down by monetary authorities into over-spending on capital goods (or equivalently moving towards patterns of production which include more time). But why are they fooled in this way? By coupling the discussion with modern psychology, we find some possible answers to this question.

Under monetary inflation, it is the investor in the equity or the high-yield debt of these undertakings who becomes subject to irrational impulse. The core notion here is prospect theory as developed for example by Daniel Kahneman (2011). He finds that if people are given a choice between certain loss or a bad bet (whose actuarial value is less than the certain loss), almost everyone goes for the bad bet. Kahneman does not go on to consider the likelihood that people do not like to admit to themselves that they are taking on a bad bet, so they fall for speculative narratives which seem to turn the bad bets into good bets. As example, when pursuing the high yield on debt securities related to shale oil, investors became irrationally certain that oil prices would stay at high levels into the long run, without due consideration of alternative hypotheses.

These speculative narratives in many cases "justify" equity purchases. They also fan booms in the carry trades—whether credit, currency, or illiquidity. These in turn go hand-in-hand with financial engineering, which enjoys boom conditions, but at the cost of growing financial vulnerability in the system whilst fostering malinvestment—investments which would not have taken place if price signalling across capital markets were undistorted by monetary inflation in the ways described and investments which do not occur for the same reason.

When thinking about malinvestment we should consider technological revolutions. Ideally, these fitful journeys into the forest of the unknown would be strongly under the control of well-functioning invisible hands. This would mean scepticism built on alternative possible scenarios to the most optimistic being fully reflected in market prices. The growth of prosperity suffers from over-optimism based on fuelling of irrational forces (by monetary inflation) leading to a hectic embrace of new technologies without their downsides continuously appraised. This is even more the case when we consider network effects—once a new technology is introduced beyond a certain point, there are considerable advantages for almost all businesses from a micro-perspective in adapting these.

In our dialogue (see question 20), we consider whether the railroad revolution was one such example of malinvestment. Ideally, the canal system would have a broader and longer dominant life in the economy and then a substantial period of similar overall importance to a grown railroad system. Fast forward to the technological revolution. Has monetary inflation via the fanning of speculative narratives and their distortion of price signalling led to over-rapid and over-extensive introduction of digitalization? It is difficult to answer this question with due perspective in the midst of a pandemic which has buoyed demand for digital products and services, causing monopoly or oligopoly profits of the tech giants to soar. (See postscript in answer to question 20, part 4). In the bigger picture "over-rapid" goes along with insufficient time for the political and legal systems to respond to the monopoly threat and mount effective defensive action, before this has become entrenched and much harder to dislodge. Would rational pricing not at least have intuitively discounted some of the serious downsides subsequently to emerge with respect to this technology, not least related to information security?

Malinvestment is hard to measure empirically due to its foundation in the counterfactual. It is possible though that disappointing productivity growth at the level of the economy at a time of rapid digitalization hints at the woes of malinvestment, even though enthusiasts of the new technology would claim that statistical measurement under-records the advances. Those claims are dubious not least given that so many of the costs of dealing with the downsides of digitalization (e.g. security flaws) are treated as gains to gross domestic product.

Could Europe Turn Against the Unsound Dollar Hegemon?

What is a big shock which might end the great asset inflation of the past decade and more?

First, the downward rhythm of prices could come to an end, and, worse, there could be the emergence of an upward rhythm. Receding non-monetary disinflation, resource shortage, sustained fall in productivity growth are possible causes. When that happens, central banks power to deliver revenue to the government via MRT fades away. Their attention (under government encouragement) will shift to inflation tax. The transition from MRT to inflation tax might occur with surprising rapidity. Upward rhythm of prices coupled with a potential emerging scarcity of capital (explained by the apparent economic obsolescence of so much malinvestment from the previous cycle) can provide the potential for new monetary inflation, this time no longer camouflaged in goods and services markets.

Second, we should consider the fading power of speculative narratives. As illustrations, perhaps events demonstrate that the narrative about the Fed being able to extend and extend the business cycle expansion meets its nemesis. There will be a time when it cannot do so. This may or not coincide with the end of the downward rhythm of prices. Or perhaps the faith in ever-emerging and everlasting monopoly power might get shaken, for example, by ferocious anti-trust action. Or the false miracles of digitalization might become exposed. And we should not ignore the fading of several once powerful narratives already in this present asset inflation—whether limit oil (the hypothesis that the pace of new discoveries is slowing and extraction becoming more difficult at the margin) which helped power oil prices above $100 per barrel, or emerging market economies catching up with the advanced economies.

The virulent asset inflation of the second decade in the twenty-first century turning into bust is not a sufficient condition for liberation from the tyranny of unsound money. That would require the strengthening of political forces which could bring about a sound money revolution. If this were to occur in the US, the dollar hegemon would change fundamentally from an agent of unsound money as in the past century to a powerful engine of sound money throughout the globe including Europe. If the US fails to lead the way, is there any prospect that Europe will independently end its present regime of unsound money—the monetary union as established by the Maastricht Treaty and subsequently deeply corrupted? We discuss this in the final sections of the dialogue which follows. There is indeed a pathway to Europe heading the journey to sound money and this most plausibly would include a role for gold in anchoring a new euro. It is possible that Europe's success in sound money implementation would unleash forces both political and economic which would bring an end to the unsound regime in the US hegemon, whose power in any event would diminish. The history of the twentieth century instructs us that seemingly momentous obstacles of the present status quo can disintegrate at short notice.

References

Brown, B. (2017). A Modern Concept of Asset Inflation in Boom and Bust. *Quarterly Journal of Austrian Economics, Spring, 20*(1), 29–60.

Fischer, S. (1977). Long-Term Contracts, Rational Expectations, and the Optimal Money Supply Rule. *Journal of Political Economy, 85*(1), 191–205.

Friedman, M. (1966). *Essays in Positive Economics*. Chicago: University of Chicago.

Friedman, M. (2006). *The Optimum Quantity of Money*. New Brunswick: Aldine Transaction.

Friedman, M., & Schwartz, A. (1963). *A Monetary History of the United States*. Princeton: Princeton University Press.

James, H. (2012). *Making the European Monetary Union*. Cambridge, MA: Harvard University Press.

Kahneman, D. (2011). *Thinking Fast and Slow*. New York: Farrar, Strauss and Giroux.

Rothbard, M. (1963). *America's Great Depression*. Auburn: Mises.

Part II

Dialogue

2

Phobia of Deflation

Question 1

Simonnot: How can we explain the deflation phobia of our rulers?

Brown: "Deflation" for our "authorities" means a persistent fall in prices as measured by the consumer price index.

For some, deflation carries the stigma of wage cuts. Mixed in with this may be Keynesian folklore about the futility of cutting wages during the Great Depression of the early 1930s.

Even some of those who reject the folklore, arguing instead that real wage cuts especially in highly cyclical sectors are part of the recovery process from recession, accept the notion of "money illusion": it is supposed to be difficult to get real wages to move down in some segments of the labour markets as required for overall economic re-balancing (and in line with supply and demand) if individuals are resistant to cuts in their nominal wage rates; hence a little inflation may oil the path of the economy.

Then there is the perception that "deflation" means that debt burdens increase in real terms and this can cripple the potential dynamism of the economy.

Finally, there is the "modern concern" (under the 2% inflation standard since the mid-1990s) that deflation means market interest rates even when low or zero in nominal terms remain significantly positive in real terms, whilst in practice at times (such as severe cyclical weakness) the "equilibrium real rate" should be negative.

All of this is deeply mistaken.

In a well-functioning capitalist economy under sound money there would be periods when prices tended to fall and others when they tended to rise—albeit with some regression to the mean when considered over the very long run. As a matter of historical fact, several episodes of great increase in prosperity have featured persistently falling prices (e.g. the US through the "gilded age" in late nineteenth century). And who in the age of Amazon (instant information available to everyone on comparative prices), coupled with digitalized labour markets in which trade unions have lost bargaining power, thinks there is still such a thing as "money illusion" or "wage rigidity"? Central banks in fighting a natural downward rhythm of prices create asset inflation which culminates in waves of bankruptcy and financial distress.

Finally, sound economic recovery does not depend on various forms of monetary stimulus; rather, the stimulus distorts the recovery, inducing early on asset inflation and malinvestment whilst potentially weakening the power of creative destruction. Better for a pro-cyclical move of goods (and services) prices to lead the way to recovery—prices fall to an an abnormally cheap level in the weak phase of the cycle such that households and businesses can see a strong likelihood of higher prices in the future, meaning it is advantageous to bring forward spending. Surely the most recent cycle (from US peak in November 2007 to peak in February 2020) has demonstrated that the most radical policies in fact go along with the slowest economic recovery ever from Great Recession (2008–9) and Crash.

Question 2

Simonnot: Who hasn't learnt about the declaration of William J. Bryan to the Democratic Party convention of July 9, 1896 in Chicago: "You will not crucify humanity on a cross of gold". This populist leader wanted to stigmatize the deflationist policy of the government at that time. That was in the era of the gold standard. Would you say, nonetheless, that deflation phobia has got worse since the abandonment of the gold standard in 1914: and for what reason.

Brown: Yes, deflation phobia has got worse since the collapse of the gold standard. When Bryan made his comment many contemporaries would have realized that the growth of real wage rates and the economy had been strong (in fact, the strongest ever in US history) during the period from the mid-1870s to the late 1880s despite a persistent fall in prices.

And as a matter of historical fact, Bryan was incorrect. The downswing in prices from the mid-1870s had already come to an end by the mid-1890s; the rate of increase in above-ground gold supplies accelerated under influence of new discoveries and improved mining technology (themselves stimulated by the long previous fall in the price of goods in general relative to the fixed gold price).

Moreover, Bryan's populist fury against gold surely fuelled some capital flight out of the dollar during the early and mid-1890s meaning interest rates in the US were unnaturally high and contributing to the poor overall business conditions about which he complained (see Brown 2020; Shiller 2019).

In general, under the gold standard there was widespread realization that price downswings even extending over many years would ultimately be reversed. Over the very long run, there was a well-known tendency for prices to "revert to the mean". Lack of any such tendency under fiat money regimes could be a factor in the intensity of deflation phobia there; no confidence exists in mid-winter that less dark days lie ahead.

References

Brown, B. (2020). Book Review: Narrative Economics: How Stories Go Viral and Drive Major Economic Events. *Quarterly Journal of Austrian Economics, 22*(4).

Shiller, R. (2019). *Narrative Economics: How Stories Go Viral and Drive Major Economic Events*. Princeton: Princeton University Press.

3

The Great War and the End of the Gold Standard

Question 3

Simonnot: Perhaps Bryan was wrong. But he became famous nonetheless thanks to his polemic figuring the crucification of humanity on a cross of gold. In the same way Keynes's description of gold as a "barbaric relic" has buried itself in the collective conscience and springs into any serious discussion about the gold standard. We must take account of the power of persuasion of the demagogues.

Soon after Bryan's speech, humanity was well and truly crucified but on a wooden crucifix taking the title of the famous novel of Roland Dorgelès published in 1919. The bronze crosses in cemeteries were melted down to make cannon. In parallel, gold and silver coins disappeared from circulation. Right from the start of the hostilities, people wanted to retrieve the gold they had previously handed over to banks in exchange for notes believing as an act of faith in the pledge of immediate and absolute convertibility. This pledge could not be fulfilled by banks which had less than 100% reserves in gold. It was necessary therefore to close the gold windows—an action which we find repeated by the Nixon Administration in 1971 with respect to the sole gold window then of the US Treasury. In the pre-1914 gold standard, there were many banks with windows where one could exchange notes for gold at the legal par rate without having to use the central bank's window.

Do we know how much gold was still held by banks outside the central bank in August 1914? Could the closing of gold windows have been avoided in Europe (even in Switzerland they were closed at the start of the conflict)? Would the war have taken a different course if the gold standard had been maintained? Would it have been better for the US to let the gold price float against the dollar as you suggest in A Global Monetary Plague (2015)? Would that step not have undermined the fractional reserve banking system?

Brown: I agree with you about the force of persuasion of anti-sound money demagogues.

Yet demagoguery can also be used in reverse by the advocates of sound money. (And I love your citation of the bronze cross—it reminds one of the trains carrying the war dead back on the opposite side of the track to those taking the enthusiastic new recruits to the battlefields as described by Remarque (2010) in *All Quiet on the Western Front*.) What about the "barbarism of fiat money"—its destruction of freedom and long-run prosperity; or the sub-title of our dialogue "the tyranny of unsound money". And we should note that under fiat money barbarism, the demand for gold as ultimate safe-haven/protection has been many times greater than essentially monetary demand under the gold standard (equivalently the real price of gold today is 2–3 times higher than on average in the 1875–1914 period and correspondingly the growth of above-ground gold supplies (including jewellery) hoarded in vaults and elsewhere has been explosive). Modern demand for the "barbaric relic" is a reflection of fiat money barbarism.

Back to your core question: was it possible in 1914 that the belligerent countries could have stayed on gold, and how would this have influenced the course of the war: And to follow on, was it at all practical for the US to float the gold price as I suggested given the constraints of fractional reserve banking.

As a matter of history, some major military conflicts have occurred without suspension of the gold standard. Think of the Russian-Japanese war and (I stand to be corrected) the Franco-Prussian war (from memory of my studies France remained on gold throughout). Could any of the belligerents in 1914 have stayed on gold? The extent of gold withdrawals (hoarding of coins and conversion of notes) during the final days of the pre-war crisis suggest that an important section of the public was acutely anxious about the struggle which might lie ahead, notwithstanding the promise of the political leaders that all would be finished by Christmas. The spectre of national bankruptcy in which massive war debts and fiat money would be written off by inflation had entered the intuitive zone.

If any belligerent country could have tried to stay on gold in August 1914 it was Britain. Indeed, in the weeks ahead of the outbreak of war there had been huge capital inflows into London, as short-term lending in sterling to foreigners was not rolled over (correspondingly the US dollar slumped against the pound). As the war turned out badly (the Battle of the Somme 1916), huge pressures would have developed in British financial markets, amidst a haemorrhage of gold, which might have added to the political pressures within Britain for a negotiated settlement. Instead, the pound's exit from gold in August 1914 made it feasible for Lloyd George (Prime Minister from December 1916) to preach war until absolute victory and to work against the feeble attempt of the Wilson Administration to bring about a peace settlement in late 1916 (see Brown 2011).

In fact, the US, which as a neutral (until April 2017) remained on the gold standard (see Brown 2013), had enabled Britain and France to unload unlimited amounts of gold (in the U S) at the official conversion price into US dollars. The result was dollar inflationary finance (courtesy of US savers) for the Entente—essentially dollars were printed to pay for the French and British gold—which made a negotiated peace even less plausible in late 1916.

Was a floating of the gold price in the US feasible during say 1915–16?

US nationally chartered banks in the years before the Federal Reserve was launched (1914) had their reserves in effectively the equivalent of Treasury bills, not metallic gold. And under the Federal Reserve System, reserves (of the banks) from the start were almost entirely in deposits at the Federal Reserve banks. Hence, a fall in the dollar price of gold in the free market would not have created pressure on the banks; and individuals would not have been inclined to demand gold in exchange for currency or deposits at the banks (or ultimately at the Federal Reserve) where the official price would still apply to conversions rather than the now lower free market price; there would have been a big accounting loss in the Federal Reserve system (ultimately part of the government accounts) as regards its holdings of gold if valued at the free market price—but surely the accountants would have continued to use the official price (justified in any case by no commitment to convert dollars into gold at the market price).

The international gold standard was not restored in the 1920s; instead there was a gold exchange standard. The main features of this included the US dollar fully convertible again into gold coin (suspended during US belligerency 1917–18), Great Britain fixing (in 1925) the sterling price of 400 oz gold bars (but no promise, as pre-1914, of converting on demand pound notes into gold coin at par) and Germany pegging (in 1924) the Reichsmark to the dollar. A key obstacle in the way of the restoration of a full gold standard (in which gold coins circulated and all notes could be converted into gold) outside the US was a shortage of gold, especially in the case of the European belligerents—so much had been requisitioned and (in the case of Britain and France) shipped to the US in wartime financing.

If hypothetically the dollar had been floated against gold during 1915–16 and its fallen dollar price had discouraged shipments, there would have been a much easier prospect of restoring a full gold standard in Britain and France following the war. Restoration would require abundant gold holdings available to the national monetary system in question, whether as gold coins already minted still in the hands of the public, gold stocks held by government (including the central bank) and gold reserves which banks could convert into paper money on demand.

In the US, the question would have been whether to fix a gold parity for the dollar after the war which was the same as pre-war or partly towards the floating rate hypothetically in 1916 (say $10–15 per ounce compared to $20.67 official price). The attraction of the latter course would have been to encourage a return of prices for goods and services to pre-war levels (from higher levels reached during the period of US belligerency, albeit that the cumulative rise in prices during the period of neutrality would have been much less with gold inflows curtailed). A disadvantage, though, from the viewpoint of the Federal Reserve (and the political authorities to which it was answerable), would have been a curtailment of any scope for a national US monetary policy, given that the margin of its free reserves above the legal obligation related to its note issuance would have diminished sharply (see Koning 2009).

For the record, Switzerland, which did float the gold price during the war (meaning that the Swiss franc rose to a big premium against the dollar compared to parity) in response to huge capital flight from Germany—the Swiss National Bank no longer supplying francs at par against gold presented to it—returned to a gold standard after the war at pre-war parity.

Observation

Simonnot: In light of what you say, one can understand better how so many enlightened writers of the "Belle Epoque" (1871–1914) period (most of all Norman Angell and Ivan Bloch) had predicted at the start of the twentieth century that henceforth war was impossible for economic and financial reasons. They had overlooked the fact that belligerents could finance expenditures of war by over-indebtedness and monetary inflation—effectively by printing money.

References

Brown, B. (2011). *Monetary Chaos in Europe*. Oxon: Routledge Revivals.
Brown, B. (2013). *The Global Curse of the Federal Reserve*. London: Palgrave.
Koning, J. (2009). *How the Fed Helped to Pay for World War One*. Auburn: Mises Institute.
Remarque, E. (2010). *All Quiet on the Western Front*. Future Classics, Vintage.

4

From Birth of Dollar Hegemony Towards the 1929 Crisis

Question 4

Simonnot: Did the "establishment" of the Gold Exchange Standard at the Genoa Conference (April to May 1922) play a role in the Great Crisis of 1929? If so, which?

Brown: The Gold Exchange Standard declaration of the Genoa Conference did not make the Great Crisis of 1929–31 inevitable; but once it erupted, the crisis blew that Standard apart.

The key monetary contributor to the crisis was the inflationary Federal Reserve policy through 1921–27. If by some miracle Britain, France and Germany had found their way back to a full gold standard (rather than forward to the Gold Exchange Standard or Dollar Standard), then it is possible (but far from certain) that an external constraint would have emerged with respect to US monetary inflation. In reality, the Genoa Declaration was not the main obstacle to that occurring.

Yes, occasionally exchange rate stability (notably of sterling) within the context of the Gold Exchange Standard was a justification (from the viewpoint of Governor Strong) for a particular interest rate policy decision (or open market operation) by the Federal Reserve. However, in the bigger picture its stance in the years 1921–27 would have been inflationary anyhow. Briefly, the Fed reacted to the political fallout (which included hostility in Congress, manifested by relevant committees holding sessions which featured testimony from top officials) from the steep recession of 1920 (which it had helped to induce and intensify) by pursuing easy policy throughout (see Meltzer 2003). This was not apparent to all as rapid technological progress through these years meant that the natural rhythm of prices was downwards (think electrification, the mass assembly line, radio and telephone, plus a growing glut of commodities globally).

Hence, when the Benjamin Strong Fed sought to stabilize prices and avoid political push-back from a new episode of "price deflation" (an aim which Strong did not admit to and in fact argued against before Congress—see Brown 2015), it was in fact manipulating rates downwards to an average level surely well below neutral and inducing powerful asset inflation. A key aspect of that asset inflation was a massive lending boom (carry trade in today's terms) into the Weimar Republic, which was viewed as an economic miracle in the aftermath of the hyperinflation and stabilization of the mark according to the Dawes Plan in 1924.

Suppose hypothetically the Fed during these years had pursued sound money, what would that have meant for the gold exchange standard?

In the case of Germany, a vast credit bubble which ultimately turned to bust would not have formed; it was the economic and political collapse in the Weimar Republic, a direct consequence of that bubble and bust, that swept away the Gold Exchange Standard including the free convertibility of the reichsmark into the dollar at a fixed exchange rate. In the case of Britain, if sound money in the US fostered no political will to defend sterling resolutely at its pre-war parity, then that country most likely would have ultimately re-fixed its currency against the dollar at a substantially devalued parity (compared to 1914). The germ of beggar your neighbor currency policy, as evident implicitly in contemporary British policy debates, was already present in the 1920s as a potential menace to global economic prosperity. It was the German collapse which triggered the floating of Sterling (taking the form of a huge decline against the US dollar) in 1931—a total break with the Gold Exchange Standard.

Question 4, Part 2

Simonnot: What do you mean by the neutral rate of interest?

Brown: If interest rates in the market (averaging out short-term fluctuations) remain close to the neutral rate (changing all the time and unknown) over time there would be no substantial monetary inflation. Yes, prices would rise and fall over time in line with "natural rhythm" (as driven by the business cycle, swings in productivity growth, etc.), but they would tend to regress to the mean over the very long run. Absence of asset inflation means in everyday terms no sequence of bubble and bust. Note that under a sound money regime no one spends time estimating the neutral rate of interest—indeed this may be an impossible feat. Actual rates are floating, without any official intervention in the form of rate pegging or broader rate manipulation. This is in the context of the monetary system being well pivoted to the monetary base (whose growth is determined by automatic or constitutional rules). The automatic rules for determining the supply path of a well-pivoted monetary base, not estimates of neutral rate and related misguided interest rate policy, are the foundations of sound money.

Simonnot: And what do you mean by asset inflation?

Brown: How to define asset inflation? This is the twin of goods and services inflation—both driven by (or stemming from) monetary inflation. The key aspect of asset inflation is a strengthening of irrational forces in the marketplace as evidenced by "desperation for yield" and "positive feedback loops" (in which capital gains fuel euphoric expectations). In asset inflations carry trades boom (risk-arbitrage from low interest monies into high interest monies, liquid assets into illiquid, low risk credits into high risk, short maturity government bonds into long-maturity) with investors pretending to themselves that the risks taken on or the liquidity given up is small. There is much speculative storytelling with investors discarding their normal rational scepticism, momentum trading and financial engineering (e.g. increasing leverage, camouflaged wherever possible, so as to raise equity values, essentially depending on abnormal strength of irrational forces).

Question 4, Part 3

Simonnot: If there had been no Gold Exchange standard, would the course of US monetary policy have been less damaging?

Brown: Take first the situation between the US dollar and sterling.

Certainly the critics faulted Benjamin Strong for deliberately easing Fed policy at two key junctures (1924 and 1927) to help with the task of getting and then keeping sterling on the gold exchange standard (in fact gold bullion standard which resembled in effect a dollar standard as explained in answer to question 3). There were no "rules of the game" of the gold exchange standard which forced the Fed to act in that way. And as a practical matter, with gold held by the Fed far above the legal minimum required (related to liabilities outstanding) this institution had considerable scope to set monetary conditions independently of current gold flows.

Governor Strong could have told his friend at the Bank of England (Norman) that the answer to the pound's weakness should lie with British monetary policy not with demands that the US abandon sound money. The Bank of England should allow bouts of weakness to exert their full influence on interest rates (via contraction of the monetary base in Britain); accordingly, these would move sharply higher on occasion, convincing markets that the British authorities were not undermining the new standard. Commitment meant that the authorities would not act to thwart a downward adjustment of prices in the British economy if that is what monetary flows under the fixed exchange rate with the dollar brought about (and it is far from certain that this would be the case).

As regards the famous (or infamous) easing of Fed policy in 1927, the trigger to this seems to have been foremost Strong's concern to shore up a faltering US stock market (he described this as a coup de whiskey for Wall Street to Emile Moreau, the Bank of France governor) (see Pollock 2013). In fact, Reichsbank President Schacht begged Strong not to cut the discount rate for fear that this would intensify the flood of speculative funds into Germany. (Early in 1927, the Reichsbank had taken direct monetary action to burst the Berlin stock market bubble, which crashed subsequently in May of that year.)

Question 4, Part 4

Simonnot: Isn't it also necessary to take account of the decision of Winston Churchill, then Chancellor of the Exchequer, to restore (28.4.1925) sterling to its pre-war parity of \$/£4.86? Subsequently, Churchill confessed to his doctor that it was the biggest blunder of his life. And in "The Economic Consequences of Mr. Churchill" John Maynard Keynes poses the question "why did he do such a stupid thing?" Let's remember that in the context of an actual continuing fall at that time of British prices the pound had climbed on the eve of Churchill's decision to \$/£4.81 (it was \$/£ in February 1920). Should one not indeed have profited from this situation to re-establish the pound in its previous glory (5 centimes more or less difference from actual market rate)? And wasn't it praiseworthy to permit the Bank of England to respect the exchange rate commitments that it had made vis-à-vis holders of sterling?

Brown: What was Churchill's biggest blunder?

One might have thought the Dardanelles campaign of 1915 in which 250,000 Allied soldiers lost their lives in the ill-fated mission he approved as Britain's Admiralty Chief (a Cabinet position). How could Churchill have thought "returning sterling to gold" was a bigger blunder?

There is only one way to make sense of this: that sterling's return to gold in the form Churchill selected was a significant factor in the US following the fatal path of monetary inflation which culminated (via fantastic credit bubble and then bust) in German economic and political collapse, opening the way to the Second World War. Biographies do not suggest that Churchill was ever aware of this possible cause for remorse. The issue, however, is surely important to consider in serious counterfactual history of these years.

Formally, Churchill put the pound on to a gold bullion standard at the pre-war parity to the US dollar. The rise of the pound ahead of that was largely speculatively driven—with markets anticipating Churchill's decision. And yes, the rise in the pound did press wholesale prices down (in Britain), useful preparation for the move. Whether sterling was overvalued at 4.86 in fundamental terms according to purchasing power parity (taking account of a wider span of prices than wholesale) in 1925 has been extensively debated (see Gerlach and Kugler 2015) with generally non-striking results. In broad terms, estimates range from overvaluation of 5% or a little more, to slight undervaluation.

This all begs the broader issue. Under a fixed dollar–sterling exchange rate system where money flows are not sterilized by the British authorities and all actors (producers, consumers, traders) have full confidence in their commitment to the parity, flexible adjustments downwards or upwards of prices (of goods and services) will be part of the process for guiding the real exchange rate (the fixed nominal exchange rate adjusted for relative fluctuations in prices) along an equilibrium path, without anyone having to make bold estimates about where this lies.

Looking through form to substance, Churchill in effect put the pound on a dollar standard (at pre-war exchange rate parity). The US already had considerable scope to run an independent monetary policy. The vast sales of gold (by Britain and France) in the US during the period of neutrality had swollen the gold holdings of the Federal Reserve. In consequence, at its discretion it could now manage huge holdings of government debt (in open market operation) given the large surplus over legal requirements (so-called free gold reserves). Changes in legislation facilitating Fed holding of government debt had also occurred once the US entered the war. In all, gold flows no longer exerted a constraint on Fed monetary operations under normal circumstances (technically there were large free reserves of gold at the Federal Reserve). Britain's own monetary policy would have to take its lead from the US, given its commitment to the fixed parity for sterling against the dollar.

Benjamin Strong, however, at times took deliberate monetary action to spare the Bank of England having to effect the tough tightening of monetary policy that would have defeated speculative attacks on sterling. In general, Strong's policy of monetary inflation spared the Bank of England from having to allow monetary conditions to bear down on domestic prices if need be. ("Need be" because who knows whether a stronger commitment to sound money in Britain at that time, albeit signalled initially by monetary toughness, might have strengthened long-term capital inflows, both into sterling and into UK real assets, meaning a sustained fall in British prices would not be essential to sustain parity.)

Could Churchill have insisted on British monetary policy being run such as to build confidence in the restored parity, meaning no truck with Keynes and fellow-thinkers who criticized the return to gold?

Keynes at this stage was not on record as against the gold standard (see conclusion to this dialogue). However, he argued that the pound should have been devalued first, and he criticized the US for not having allowed gold inflows to increase the money supply to the extent as would have happened under the automatic rules of the full pre-1914 gold standard. That latter criticism was at best ingenuous. With no large or medium-sized country except for the US on a full gold coin standard, mimicking the automatic rules of the pre-1914 gold standard had little sense or meaning from a US or global perspective. In any case, the huge sales of gold in the US by France and Britain during the period of US neutrality in the First World War had resulted in the Fed's gold holdings being well above the legal minimum as specified in terms of its notes and deposits outstanding, meaning that there was now no strict in-built link between gold inflows into the US and monetary base.

As the future was to reveal, Bank of England chief Montagu Norman was an "appeaser" (see question 6), consistent with him in this flashback having no deep commitment to a founding block of free society—sound money. His ostensible backing for Sterling's "return to gold" was in a highly corrupted form. His thinking appears to have been in line with the Treasury (and with Keynes) on the point that the US should pursue an "expansionary" (in effect inflationary) monetary policy so as to contribute to monetary stabilization in Europe and in particular giving a helping to hand to sterling's "return to gold". They had no thought or premonition about how inflationary Fed policy, by generating a global credit bubble whose epicentre would be US lending into Germany, could destroy the dawning international order including the infant and fragile German democracy. Instead their concern was to provide scope for the British monetary authorities to manage interest rates for broader economic purposes (such as accelerating cyclical expansion), an idea which the Fed, as the central bank of the new monetary hegemon, had put into practice in the aftermath of the steep 1919/20 recession. No mention by the British advocates of more US monetary inflation that the US already had experienced a great monetary inflation during the First World War (including the period of US neutrality) and that the overhang from this, in terms of malinvestment and continued mal-signalling of capital market prices, was likely persisting into the 1920s (a factor in why the eventual bust was so great) notwithstanding the sharp recession of 1920–21. A new dose of monetary inflation, even if ostensibly milder, would surely not aid the healing process. The recession could not on its own have repaired the signalling function of capital markets; this would depend on a sustained period of sound money—but that was not to be. For example, over-sensitivity to narratives without due scepticism and positive feedback loops of unusual strength (from capital gains to expectations)—all aspects of asset inflation—could still be "built in" to market reflexes, ready to create extreme malfunctioning when monetary inflation resumed.

We could turn Keynes's polemic "The Economic Consequences of Mr. Churchill" with its theme of "how could he be so stupid?" on its head to "What was Mr. Keynes thinking?"; US monetary inflation was the curse of this age. The polemics of Keynes against gold in the context of sterling's "return to the gold standard" at the 1914 parity (he was not yet writing against gold money in principle), like those in different form and age by Bryan (see question 2) (who similarly did not attack gold in principle but rather the decision to demonetize silver—effectively abandoning bi-metallism), had market and economic impact, damaging for the country where sound money was under attack (by stimulating flight of capital, which meant interest rates had to rise so as maintain exchange rate or gold parity; this market power of Keynes' words depended on his ideas empowering forces in the political arena). The damage of Keynes's polemics spread much further afield. They came at a time when the Fed was already pursuing monetary inflation. And they provided a globalist veneer of respectability for the economic propaganda of National Socialism in Germany.

We have discussed already how the Fed took an inflationary course in the aftermath of the 1920 Great Recession. This had global consequences given that the US was now the monetary hegemon in the new regime emerging to replace the pre-1914 gold standard, whether global dollar standard or gold exchange standard. And this raises the larger point. Churchill had a more important implicit choice to make—whether to go along with regime change as now occurring, and have the pound join the dollar standard (at the pre-war parity for the dollar–sterling exchange rate as then determined by gold coin arbitrage), or whether to take the pound back on to a full gold standard (with circulating gold coin).

If a full gold standard, should the pound return at pre-war parity or should it have its gold content cut (and so a devalued parity against the dollar)? Given the post-war shortage of gold in Britain (after so much had been sold during the war), the return to a full gold standard would have required somehow the British monetary authorities building up their gold reserves. In principle, this could be done by the floating of a mega-loan in New York (the proceeds converted into gold in the US), but the prospects for a successful issue were not great given the huge amount of Allied war debt to the US and doubts about its future solvency. A devaluation of the pound might have been a catalyst to a huge balance of payments surplus for Britain (both on current and capital account of the balance of payments) and a related accumulation of gold, but there was considerable inflation danger along the way and potential US retaliation (in the form of tariffs or quotas). The Smoot-Hawley tariff was successfully making its way through Congress before the 1929 Crash.

Alternatively, Britain could have attracted huge capital inflows (and gold accumulation alongside) by rigorous pursuit of sound money policies hopefully accompanied by economic renaissance. (By contrast, continuing doubts as to the soundness of British monetary conditions, encouraged by episodes of the authorities opposing an automatic tightening of the money market in response to any drain of gold and foreign exchange, would strengthen the obstacles to free market forces including creative destruction.) The British pound as a sound money with relatively high interest rates could have posed significant competition for the US dollar undermined by the Benjamin Strong monetary inflation. In turn, as the pound's reputation grew, the flow of gold to Britain from the US (the counterpart to a global monetary shift towards sterling) might have been on a sufficient scale to cut short the Strong monetary inflation. That would have been good news for all, including the US and Germany.

Indeed, a powerful argument even from a strictly domestic viewpoint (in London) for a return by Britain to a full gold standard would have been that this would reduce US monetary hegemony (which was proving to be inflationary) in the new order (meaning that the US had less scope to impose monetary inflation or other types of monetary error on the global economy). The greater potential gold flows in and out of the US, for example, would have constrained the scope for independent (and in fact inflationary) US monetary policy. Britain might have become a component of a self-regulating gold standard world rather than a US monetary satellite.

There was an obvious attraction in trying to get such advantage without a high amount of monetary pain first—hence the superficial attraction of the pound returning to a full gold coin standard at a devalued rate. That option was in any case far from certain success. One particular risk, in addition to the US trade retailiation danger, was that capital inflows into Britain following the devaluation might disappoint the expectations that these would adequately replenish gold reserves. If one devaluation, with its related inflation tax on holders of the pound, why not further devaluations? Attempting to start a new era of pound soundness with a windfall tax on its (monetary) customers might not be such a great idea, where trust is the "name of the game".

The option of a full return to the gold standard for sterling (meaning sterling convertible into gold coin not just bullion bars of 400 oz) in whatever way (either with or without devaluation first) would have been contrary to the Genoa Conference's declaration in favour of the Gold Exchange Standard (in which senior British Treasury officials had played a lead role in framing), but surely that was just a detail for a strong Chancellor with an expert advisor chosen for his or her ideological commitment to sound money. This was not the situation in London at that time, the true pity of Mr. Churchill's sterling policy.

Let's proceed to consider the situation between the US dollar and the Reichsmark. Here it is plausible that the gold exchange standard contributed to financial instability, but this was on the premise of the US pursuing unsound money. Given the fixed parity between the mark and the dollar, the Reichsbank could not tighten domestic monetary conditions in line with the fantastic economic boom in the Weimar Republic (1924–27) and evidence of asset inflation (including not just German stock market, but also German loan market and Berlin real estate).

If the mark-dollar rate had been floating, then the Reichsbank could have tightened policy irrespective of US monetary inflation and this would have been accompanied by the mark rising to a temporarily much higher level. The boom–bust cycle in Germany would have been lessened. Of course, floating the mark was a political no-no at the time; it would have been a direct break with the Dawes Plan and could have triggered highly destabilizing inflation fears given the recent hyperinflation (1922–3).

Question 4, Part 5

Simonnot: You use in your answers to this question the term "monetary hegemony". Is this a figure of speech (the transposing of a military or political term to our subject) or is it a concept which has its own meaning for economists (like monopoly)? And in what way does it apply to the dollar of this period?

Brown: A crucial aspect of hegemony in international monetary economics is the power of a given monetary authority in one country to influence monetary conditions outside. As you say, the origin of the term is in military analysis, but the concept has spread into economic analysis. There is no one standard definition which all economists would accept and there are indeed considerable nuances in the literature (see Eichengreen 1987a, b).

Under the pre-1914 gold standard, there is no strong case for talking about monetary hegemony, at least according to the concept presented here (see Spahn 2001; Green 2018; and Eichengreen, 1987b for alternative views). World gold supplies set the path of the monetary base for the whole global system. There was no role for monetary policy making by any national (or for that matter supranational) authority. (There could be periods where persistent large net capital flows into one country responding to unusual investment opportunity could go along with relative monetary ease there for a considerable time.)

The point here is controversial. After all Keynes maintained that pre-1914 "the sway of London on credit conditions throughout the world was so predominant that the Bank of England could have claimed to be the conductor of the international orchestra". And some economists have taken their cue from this remark (see summary in G. Green 2018).

The facts do suggest that the Bank of England did indeed have some limited scope to influence conditions in the sterling money markets. But if this occurred on a sustained or powerful basis contrary to the gold flows consistent with the automatic rules of the gold standard, the Bank would have had to change course. Hence, hegemony in the Keynesian description seems to be a description of a dance in monetary tactics rather than of monetary power relationships.

The "seizing up" of the international gold standard at the outbreak of the First World War, the virtually simultaneous launch of the Federal Reserve, and the vast depletion of European gold reserves (sold in the US to pay for supplies of war materials) changed all this. The Federal Reserve now had considerable scope to set the path of monetary base growth in the US independently of fluctuations in gold reserves. The Fed's holdings of the yellow metal had swollen tremendously during the period of neutrality in ways which created a large margin of "free reserves" even despite matching monetary base growth. That margin, together with legislative changes once the US entered the war, enabled this institution to undertake huge open market operations in Treasury debt (see Koning 2009). In the post-war years potential flows of gold in and out of the US had diminished given that foreign countries were (from 1919) largely using dollar reserves rather than gold to hold their exchange rates at parity with the US currency or otherwise manage their floating exchange rate. A national US monetary policy was now feasible. At certain points, though, gold flows out of the US, so long as the US dollar remained fully convertible into gold (as from 1919–1933), could set limits to safe monetary base growth (in terms of not endangering convertibility).

The US became the global monetary hegemon already in 1919 (let's exclude from present discussion the special situation during the First World War). In the pursuit of its national monetary policy, the Federal Reserve had serious influence over global monetary conditions—far in excess of what any other central banks possessed. It was using and brandishing a supplementary tool of monetary management (albeit constrained by monetary base growth, itself determined by the Fed)—interest rate policy designed to achieve objectives such as stimulating the recovery phase of the business cycle (see introduction to this dialogue). The tool was an important component of hegemony. All this runs counter to the view of Kindleberger (see Meardon 2013) that there was no hegemon in this period and that was the problem (for global monetary stability). Let's explain the difference in viewpoint.

The hypothesis of US monetary hegemony at this time is closely associated with the Fed resolving after the Great Recession of 1920–21, for which it received much blame, not to allow any decline in goods prices overall, such as would have occurred under a full gold standard. There was great political push-back to stabilize prices rather than allowing these to fall under the influence of the contemporary industrial revolution (and associated spurt in productivity growth) and commodity glut. And at least on two occasions through the 1920s, the Federal Reserve forcefully injected monetary base into the system either to drive economic recovery (as in 1921–22) or resist a threatened asset market pull-back (1927).

These inflationary conditions in the US were the decisive factor in stimulating the colossal credit bubble in the Weimar Republic. The global monetary environment and its huge dangers were determined by the Federal Reserve. The Bank of England was not even a minor player—with its efforts all devoted to avoiding any domestic monetary contraction in its battle to sustain the restored parity between the dollar and sterling.

For Kindleberger, monetary hegemony meant something else—the power to manage and determine international monetary relations as between governments and central banks (see Meardon 2013). On this definition there was no monetary hegemon in the interwar period and he argues that this situation meant there was no international lender of last resort in crisis.

Hypothetically, Kindleberger suggests that without a powerful monetary hegemon there was no safety break to avoid the catastrophe of the German banking crisis in 1930–31. Britain, once the leader of the orchestra, was no longer up to the task (in fact, at the moment of maximum crisis it turned inwards and embarked on a beggar your neighbour devaluation)—and the US was not in tune with its responsibilities as a now lead player. Hence, his contention that the system works best when there is one super-powerful hegemon, rather than two or several lesser hegemons, according to his definition.

Kindleberger's concept of monetary hegemony rests heavily thereby on ideas about saving the system and global lenders of last resort. These smack largely of benign intervention rather than nurturing the invisible hands of free market capitalism.

Moving beyond the historical example of the 1920s, how can we best define monetary hegemony for the purpose of analysing contemporary international economic and financial outcomes?

Hegemony is starkly evident in the case of countries which peg their currencies to the US dollar. The holding of the peg depends on the authorities there convincing all that convertibility of their currency into the US dollar (without exchange restrictions) at the given parity is the essence of their monetary regime. If successful, that means there is no national monetary policy. Monetary conditions are set by the US link. That was the case for Germany between 1958 and 1968 under the Bretton Woods System, subject to some reservations regarding the revaluation of the Deutsche mark in 1961.

In today's world, most currencies are floating against the US dollar, including the key rates of the yen and euro (and previously the Deutsche mark). What does dollar hegemony mean here?

First, most monetary authorities around the world are sensitive to the course of their exchange rate against the dollar. If the pursuit of their national monetary policy goes along with an exchange rate fluctuation which causes considerable stress to a politically important group within their country, then they would bend so as to alleviate conditions. In this sense, the national monetary authority has limited scope to pursue a monetary policy stance at divergence to that of the US. For example, if the latter is involved in an inflationary binge ahead of election time (such as the George W. Bush Administration from 2003–04), the foreign monetary authority in defying this could cause the national currency to head for the sky. Such defiance may well be politically impossible.

Second, US monetary policy is a determinant of speculative temperature around the globe. If the Federal Reserve is pursing monetary inflation which features strong asset inflation—stimulating powerful carry trades as dollar-based investors reach for yield by taking aggressive positions in credit risk, term risk, currency risk, illiquidity and also become unusually receptive to various speculative narratives (which can bolster their perceived returns from going into risk-assets)—this can have profound effects on asset markets also throughout the non-dollar world. The widespread corruption of asset market price signalling means scope for considerable mal-investment globally, not just in the US. Risky credit, equities and real estate in emerging markets and elsewhere (Europe and Asia for example) become hot, albeit that much of this is hedged back into dollars by the investors concerned. The non-dollar currencies with yields higher than in the US get bid up in the currency carry trades beyond what could be rationally justified (perhaps related to narratives which under sober rationality would not be widely believed—but the monetary inflation encourages irrationality).

Yes, the foreign monetary authorities could try to shelter their economies from this speculative tide by even tightening domestic monetary conditions and allowing their currencies to rise to the sky in the short run. But as we have seen, there are very strong political forces which would work against that. Rather than accept a perhaps lengthy contraction of the traded goods and services sectors, as a cost of the defense effort against the US monetary menace, why not bend domestic monetary conditions in the inflationary direction of the Federal Reserve?

The ultimate basis of the dollar hegemony as described here is the size of the US economy (or perhaps more accurately of the US dollar zone, which includes the US and all countries whose currencies are pegged to the US dollar) and the partly related predominance of the dollar's role as an international money. Many investors outside the US "think in US dollars": this is their reference currency and along with that much of their borrowing and lending is in that currency. Other factors in the predominance include relative confidence in US monetary authorities (e.g. presently travelling less far into the forest of non-conventional monetary policies than Europe and Japan; in the past, a gold link of sorts as under Bretton Woods would also work in that same direction) and also the depth or liquidity of US asset markets.

Question 4, Part 6

Simonnot: But how does the great power in question (here the US) profit from its monetary hegemony? Is it from running a deficit without tears as Jacques Rueff maintained? Or are there other advantages? Are there not some disadvantages from being the monetary hegemon—for example, an obligation to take account of how domestic policy decisions spillover abroad, even if Connally claimed in 1971 that the dollar is our money but your problem. Another downside (of hegemony) is having to run a current account deficit so as to provide the world with dollars, culminating in a weakening of the dollar (Triffin paradox). Just as geopolitical hegemony requires additional military expenditure doesn't monetary hegemony impose a cost which counterbalances its eventual advantages?

Brown: The most profound way in which the US could gain from its monetary hegemony would be to use this towards exporting a sound money regime to the rest of the world.

Take the case where the US were indeed under a sound money regime—meaning a well-pivoted monetary base growing at very low rates, interest rates freely determined without intervention both in short and long-term markets, and prices of goods and services fluctuating both downwards and upwards but with a tendency over the very long run to revert to the mean.

Then most countries would decide to peg their currencies to the US dollar. Why suffer the costs of exchange rate volatility and the challenges of establishing independent sound money conditions for smaller currencies, when the benefits of soundness could be achieved as a member of the dollar zone? The US economy and foreign economies would gain from the end of currency wars (competitive devaluations) and from the general flourishing globally which would go along with the spread of monetary soundness.

As the hegemon, interest rates on the dollar would tend to be somewhat lower than those abroad. This premium on foreign interest rates would reflect differentials in liquidity, and residual devaluation risk however tiny. Hence, there would be an added advantage for the US of a somewhat lower cost of capital—meaning a stronger momentum in the long run of capital accumulation. This would spur the rise of general living standards within the US.

In sum, dollar hegemony when applied towards sound money, benefits all, both in the US and abroad. But we can identify some specific benefits for the US.

Connally's remark (in your question) about the US dollar being our money but your problem demonstrates a total incomprehension of these points—a blindness of the Nixon Administration (in which Paul Volcker as under-Secretary of Treasury was a prime mover on currency policy—see Salerno 2019) which was to cost the US (and the globe) dearly.

Yes, as Connally implicitly noted, the US had considerable scope, in view of its monetary hegemony, to launch inflationary monetary policies (towards pump-priming the US economy in the run-up to the 1972 elections). A smaller less powerful country doing the same thing would have experienced an immediate currency collapse adding to immediate inflation pressures domestically.

The US by contrast was able to delay the dollar's fall (given the fixed exchange rate system prevailing anchored on the dollar and in any case the reluctance of many foreign countries to experience sharp currency appreciation). But the monetary inflation created by the Arthur Burns Fed in the years 1970–72 came home to roost with the highest peacetime inflation and the greatest recession plus asset market slump from 1973–75 since 1929–33. The slumps outside the US which fed back to the US (making the slump there even worse) owed their severity to how far foreign countries had followed the US monetary lead as set by Messrs. Connally and Burns (albeit that the latter had been against the closing of the gold window in 1971—see Salerno 2019).

There is another way in which the Nixon-Burns inflation and the export of this to the rest of the world came home to roost. Far from the dollar being the foreigner's problem only, US citizens would suffer huge opportunity loss from

4 From Birth of Dollar Hegemony Towards the 1929 Crisis

monetary wildness due to damage insurance claims. These would emerge in the form of opportunity loss related to the depletion of US gold reserves in the years 1962–71 under the Great Monetary Inflation (which continued through to 1978 with brief remissions). Also, one should consider the opportunity loss of US citizens who were legally prohibited from holding gold during these years—a prohibition which contributed to the severe undervaluation at that time of the yellow metal (and thereby cheap insurance for foreigners against US monetary havoc).

European central banks (Germany, France and Italy) were at the forefront of those turning dollars into gold at the US Treasury window (which remained open until August 1971 despite the freeing of the gold market for non-US private transactors from early 1968). In effect, foreign countries could take advantage of a vastly undervalued gold price given the inflation that the US was unleashing on the globe and the global monetary chaos in its wake. Eventual huge rises in the price of gold meant that foreign countries who had built up gold in part as an insurance against wild US monetary policy and its consequences obtained handsome compensation (the counterpart being US citizens who had given up some potential gains on their government's gold reserves).

The optimist on the global monetary future could say this re-balancing of official gold stocks from the US to Europe as driven by US monetary inflation in the 1960s could make an international gold standard again possible for the first time since 1914 (at a much higher gold price). All, including the US, could be the gainer from that. Well, perhaps "everything is for the best in the best of all possible worlds", but this was certainly not the intended destination of policy makers in the US hegemon!

Let's consider the issue of the US tending to run current account deficits as the counterpart to global demand for dollar investments, a feature of the dollar hegemony. These deficits should not be seen as a cost for the US. Rather, they reflect the greater investment which takes place in the US in consequence of overseas accumulation of dollar assets; and as above this goes along with greater US prosperity (greater amount of capital per unit of labour). A permanent US current account deficit reflecting an advantage of the US in attracting capital which flows into greater than otherwise capital spending should not obviously trigger dollar weakness at any point.

There is no long-run cost which the US must bear to support these benefits of monetary hegemony (different from the case of military hegemony which must be based in part on defence spending). Rather, there is essential self-discipline. The US would have to abstain from periodic bouts of monetary inflation or more permanent monetary inflation. Historically this has not been possible. Political forces in the US have brought about generally unsound monetary conditions. Often these have been triggered initially by the pursuit of short-term election gains for the Administration in power.

Also, throughout the 100-year history of US monetary hegemony there has been an almost continuously dominant view in the US political system that "monetary management" can produce better results than a pure sound money regime. And there have been long periods of explicit monetary inflation pursued towards holding down the cost of government debt.

The historical record has shown that the US has lost from its abuse of monetary hegemony to pursue unsound monetary policies and export these to the rest of the world, whatever the short-run gains which could be identified. In the 1922–27 period, the Fed's stimulatory policies created a vast global credit bubble; the fantastic boom and bust of credit and assets in the Weimar Republic, directly a result of Fed policies, was a hugely powerful catalyst eventually to Great Depression in the US (and some would say world war).

Though there were sub-periods during the great US monetary inflation of 1962–78 when the US might have seemed to be making gains at the cost of foreign countries, the overall outcome for the US and the globe was almost certainly worse than what would have transpired under sound US monetary conditions. And we could say the same about the almost two decades since Greenspan and Bernanke, under the direction of the Bush Administration, resolved to breathe inflation "back into the US economy" in 2003.

References

Brown B. (2015). *A Global Monetary Plague*. London: Palgrave.
Eichengreen, B. (1987a). Conducting the International Orchestra: Bank of England Leadership Under the Classical Gold Standard. *Journal of International Monetary Finance, 6*, 5–29.
Eichengreen, B. (1987b). *Hegemonic Stability Theories of the International Monetary System*. NBER Working Paper 2193, March 1987.
Gerlach, S., & Kugler, P. (2015). *Back to Gold: Sterling in 1925*. CFS Working Paper no. 515, Goethe University.
Green, G. (2018). *Monetary Policy Spillovers in the First Age of Financial Globalization 1884–1913*. Bank of England Working Paper 718, March 2018.
Koning, J. (2009). *How the Fed Helped to Pay for World War One*. Auburn: Mises Institute.
Meardon, S. (2013). *On Kindleberger and Hegemony: From Berlin to MIT and Back*. Bowdon College Working Paper 29, September 2013.

Meltzer, A. H. (2003). *A History of the Federal Reserve*. Vol. 1: 1913–51. University of Chicago.

Pollock, A. (2013). *The Fed Is as Bad as Knowing the Future as Everyone Else Coup de Whiskey in 1927* (Statement Before House Committee on Financial Services) September 2013.

Salerno, J. T. (2019). *Paul Volcker: The Man Who Vanquished Gold*. Mises Wire.

Spahn, H.-P. (2001). The Hegemony of the Pound Sterling in Gold Standard. In *From Gold to Euro* (pp. 97–125). Springer Verlag.

5

Explaining 1929

Question 5

Simonnot: Let's turn now to the crisis erupting in 1929. According to the well-known account of Milton Friedman, the Fed could have avoided the cataclysm by increasing the supply of money. This thesis has subsequently had an influence not just on economists but also on policy makers whether in government or central banks. At a ceremony in honour of the 90th birthday of Friedman at the University of Chicago in 2002, Ben Bernanke, who was not yet Fed Chair but a Fed Governor, declared "I would like to say to Milton and Anna (Anna Schwartz, co-author of Monetary History of the US), regarding the Great Depression you are right, we did it. We are very sorry. But thanks to you we won't do it again" (see Bernanke 2002). And in fact, as Chair of the Fed, Bernanke turned to administering the Friedmanite kitchen recipes. Certainly one must give credit to Friedman for having contributed to the demolition of the idol of Keynesianism—which nonetheless is still worshipped in large parts of the world. But one must ask if one has not fallen from the Charybdis of Keynesianism to the Scylla of Friedmanism. Should the Friedman analysis of the Great Depression not be put radically in question, just as that of Keynes, which still has great influence?

Brown: That comment of Professor Bernanke to Milton Friedman on his 90th birthday is chilling ("You are right; the Great Depression was our fault; we are very sorry, but thanks to you, we won't do it again"). Not least, the use of "we", as if the Fed is some timeless community or state within a state with a collective mind, rather than a procession of diverse monetary bureaucrats, appointed by a succession of presidents each of whom had firm expectations as regards the likely nature of policy-decisions by his chosen monetary chief (and deputies). But let's get on to the main point; chilling, because the Fed did repeat a version of the same mistake in the years before the 2008 crash and Great Recession (and ahead of the next Crash and Great Recession) as in the years before the 1929 Crash and Depression (unleashing a great monetary inflation camouflaged—partly in the case of 1996–2007, wholly in 1922–29—in goods and services markets but not asset markets).

Friedman did not recognize that grand mistake. Instead, he writes about a much more problematic mistake: could the Fed have done more when the Crash and severe economic downturn arrived (never mind whether it was responsible for the arrival) to make it less severe?

Let's review first the "grand mistake" of Fed policy in causing the calamity; some of this already appears earlier in our dialogue. Murray Rothbard whose book *America's Great Depression* was published in the same year (1963) as Friedman and Schwartz's *Monetary History of the US* gives a very full account. In the aftermath of the deep 1920 recession, the Fed sought to stabilize prices, resisting any tendency for them to fall under the influence of rapid technological change or abundant new supplies of commodities or whatever. Artificially low interest rates played an infernal role in generating asset inflation (goods inflation disguised due to the factors mentioned), which emerged in real estate, equity markets, domestic credit markets (including fantastic financial engineering—specifically leverage), and crucially the international lending boom into the Weimar Republic (which after 1924 was perceived as a miracle—the "wonder-economy").

At the edges, constant nagging by Bank of England Governor Norman that his friend (Governor Strong) should help out the sickly pound (only sickly because Norman would not allow monetary conditions in Britain to tighten automatically in line with an "external drain") by running an easy monetary policy had some influence, though debatable how much. Fed policy would have been inflationary anyhow. When the asset inflation turned to asset deflation, the centre of the storm became Germany, the epicentre of the previous US-led asset inflation. The storm became pitch black, given the disastrous course of politics in that country (especially from the September 1930 general election onwards). The default of Germany (most of all its standstill on all foreign credits) in September 1931 was cataclysmic to the global financial system, as was the ensuing mega-devaluation and floating of sterling, precipitated by a flight of capital from Britain (the catalyst to this was the role of London banks in recycling loans into Germany which now had become frozen).

On top came the disastrous decision of the Fed to make a big hike of interest rates in autumn 1931 so as to pre-empt any more serious run on the dollar's gold status in the wake of the pound's floating; the Austrian school and monetarist historians agree that there was no justification for that hike in rates and that the gold reserves of the Federal Reserve banks would have remained quite adequate (to sustain the pledge of gold convertibility for the dollar) without it.

Friedman and Schwartz (1963) maintain that if the Federal Reserve had been a more assiduous provider of liquidity to failing banks in the US from the second half of 1930 and continuing through 1931 and into early 1932—and if in addition it had been an aggressive monetizer via purchases of government bonds (such open market operations did actually start in spring 1932, very belatedly according to Friedman, but still effective in generating a fitful recovery)—then there would have been no Great Depression. This is an extraordinary counterfactual assertion. The financial collapse in the Weimar Republic was a heavy blow to big US bank solvency and liquidity (US banks had been at the front of the lending boom, whether directly or to other banks which had been lending into Germany). And by this stage, the slide in US equity and real estate values added to the woes of general insolvency in the US banking system.

Yes, a Hoover-type moratorium in April 1931 rather than 1932 might have alleviated the crisis; but that did not happen and it did not come into Friedman's wonder-recipe. Strangely, Friedman does not even mention as significant the German crisis. Far from agreeing that the years (1924–27/28) leading up to the 1929 Crash were a period of monetary inflation, most apparent in asset inflation, he and his co-author describe them as the high tide of monetary policy making by the Federal Reserve.

Friedman claims that if the money supply had increased rather than being allowed to fall by 30% between 1930 and 1932 there would have been no depression. But first was it possible to achieve that monetary outcome, given that the money supply to monetary base ratio would likely have plummeted; and even if achieved, why should that have arrested the serious decline in spending, given all the other adverse factors. Perhaps this was not mission impossible; but the outcome is highly problematic, making it impossible to recommend for the future with any grounds for optimism.

There would be much more hope in the adoption of sound money policies which do not allow monetary inflation including asset inflation to get underway in the first place. Optimists on humanity can argue that German historical experience of that era was a once-only hell; and the Fed's grave monetary errors through the 1920s which were an essential pre-condition of that inferno should not keep recurring as has been the case during the past century. Pessimists have strong grounds for disbelief not least given the widespread denial of these errors both historically and contemporaneously.

Question 5, Part 1

Simonnot: Just to be precise, what do you mean by monetary base?

Brown: Monetary basis is in today's US context defined as the total of currency in circulation plus reserves held by the banks with the Federal Reserve. Under the gold standard, by contrast, if one tried to define the monetary base, it would be on a global basis and include above-ground gold supplies.

Simonnot: Above-ground gold supplies? Does that include jewellery and works of art in gold?

Brown: The standard answer would be to exclude jewellery, etc. Nonetheless, this wider demand for metallic gold (including jewellery) was one factor in the long-run tendency for prices of goods and services under the gold standard to revert to mean. Big price falls in other items of consumption would lead to less demand for jewellery (whose relative price given the fixed gold price would rise), and so some jewellery would be melted down into monetary gold, adding to the supply of money (helping to reverse ultimately the price falls): conversely for big price rises. In any event, under the gold standard no one was studying monetary base data as far as I know either for the global system as a whole or less meaningfully for one country (though in the US context, Milton Friedman and Anna Schwartz do retrospectively analyse a specifically US monetary base).

Simonnot: In *A Global Monetary Plague* (pp. 110 and 143) (Brown 2015), you write that the monetary base should pay no interest so as to function as a hot potato. A hot potato is a potato which the "holder" tries to get rid of as fast as possible so as not to burn his fingers. Is that how one should understand the nature of the monetary base?

Brown: Maybe hot potato is not the best description. My point is that monetary base when it pays no interest is expensive to hold (in terms of opportunity cost—interest income foregone). This expense means that holders actively try to economize on their holdings. And so, fluctuations in the money market rate of interest have direct impact on demand for monetary base (an increase means higher opportunity cost and holders try to economize more and conversely). Changes in money market interest rates are hence the means by which supply and demand for monetary base are in continuous balance. By contrast, once monetary base pays the "market interest rate", the latter in effect becomes a diktat of the central bank (interest rate pegging). And monetary base becomes virtually (but not totally) indistinguishable from say short-term Treasury bills. There will be no robustness to any estimated income-velocity of monetary base over the very long run as is a condition of this being the pivot of the monetary system.

Question 5, Part 2

Simonnot: A follow-on to the New Deal rarely mentioned by the apologies for Roosevelt and his "Keynesian policy" (as conducted before the publication of the General Theory 1936) is the recession of 1937–38. Alfred Sauvy was one of the few French economists to draw attention to it. He writes (Sauvy 1972): "In 1937–8, the US suffered a severe economic downturn in one year, from May 37 to May 38, industrial production fell by 35%, more quickly than in 1929. Yet historians have put a veil over this disaster". Unfortunately, he made this wise remark only in a note in small print at the foot of a page. How do you yourself explain this recession? What were its consequences and why have they been so hidden?

Brown: The severity of the downturn owed much (but not all) to the sudden passage of asset inflation which built up under the aggressive monetary stimulus from 1934–36 into asset deflation. That stimulus had taken the form of a massive increase in the monetary base which accompanied and followed the 1934 devaluation of the US dollar. In fact, the increase in monetary base as a proportion of GDP was comparable to that under Bernanke's QE policies from 2009–13. But nobody called it QE at the time. The increase was passive—the counterpart to huge capital inflows to the US after the devaluation—reflecting in part capital flight out of France and the rest of the gold bloc on speculation that this would fall apart and in part closing of previous speculation against the dollar. The Federal Reserve, cooperating with the Treasury, allowed the US official purchases of gold to add to the monetary base. There was no sterilization.

This all went along with the emergence of hot speculative temperatures in the US equity market and commodity markets through 1935 and especially 1936; goods and services prices re-bounded—likely by significantly more than just a benign cyclical rebound. There was evident growing concern about excess speculation and inflation and much chatter about how the Fed should tighten monetary policy; talk even circulated that the President could cut the price of gold. In late 1936, the Fed started slowly to normalize monetary policy, by hiking reserve requirements (thus reducing excess reserves), though money market rates hardly rose at all. Treasury bond yields started to climb.

By early 1937, the stock market started to experience considerable volatility and overall peaked, moving down decisively in late winter and early spring.

The Roosevelt Administration responded by exhorting the Fed to stabilize the bond market (interventions there brought the yield back down from its March 1937 peak at around 2.8% for 10-year Treasury issues) and repudiating any talk of dollar revaluation against gold. Equity markets stabilized and moved upwards through late spring. But then a sudden crash occurred in late summer against the background of economic data (and corporate news) which suggested a serious emerging downturn (in fact the NBER dates the start of the recession as May 1937). Alongside, geopolitical risks increased with Japan's invasion of China and the German re-militarization of the Rhineland: these were significantly negative for business confidence and thereby for capital spending decisions. The asset market deflation together with the economic slowdown worked on each other to produce an intense overall cyclical downturn driven by a plunge in capital spending.

The intensity of the recessionary forces gathering through spring and summer 1937 (these included the Supreme Court voting that New Deal labour union legislation was constitutional and dismay at big proposed rises in corporation tax following the landslide re-election of President Roosevelt the previous November) meant the monetary reversal (already in spring 1937 the Fed had moved back to ease) was not successful in bringing an extension of the economic expansion. Note also that there was little or no scope for monetary stimulus from the shrunken democratic world outside the US.

Bottom line: the earlier strong monetary stimulus played a key role (via the generation of asset inflation) in the severity of the 1937–38 downturn. The passage of asset inflation into deflation, whenever that occurred, would precipitate or aggravate a downturn of capital spending. The timing of that passage, however, depends also on factors unique to each business cycle, as detailed above.

Simonnot: What were the consequences of the Roosevelt recession?

Brown: The Administration doubled down on Keynesian economic policy (increased spending and budget deficits); the Fed abandoned the aim of monetary normalization. It is hard to judge the role these played in the subsequent strong recovery, as by now European re-armament was a big factor in overall spending and market action. Milton Friedman blamed the recession on Fed tightening; the Keynesians blamed the Administration for raising taxes through late 1936 and early 1937. Both diagnoses are likely wrong, identifying at best only a small part of the overall explanation, but they formed part of an intellectual folklore of the different economic camps.

Simonnot: Why was the recession hidden?

Brown: I don't think there was any hiding. If one reads contemporary accounts, as the annual report from the BIS, everyone at the time knew a serious recession in the US was taking place. Perhaps one factor in low prominence was the lack of global dimension; there was no simultaneous big recession in France and Britain (but yes, the contemporaneous Canadian recession was very severe). And Japan/Germany by then were out of the international economic order. Keynes apparently lost big in the market downturn—as always, he had backed his view of the world by speculating in markets; he could not foresee that the Roosevelt reflation of which he strongly approved would fail.

References

Bernanke, B. (2002). On Milton Friedman's 90th Birthday. Remarks by Ben S. Bernanke before the Conference to Honor Milton Friedman, University of Chicago, November 8, 2002.
Brown, B. (2015). *Global Monetary Plague*. London: Palgrave.
Friedman, M., & Schwartz, A. (1963). *Monetary History of the United States*. Princeton: University of Princeton.
Rothbard, M. (1963). *America's Great Depression*. Auburn: Mises.
Sauvy, A. (1972). *De Paul Reynaud a Charles de Gaulle. Un economiste face aux hommes politiques 1934–67* (p. 21). Tournai: Casterman, 1973.

6

How Gold Financed Nazi Germany

Question 6

Simonnot: We have already discussed the hypothetical case of how a survival of the international gold standard in 1914 would have shortened the European conflict, making it less murderous and less costly. Could we say anything similar about the war starting in 1940? Recall that in Nazi Germany the holding of gold was banned for individuals, as in Roosevelt's America or in the France of John Law in 1720.

Brown: How did the operation—or non-operation—of the gold standard influence the course of the Second World War?

Without doubt, as you suggest, the almost totally fiat regime around the globe in the Second World War (the exceptions being the limited monetary gold "convertibility" of the US dollar and the wider gold convertibility of the Swiss franc) did permit the raising of inflation tax (albeit with inflation suppressed by price controls and rationing) on an unprecedented scale. Thinking of gold's role in extending, starting or deepening the Second World War, it makes sense to focus on two specific issues.

First, there was the transfer of Czechoslovakia's gold reserves to the Reichsbank in May 1939. The Czechoslovak government held its gold in London (placed there technically via the intermediation of the Bank for International Settlements) and when Germany occupied Prague in March 1939, setting up a protectorate over the Czech Republic, the Bank of England recognized Berlin as the ultimate master of this gold. The Governor of the Bank of England, Montagu Norman, a friend of Hjalmar Schacht since the early 1920s and godfather of his son (a friendship which survived Schacht's growing orientation towards the National Socialists, his resignation as Reichsbank President in 1929 in belated protest against the Young Plan, his re-appointment in 1933 as Reichsbank President by Hitler), approved the transfer—intervention of Schacht, Minister without portfolio since January having "resigned" from the Reichsbank, is noted by Blaazer (2005)— and circumvented attempts of the British and French finance ministries to prevent this happening. From many accounts that transfer of gold played a key role in the German military buildup (not least in the hoarding of key commodities) in following months (otherwise Germany was virtually bankrupt), making a crucial difference to the early war outcomes.

Second, there was the continuous monetization in Switzerland of looted gold, whether from official entities, or private persons (including concentration camp victims), by the Nazi regime. The role of the Swiss National Bank and Bank for International Settlements in making this all possible has been well documented (see Brown 2018). The US did try to put breaks on the flow, not least by freezing Swiss dollar deposits (which sold for most of the 1941–44 period at far below official parity—that is, the Swiss franc expensive); Nonetheless, the Swiss franc's international role, especially in Latin America, facilitated the use of gold by Germany.

Comment

Simonnot: As to the Bank of France, as you now, it succeeded in sheltering its gold.

References

Blaazer, D. (2005). Finance and the End of Appeasement: The Bank of England, the National Government and the Czech Gold. *Journal of Contemporary History, 40*, 25–39.

Brown, B. (2018). *The Flight of International Capital*. London: Routledge.

7

Bretton Woods: The False Gold Standard

Question 7

Simonnot: We come now to the Bretton Woods agreements, signed 22 July 1944, when war was still raging in Europe. Three quarters of gold stocks held by central banks are (at this time) in the hands of the US. Would it have been possible to restore a true gold standard and to avoid the setting up again of the Gold Exchange Standard? Did we narrowly escape Keynes's designs for the "bancor"? The parity of 35 dollars per ounce of gold, imposed by Roosevelt on 30 January 1934, did this make sense?

Brown: Yes, Keynes's proposal for an international unit of account (and in some sense official money) the Bancor got nowhere at Bretton Woods. But, overall Keynes was successful in putting his imprint on the post-war global monetary system. The architecture was founded on a hostility towards free capital movements internationally, which can be traced to the view (shared by Keynes and championed by Nurkse (1944)) that speculative movements of money had been the root of disorder in the pre-war decade. It was only with the scrapping of all currency exchange controls by West Germany in the late 1950s (until then only US, Canada and Switzerland were without controls, the Canadian dollar floating) that a free global monetary order started to return. At its core was the Deutsche mark–dollar exchange rate. This was fixed but subject to adjustment, as in 1961 and 1969 (DM revaluations). By the start of the 1970s, this core was virtually broken. Indeed there had been an emergency floating of the DM ahead of its revaluation in Autumn 1969. There was broader frailty evident by then in the monetary "order" which had emerged at the end of the 1950s, including the partial closing of the US Treasury's gold window in Spring 1968.

So, we should not characterize the Bretton Woods System as a gold exchange standard in the sense of the inter-war years (1924–31). In particular, the dollar was convertible into gold only for non-US citizens and in practice until the late 1950s, that meant mainly for foreign official institutions given prevailing restrictions outside the US on private currency and gold transactions. Could the US have adopted a full gold standard in 1945 (as between 1919 and 1933)? Almost certainly yes; the official gold price of $35 an ounce then was far above the official price of the 1920s (20.65) when the US was on a full gold coin standard, and prices had roughly doubled since then (during the Second World War and its immediate aftermath). So $35 made sense as the conversion price (in a full gold standard), though the private demand for gold coin inside the US after so many years of restrictions (on private gold holding by US citizens) would have been unpredictable.

Could the defeated powers, Germany and Japan, have adopted full gold standards when they stabilized their monetary systems after episodes of hyper-inflation? This seems implausible, given the scarcity of gold or foreign exchange reserves in those countries. But after a subsequent decade or more of economic miracle and with the potential for huge capital inflows and trade surpluses under the regime of fixed exchange rates with the US dollar, the gold standard option surely existed further ahead. Preparation for this would have included the official accumulation of gold—which in fact happened through the 1960s in the case of Germany and France (courtesy of the US—see Question 4 Part 6). France's moment (for returning to gold) came and went briefly under President de Gaulle in the mid-1960s. In Britain, gold standard resumption never became a live political issue and would have required anyhow steps to build up gold reserves. Instead, through much of the 1960s Britain was pursuing inflationary monetary policies inconsistent even with sterling's fixed parity against the dollar (sterling eventually devalued in 1967) even despite the growing dollar inflation. Anyhow, "a return to gold" by the UK would have required the government to float a huge international loan for the purpose of buying up metallic gold reserves (at the US Treasury gold window): but how to navigate that in the 1960s when Washington was preoccupied with the so-called US balance of payments deficit (in fact a manifestation of US monetary inflation).

In sum, the gold exchange standard was not re-instituted at Bretton Woods in the original 1920s sense of that concept (which certainly includes free capital movements). Instead the agreements there set up a fake gold exchange standard—a dollar not convertible into gold for US citizens and most major foreign currencies with fixed (but adjustable) exchange rates against the dollar but subject to exchange restrictions on capital flows. This fake gold exchange standard, like the 1920s standard, did not constrain the US to follow sound money policies (except in the sense that ultimately failure to follow these brought the breakdown of the standard).

Question 8

Simonnot: One of the "arguments" of the OPEC ministers in their shock action of October 1973, in parallel with the outbreak of the Yom Kippur War, was that the dollar had lost value. In effect, two years earlier, in August 1971, Richard Nixon, then President of the US, had closed the "gold window" and implemented a devaluation of the dollar. What was the justification for such a repudiation of the solemn commitment of the US at Bretton Woods regarding the parity of the US dollar?

Brown: OPEC's attempt to justify the strengthening of its cartel (including severe output restrictions) in autumn 1973 by the need to catch up with the fall of the dollar was laughable (in fact, much worse). In a free market for oil without a cartel, the oil price in dollars would have risen as the greenback fell—as indeed happens across the commodity markets in general (explained by demand in non-dollar countries rising in dollar terms as the greenback falls). OPEC members could have argued justifiably that long-term contract prices should reflect such reality as illustrated in the spot markets—and have refused to enter into such contracts if the buyers showed no flexibility, putting its their supply into the spot market instead of the contract market.

As regards the more general question as to whether the US in summer 1971 had justification to break its "solemn commitment" to sustain the fixed gold parity of the dollar as per the Bretton Woods system, my short answer is yes. The excuses given and the follow-on policies decided upon by the Nixon Administration were in large part false and flawed. We should recall in any event that gold convertibility of the dollar at $35 fixed price came to an end in spring 1968 and was only preserved for official transactions which would be subject to diplomatic pressures (including requests from the US that its European partners not press for huge conversions at any point especially during periods of market tension).

Fundamentally, under the Bretton Woods regime for most of its life, gold was not at its pivot. The yellow metal only got near a pivot position when restrictions on capital flows in Europe and Japan started to fall away and when correspondingly the private gold market (most importantly for non-official transactions) grew rapidly after so many years of restricted access in most countries. By this point (in the mid-1960s) it is plausible that the official gold price of $35 per ounce was far below where supply and demand for the yellow metal would be in balance without first a powerful monetary deflation in the US (meaning a big fall of US prices).

After all, there had been a big cumulative rise of US prices and global real wealth in the preceding two decades, meaning a potential explosive increase in the demand for gold to match (at an unchanged official price), especially if US citizens were to be allowed again to hold it. What should the new gold price have been to reflect all this? No one knows of course. If the Nixon Administration had sought to go down the road of "the already partially blocked gold window of the Bretton Woods structure is finally closed; now a new gold window is fully open again at say $60 per ounce", there would have been huge uncertainty about the price path for goods and services which would follow over many years both in the US and abroad—though arguably lower than what transpired.

Reference

Nurkse, R. (1944). *International Currency Experience: Lessons of the Interwar Period*. Geneva: League of Nations.

8

The Strategic Choice for Germany

Question 9

Simonnot: What have been the consequences of Nixon's monetary system coup? How can we describe the exchange rate regime which it generated?

Brown: The real drama in summer 1971 was President Nixon and his Fed Chief deciding to persevere with a policy of great monetary inflation, all very much with the November 1972 elections in mind and conditioned by the apparent sluggishness of the cumulative economic upturn to date since the 1969/70 recession. (Over subsequent years the data during that recession have been revised so much that it is dubious whether this existed.) In fact, the key date in signalling the final collapse of the Bretton Woods edifice was the earlier decision of the German government and the Bundesbank to float the DM free of the dollar in May 1971. Contemporaries viewed that date as the beginning of the final end for "the Bretton Woods system" including its core component, the fixed DM–dollar rate.

The only way in which the US could have coaxed Germany back on to the dollar standard was to restore confidence in the Federal Reserve steering a non-inflationary path—and the job (of coaxing) would be difficult given the lack of commitment to dollar–gold convertibility even at a future date. Perhaps Bonn was prepared to give Washington the benefit of the doubt on this at the Smithsonian (December 1971); but a little more than a year later that confidence had melted away. The free float of the mark against the dollar—no longer in the sense of a transitory development until a new fix but of

© The Author(s) 2020
B. Brown, P. Simonnot, *Europe's Century of Crises Under Dollar Hegemony*,
https://doi.org/10.1007/978-3-030-46653-4_8

the new status quo—was the revolutionary change in the global monetary system at this time. The belief amongst responsible German monetary officials (including their political chiefs) was that the new doctrine of monetarism could salvage monetary stability at least for Germany (and perhaps a wider European DM area) in a world without a gold anchor where the US hegemon was prone to monetary inflation.

Japan, by contrast to Germany, was highly reluctant to break with the dollar standard, meaning no change in the yen–dollar parity, even after the "closing of the gold window" and even given all the signs that the Nixon Administration and its Fed were pursuing a highly inflationary path. But the Nixon Administration was determined to crush Japan's opposition to revaluing the yen, not least given all its rhetoric about unfair competitive advantages of foreign countries. The biggest "offender" (and the biggest trade surplus) was Japan.

In principle, Tokyo currency diplomats could have made the case that huge money inflows into Japan would boost prices there and that the country would lose competitive advantage (alongside a real appreciation of the yen even though fixed still in nominal terms versus the dollar). But President Nixon was a man in a hurry—and Tokyo gave in to the pressure to allow its currency to float upwards. Again, after the breakdown of the Smithsonian accord, Tokyo was keen to stick with the re-vamped dollar standard, but hot money flows were now irresistible whilst Washington had no interest in its partial reconstitution, embracing instead fully the "floating dollar" concept.

Some in the Nixon Administration were enthusiastic about Milton Friedman's case for floating exchange rates (Friedman 1953). The floating dollar against the mark and yen, however, came about not because of such fondness. Rather the key facts were first, Germany's understandable intolerance of US inflation and second, the intolerance of the mercantilists in Washington for Japan's "unfair" trade surplus.

Friedman did not spell out the crucial potential vulnerabilities of a floating exchange rate system to unsound US monetary policies. If the US were pursuing sound money policies, the rest of the world would want to peg their currencies to the dollar and be part of a sound US currency bloc. If by contrast the US embarked on unsound policies, a floating exchange rate system would emerge, but it would be inherently unstable as huge and volatile global capital flows driven by the ebb and flow of US monetary inflation would be the rule not the exception.

Reference

Friedman, M. (1953). *Essays in Positive Economics*. Chicago: University of Chicago Press.

9

For or Against Friedman

Simonnot: Put in another way, the victory of Friedmanite monetarism was an optical illusion. Nonetheless, monetarism became the fashionable theory of the time, Friedman taking until his death the role of guru once assumed by Keynes, seeming to inspire the monetary policies of central banks from 1971–72 onwards. These appeared to give themselves targets conforming to the quantity theory of money. For example, the supply of money should increase by x% per annum regardless of the perceived phase of the business cycle.

Question 10

Simonnot: Was it possible to agree on an adequate definition of the money supply?

Brown: Practical monetarism was based on many contradictions and arguable assumptions. The idea that we could identify a broad monetary aggregate for which the demand would be highly stable and the supply strictly under the control of the monetary authority never corresponded to reality, albeit passingly there were some encouraging empirical results in this field, including Friedman and Schwartz's monetary history (see Friedman and Schwartz 1963). (In part these results may have reflected an interest rate policy inconsistent with monetarism—a point made in the introductory essay to our dialogue).

The strictest strand of monetarism emphasized the pivotal role of the monetary base and advocated the setting of firm targets (of the form x% per annum) for the growth of this. Even so, the monetary base under a pure fiat money regime featuring large-scale deposit insurance and "too big to fail banks" has very different properties from under a gold regime. In the former, the actual demand for monetary base is quite narrow—at least as regards demand for reserves by the banks; demand for currency (essentially for banknotes) might be broader under certain conditions but highly sensitive to variables such as retail payment patterns (cards vs. cash for example) and fluctuations in interest rates which deprive it of a potential pivotal role on its own. (Demand for gold under a gold standard is interest elastic to some degree, essential to its operation, but not to such an extent as to dislodge the anchor to the monetary system.) The German monetarists sought to get around these problems of a purely fiat monetary base by stipulating high reserve requirements for the banks.

We should note further that under the gold standard the supply of monetary base does not increase in Friedmanesque fashion at x% per annum, but responds to changes in real demand. So, at times of rapid growth in economic prosperity, marked by similar productivity growth and downward pressure on prices, the supply of newly mined gold would get a boost in the long run (reflecting higher profits in the gold mining industry).

Question 11

Simonnot: Could one be confident that Friedman's quantity theory of money was valid?

Brown: Friedman's guiding principles to a moderate extent overlap those of sound money advocates; they are far, however, from being in alignment with each other. He was against rate pegging, price (and implicitly inflation) targeting, and against fine-tuning (contracyclical) policies. Yet he praises the price stability of the 1920s (1921–27), describing this as the high tide of the Federal Reserve (sound money advocates deplore this period arguing that prices should have been allowed to fall); and he writes about "helicopter money" as an appropriate (extreme) tool of stimulus. Friedman warns against the abuse of power by central bankers (though strangely he did pick a hero—Benjamin Strong, no. 1 policy maker in the Federal Reserve from its creation to his death in late 1927). In practice, Friedman favoured targeting a narrow money supply aggregate (M1) which at the time when he wrote was all non-interest bearing and cash like, though far from being wholly under the control of the central bank or enjoying a reliably broad stable demand.

Could practical monetarism have evolved to a better place than the present 2% inflation standard? The answer is yes, but as we discussed in early questions, Paul Volcker and later the Bundesbank (under Chancellor Kohl) aborted the monetarist journey. For monetarism to have evolved positively, there would have been much more work on how to build and expand monetary base so that it really could be a secure pivot to the monetary system. Yes, mission impossible in part under a fiat money regime, but in a world of imperfects, better than what occurred.

Question 11, Part 2

Simonnot: Do you really think that M1 (banknotes and coin in circulation plus sight deposits) could be the base of a viable monetary policy? Isn't such a policy condemned to failure on multiple scores?

Brown: I agree with you that M1 could not be a viable basis for monetary policy in the long run. Milton Friedman thought otherwise because his econometric estimates of demand for this aggregate had been stable for a considerable time. That was in the context of a highly regulated banking system. Given the technological revolution and deregulation ahead (meaning a big expansion of alternative means of payments especially via credit cards and other payment cards) together with alternative types of deposits (outside M1) which could be used to make payments on which interest was paid, the demand for M1 came to be on a sharply declining trend and highly volatile.

Question 11, Part 3

Simonnot: Take x (between 0 and 1) as the proportion of its loans which a bank funds from its own deposits, according to the well-known adage that loans make deposits. We abstract here from the required reserves held at the central bank. We can demonstrate in this situation that the amount of loans which this bank can make on the basis of its deposits is a multiple f, where $f = 1/(1 - x)$. If $x = 1$, meaning that the bank finances the entirety of its loans with deposits, then its potential loans are infinite. Now the technological revolution (in use of money) about which you speak, doesn't that have as consequence a considerable increase in x, approaching 1, thereby increasing hugely the potential lending capacity of the banks? Isn't this what explains the birth and rapidity of this revolution? The introduction of compulsory reserves, could it really be effective in preventing such a process? Wouldn't it be better to introduce a 100% reserve requirement as advocated by Murray Rothbard?

Brown: You raise a very important issue: in a world, where the demand for fiat monetary base has shrunk far (in part related to digitalization and related monopoly power of big tech and big banks—especially with respect to credit card/payment card use) and become highly unstable, is it possible to have sound money? Without base money firmly at the pivot of the monetary system then we have the infernal condition of central bank manipulation of interest rates.

The demand for base money cannot be stabilized and sustained on an enduring basis by high reserve requirements. As we saw in Germany in particular and also in the US, the powerful bank lobby rails against this implicit tax on bank deposits and eventually gets this watered down; and in the interim there are many ways around the requirements.

The 100% reserve requirement proposal is highly problematic. For a start, if banks can find a market for deposits which have low reserve backing why shouldn't they develop business in these, so long as buyers (the holders of these deposits) are fully informed of potential illiquidity and capital loss risks (no dependence in the marketing on implicit government support, whether as lender of last resort, too big to fail, or deposit insurance). Nonetheless, were banks to be regulated so as all their deposits had to be 100% reserve backed, then much of today's credit (including bank loans) would simply migrate into non-bank institutions and non-bank-mediated markets. Alternatively, if the banks themselves could issue a category of liability (e.g. "capital accounts"), exempt from reserves as not usable directly for payments or for cash withdrawals, there would be large-scale "regulatory arbitrage" (holders of the capital notes believing that these could be converted into transaction deposits virtually on demand).

(Just as an aside, the statement that loans make deposits is misleading—except in the case of the central bank. For commercial banks there is a "client market" for deposits; if any individual bank over-lends relative to its natural deposit base, then it has to go to wholesale markets or bond markets for funding and there are natural limits here [solvency, etc.]; and even if deposits created by the original bank against the loans end up with another bank, there is no reason why the latter would be automatically comfortable in lending back. Yes, there may be comfort if there is widespread deposit insurance, too big to fail, and effective central bank guarantees of interbank transactions, but none of this is essential.)

So what is to be done?

Some structural steps can be taken to increase demand for fiat base money and to stabilize this. These include first, severely limiting or scrapping deposit insurance—meaning that banks would have an enlarged demand for cash and deposits at the central bank; similarly scrapping too big to fail; abolishing issuance of very short-term Treasury bills so as to add to the distinctiveness of central bank deposits; and of course there must be no interest paid on reserves; introducing large denomination banknotes so as to make cash holding more convenient for the public and easier to use in big retail transactions; repealing perverse legislation and tackling monopoly abuse which in effect deprive users of cash from enjoying keener prices (examples include laws that stop retailers charging customers for using credit cards rather than cash). If all this were done, the demand for monetary base would be substantially larger and more stable than under the present regime (and the multiplier between monetary base, albeit always variable, far less arithmetically than at present)—but still highly unsatisfactory compared to the gold standard regime, where gold money is a much better pivot.

Question 11, Part 4

Simonnot: In the 1930s, according to the dominant financial doctrine in France, banks should only satisfy liquidity needs of the economy, providing short-term credit for that purpose. The financing of investments was not their function but was that of self-financing, capital markets or long-term credit institutions. The creation in the US in 1933 of the Federal Deposit Insurance Corporation was considered by French banks as "immoral" in that it only induced bad habits, relieving clients of the job of finding the most prudent banks and encouraging imprudent banks to abuse the "deposit multiplier" as discussed above. As to liquidity ratios and/or solvency ratios which the authorities proposed, even if they were defined and calculated correctly, they would not be useful for serious banks and would be illusory for other who would just "window dress" to achieve them. One is far today from such wisdom, which trusted in the invisible hand to guide bankers to act in the interest of their clients whilst respecting their privacy. Could one return to that situation and how? I do not ignore the law of large numbers or the economies of scale. But is there not a relation between deposits insurance and too big to fail on the one and the ravages of the system which we come on to discuss on the other?

Brown: Yes, deposit insurance creates perverse incentives. Deposits of banks are all of the same quality (up to the insurance limit) and sell at the same price regardless of the underlying risks. The regulator (insurer) seeks to keep these risks low and uniform, but the likelihood is that the bank can outwit the regulator.

The conventional distinction that banks which market sight deposits should maintain their assets in short-maturity liquid form is unduly rigid. Ideally, a market should develop in different qualities of deposits—some very low or zero risk (as would be the case for a bank which holds very high reserve levels, ultimately 100%), and others higher risk and paying commensurate interest rates. The deposits at the latter would evidently not under all conditions be repayable at par on demand. Rather there would be a stipulation that the bank can suspend repayment at par and issue new short-maturity certificates instead. That would occur under circumstances of illiquidity and would not usually amount to insolvency; indeed, in pre-civil war US, there were periodic episodes of widespread "note convertibility suspension" when banks would suspend repayment in notes and these would rise to a premium over deposits.

Savers/individuals who did not in any way want to incur such a risk of emerging discount would concentrate their deposits in the very safe banks and get no or very low interest. For such a system to work efficiently, independent agencies (in private sector) would monitor bank balance sheets and the related businesses and issue ratings on the quality of the deposits; there would have to be a high level of transparency and of course big penalties for dishonest representation. One would suspect that under such a system, small savers would gravitate towards the very safe banks and get no interest whilst wealthier individuals and businesses would put part of their money holdings in the riskier banks. And in assessing riskiness of deposits there would be two elements—first, the level of cash reserves held by the bank; second (and ultimately more important), the equity capital in the bank (as a share of deposits) and the overall riskiness of its assets. A bank with high-quality assets (some long-term) and intense equity funding would be able to market high-quality deposits without holding anything like 100% reserves—as in all circumstances this bank would be able to raise funds.

Is it at all likely that we will get to such a free market in deposits? No, not under present social/economic conditions and given dominant popular views which now form the consensus. But none of this is set in stone. Revolutions in this area can occur, in some respects more likely during a period of prosperity than the contrary.

Question 11, Part 5

Simonnot: There is no free lunch as you know. If the rate of interest on sight deposits is zero, there has to be some degree of fractional reserve banking (rather than 100% reserves) so that bankers can earn income from "making deposits work" (hot potatoes to use your expression). By contrast in a system with 100% reserves the banker would have to charge a fee to the deposit clients (in effect negative interest rate). Now, what is the best regime for reserves at the central bank? If I have understood you correctly the interest on these must be categorically zero. But what about the free lunch here? The central bank must make these reserve deposits work somehow. (NB: We will return to the subject of negative rates as practiced recently.)

Brown: Let's take one step back. In the world of a strict gold standard, high-powered money (otherwise called monetary base), made up of above-ground gold, pays no interest. The yellow metal is non-income bearing. Yet in such a gold standard world a fully competitive banking system is possible (indeed that is the essence of "free banking"). Banks hold some reserves in gold under such a system but this does not force them into risky business models or cascade lending or anything else. Yes, there is the possibility of periodic seize-up when some bank deposits would sell at a discount—and that is exactly what happened. The key aspect here is that the public should be fully able to assess reliably the quality of alternative deposits on offer and satisfy themselves that the returns (interest) are commensurate with the assessed risks. Of course, under the gold standard historically average nominal interest rate levels were low—and so the average opportunity cost of zero-income reserves would also be low. In principle, the same would be true under a sound money fiat system if such a thing can be created. In a sound money fiat system with effective competition and transparency there would be no infernal machine driving banks into risky activity with the purpose of fooling deposit customers and authorities. As regards the central bank itself, under the fiat regime, it matches reserve deposits with holdings of government securities; this is the basis of seigniorage—the government gaining from zero-rate financing via the central bank's issuance of money.

Reference

Friedman, M., & Schwartz, A. (1963). *Monetary History of the United States*. Princeton: Princeton University Press.

10

How the Euro Was Born

Question 12

Simonnot: As to Germany, were its objectives solely monetary regarding the creation of the euro?

Brown: When Germany broke with the dollar standard (first Bretton Woods and then the Smithsonian) in the early 1970s and pursued a hard money (monetarist) regime (comparatively) in contrast to 6 or 7 more years of the Burns inflation (in the US and globally) the over-riding purpose was to find shelter from US monetary chaos (meaning high inflation), even though that was not possible altogether, given the corollary of a super-expensive Deutsche mark (and its impact on the German export sector).

Fundamentally, there was a coalition of political forces in Germany at the time (largely in the Centre-Left) that put protecting savers and the growth of middle class incomes ahead of big profits in the powerful export sector. The Social Democrats and Free Democrats fought (and won) the 1969 election on a promise that DM revaluation would bolster incomes in real terms (import prices would fall, foreign holidays would cost less), and inflation as exported by the US policies would be turned back. The Christian Democrats and their Bavarian allies (the CSU) opposed DM revaluation, the former with ties to the export sector and the latter seeking to keep the support of farmers for whom EU prices of agricultural products were fixed in US dollars.

There is little evidence that the hard DM was pursued as a matter of geopolitical design—or equivalently that Germany deliberately sought to become European monetary hegemon in consequence, though many in France for example might have seen it that way. Certainly, the hard DM became popular with the German public and briefly the Bundesbank was the most popular institution with the German public. All of that started to change once Chancellor Kohl took Germany on the journey to European Monetary Union and appointed fellow travellers to the Bundesbank who would support that process and without any serious enough "hang-ups" about sound money to form a fatal roadblock. The motivation for Germany's journey to the euro, unlike the earlier one to the hard DM, was not to defend its citizens against a threat to the soundness of the national money; in fact they were to be exposed to a new monetary danger, even if hard to detect in the mist surrounding the future reality of European monetary union.

Question 13a

Simonnot: The creation of the euro can be seen as the monetary response to the floating dollar originating from the Nixon coup. But was it not also the product of a geo-political compromise between France and Germany, the abandonment of the DM being the price Germany had to pay for France's acceptance of German unification after the fall of the Berlin Wall? Let's recall that Mitterrand, then President of the Republic, belonged, without ever admitting it, to the old school of French diplomacy, in fact on the right (Maurras, Bainville, etc.), who loved Germany so much that they would prefer there to be several, and at least two, to paraphrase the well-known phrase of writer Francois Mauriac.

Brown: The hypothesis that Chancellor Kohl agreed very reluctantly in 1990 to the train journey to EMU proceeding in exchange for President Mitterrand accepting the unification of Germany is not convincing. Crucially, the US (under the 1st president Bush) had endorsed unification, and the Soviet Empire in convulsions was ready to deal with a United Germany, not least given its financial embrace; crucially an early agreement was reached between Bonn and Moscow on the withdrawal of Soviet troops from East Germany and related financial compensation (this agreement became part of the wider "two plus four" deal including all four allied victors of the Second World War). The UK's attitude was more problematic (with PM Thatcher at first concerned about the danger of German unification). But a French–British entente to block a United Germany at this point was surely not in question.

The counterfactual hypothesis that Chancellor Kohl could have dithered on EMU, insisting at very least on a hard money design of substance, whilst still achieving German unification, is surely robust. If subsequently the Kohl government had effectively postponed (perhaps indefinitely) the stages towards EMU in the early 1990s, for whatever reason, Germany could have placated

France by reining back its designs for East European integration into the EU (Paris not keen on East integration). In reality, by the time the Berlin Wall fell (November 1989) Chancellor Kohl was already well-disposed to the idea of European Monetary Union (and indeed in June 1988 the EU Summit had confirmed the setting up of the Delors Committee to prepare the blueprint).

Some historians of EMU argue that Kohl saw monetary union as essential to peace in Europe; others maintain that a key impetus to his support for monetary union came from the dollar devaluation in accordance with the Plaza accord (see James 2012). This resulted in tremendous appreciation of the Deutsche mark as the hard international money alternative to the now again soft dollar; and within the European Monetary System this brought further revaluation of the Deutsche mark against other key currencies (including French franc and Italian lira). All this provoked much anxiety amongst German exporters, the backbone of Kohl's Christian Democratic Party. "Backbone" had extra significance given the Party's funding difficulties at the time and the subsequently revealed slush funds controlled by the Chancellor—with dubious alleged contributions at one end of the range from arms dealers and at the other a "part commission" from Elf Acquitaine as (allegedly condoned by President Mitterrand) (see Clemens 2000). The grown support of the big exporters for the elimination of currency risk in key European markets (and perhaps unspoken for a softer domestic currency) may have counted for more in realpolitik than Kohl's beliefs about the causes of war in Europe, which were highly dubious. Global monetary union under the gold standard did not prevent war in 1914. And even if we overlooked that evidence, surely monetary and wider union was required only between France and Germany, not between 10 and 20 countries, in order to maintain peace in Europe according to Kohl's hypothesis.

Question 13b

Simonnot: Did these geo-political circumstances play a role in technical details of how the euro was conceived and launched?

Brown: In retrospect and even at the time it was clear that Chancellor Kohl in part side-lined the remaining hard money Bundesbankers who might have insisted on a constitution for monetary union which would have been unacceptable to France. In particular, the Chancellor had agreed to the Delors committee (set up in June 1988 to decide on a blueprint for European monetary union) being chaired by Alexandre Lamfalussy— esteemed widely as a skilled European diplomat rather than a person of hard money conviction. In agreeing to a committee made up of central bankers and excluding finance ministers Kohl had implicitly concurred with

Mitterrand's observation that if you want to conclude an EU agricultural treaty you don't assemble a meeting of agricultural ministers; likewise here the finance ministers had to be excluded. In preference there would be a central bankers club decision—and the members would be most concerned to further their own powers (so-called independence) rather than sticking to hard money dogma or insisting on details about the limits to the monetary financing of budget deficits. All in all, Kohl had no vision of hard or sound money principle and had no steel commitment to this ideal. That made it easily possible for him to back for largely pragmatic reasons a monetary union falling far short on sound money principle whilst linking this with the wish for no more wars in Europe. A geo-political grand design is not apparent in his monetary choices.

Question 13c

Simonnot: Even so, in *Euro Crash* (2014) (p. 196) you note that Chancellor Schmidt had defended the construction of the European Monetary System in 1978 at a meeting of recalcitrant Bundesbankers by emphasizing the special obligations of Germany towards Europe due to its Nazi past. Do you think Chancellor Kohl was of the same mindset when he negotiated with President Mitterrand? This past which according to the phrase of dedication did not want to go into the past, would it eventually go into the past? (We will again take up this question when we discuss the possible construction of a new euro).

Brown: Chancellor Schmidt in telling the Bundesbankers that they should support his plans for the European Monetary System on account of Germany's Nazi past made a great error of judgement. Yes, we can understand that pro-European sentiment in Germany can be based on such feelings of guilt. Surely, however, these do not justify German collaboration (or essential enabling) in driving a deeply flawed process of monetary integration as correctly pointed out by some Bundesbankers, even if these same critics lacked sensitivity to the Nazi past or were even complicit in it. The bad consequences for Europe in general, not just Germany, would surely not be atonement. A poorly construed monetary union could cause Europe to disintegrate despite all Schmidt's good intentions.

Did Chancellor Kohl share similar sentiments as Schmidt in his key support for the process of monetary union in Europe in defiance of some hardline views at the Bundesbank (which were eventually reduced or eliminated by his power of appointment at the top of that institution)? I can find no evidence of this. His dragging of President Reagan into a highly controversial visit to the Bitburg military cemetery (May 1985) where it emerged that SS troops were buried would surely not have occurred under Chancellor Schmidt. Moreover, Mitterrand's ambiguous history regarding his past role in Vichy France was hardly the basis for the two statesmen to join in a common revulsion of the Nazi past as the big reason for "Europe", meaning now monetary union. Rather, the German Chancellor and the French President used their joint revulsion against war as their clarion call for Franco-German progress towards monetary union: hence the visit of the two heads of state to Verdun where they held hands (September 1984).

References

Brown, B. (2014). *Euro Crash*. Basingstoke: Palgrave Macmillan.
Clemens, C. (2000). A Legacy Reassessed: Helmut Kohl and the German Party Finance Affair. *Journal of German Politics, 9*(2), 25–50.
James, H. (2012). *Making the European Monetary Union*. Cambridge, MA: Harvard University Press.

11

Trichet in Front of Trichet

Question 14

Simonnot: In a confidential memo, dated 13 February 1992, by Jean-Claude Trichet, then Treasury Director, to Pierre Bérégovoy, French Minister of Finance, which I published in "39 leçons d'economies contemporaine" (Gallimard 1998), one can read three remarks, verbatim:

First, the Bundesbank will only change its monetary policy when it is totally reassured that the threat of inflation in Germany has faded (this appears to me, unfortunately, not likely to be the case in the short run).

Second, whatever France does (EMS, not EMS … Maastricht, not Maastricht), our rates are tied to German rates through capital market dynamics totally independently of France's wish for independence or any wish for domination by Germany.

Third, in so far as Germany does not merit (or stronger than that) being the anchor of the system (EMS) our country must do everything to convince international investors that we are ourselves candidates to be the anchor, that the franc is a candidate for revaluation against the Deutsche mark and that it will have the right one day—as near as possible—to have long-term rates below German long-term rates.

In refusing any dialogue in advance and narrow cooperation (more due to institutional inabilities than bad will politically in my opinion) Germany does not offer any other concrete choice to France than to seriously contest the Deutsche mark's anchor role in the system.

Given the crucial role which Jean-Claude Trichet played first of all in the construction of the euro and then in the management of the ECB as its

President, a role which you underscore well in your own works, how do these reflections which as far as I recall are dated February 1992 strike you? Don't they indicate the ambition of the high-up French technocracy from that time Germany in its role as monetary standard for Europe? Don't they at least reveal to you his desire that France be treated in the financial markets as equal to the Federal Republic of Germany? The French example—was that not followed after the creation of the euro by other countries still less deserving of such treatment on financial markets? (We will return later to the roles of Trichet and Draghi after the crisis of 2008.)

Brown: The passages you quote from the memo of Trichet to Bérégovoy reveal a deep resentment of the anchor role which the Deutsche mark had within the European Monetary System—and this can be explained by dissatisfaction at the satellite nature of the franc (and franc interest rates) under this arrangement. (We don't know how high up this memo was in the Minister's reading list just a year before his suicide amidst the engulfment of the Credit Lyonnais scandal in which Trichet was subsequently charged but acquitted just prior to his becoming president of the ECB.)

It was surely wishful thinking on Trichet's part, though, to imagine that the franc could take over the mark's anchor role. This was based on two facts which France could not replicate. First, monetary base had successfully operated as the pivot of the German monetary order; a stable demand for this had allowed the Bundesbank to practice monetarism with some success, where the target was x% expansion of the monetary base. France had no such history of monetary base as pivot. Second, the large size of the German economy, and the dominance this had in the trade shares of neighbouring economies, meant that their currencies were natural satellites of the Deutsche mark. (In turn if we group Germany and these natural satellites together into a "DM area", this latter had a big share of French trade, much larger than the share of the French economy in consolidated DM area trade). The French franc had no such predominance (polar position) based on economic geography (trade shares).

If Trichet had been serious about ending the satellite status of the French franc with respect to the Deutsche mark, then one option was to have a freely floating currency; and simultaneously to take measures such as to put monetary base at the pivot of the French monetary system (e.g. high reserve requirements). Then the French franc might have grown into an alternative hard European money albeit smaller than the Deutsche mark but larger than the Swiss franc. All of that would have taken time, and was not certain of success; it may have been that pivoting the monetary base in France just was not possible. Even if achievable, there could have been large exchange rate instability—and so France could not escape monetary turbulence outside its borders.

An alternative option was to take France into a monetary union or other type of monetary bloc in which there were strict automatic monetary mechanisms to ensure overall soundness and to constrain abuse of potential power by the largest member. Evidently, Trichet went along with this second alternative in the context of a European monetary union. Europe seems to have been his uppermost concern rather than soundness; and "Europe" for so many French (including, it seems from the above memo, this top official) had an inherent dualism which Mitterrand understood so well—yes, France in Europe, but also Europe in France (see Fabius 1995). In another age (in fact, as was the case for de Gaulle and Rueff), striving for a non-satellite status for the French franc could have meant rebuilding a global monetary order based on gold. This, however, had no place in Trichet's plans.

Question 14, Part 2

Simonnot: Just one clarification: when you say, "First, monetary base had successfully operated as the pivot of the German monetary order", can you enlarge on why this had been so in Germany and not in France.

Brown: To my knowledge there was never any "experiment" in France with monetary base control. If there had been, would it have worked well (in terms of monetary base being well pivoted—meaning a large and stable demand for this aggregate)? I suggest probably not, given the low or convoluted reserve requirements in France; moreover, there was a huge global demand for DM banknotes (e.g. in East Germany, the other Warsaw pact countries in Eastern Europe, and the Soviet Union) which plausibly added to the stability of demand for German monetary base.

Simonnot: Bravo. What you say about the instability of monetary base in France is confirmed textually in the same confidential note of Trichet to his minister dated 13 February 1992.

1. Gradual economic slowdown continues.
2. As regards the credit aggregates, it seems that they slow coincidentally with the economy rather than leading.
3. By contrast, as regards the monetary aggregates the reduction is much stronger, M1 and M2 are shrinking whilst M3 gains by 4.1% (quarterly rate centred on November).
4. From the evidence as regards the monetary aggregates, the powerful monetary forces are add-ons to the economic slowdown. M1 is run down as funds leave sight deposits to go to savings instruments which pay interest.

M3 experiences some important "pulsations" which are linked to the phenomenon of the negative yield curve and the craze (or near craze) for money market SICAVs (funds); after having grown significantly more rapidly than nominal GDP in recent years, we now see this aggregate growing at a more modest pace inferior to the growth of nominal GDP.

This monetary instability, was it unique to France, or was it general with Germany as the exception?

Brown: Yes, Germany was the historical exception at this time in having stable demand for monetary base (key favourable factors included high reserve requirements, low in the scale of financial innovation, huge global demand for DM cash). It may well not have continued that way even without the birth of the euro. The German banking industry had growing success in getting the Bundesbank to reduce high reserve requirements and in any case opportunities increased to avoid these by shifting deposit business to the euro-DM market in Luxembourg.

Simonnot: Just to make a small diversion to the present day (2020), the decision of the ECB to discontinue issuing 500 euro banknotes, for the stated reason of combatting money laundering, will surely not help bolster the stability of M1 (its velocity) in the euro zone?

Brown: As you say, restricting the supply (or abolishing ultimately) of 500 euro notes is a bad step if the aim is to ultimately restore monetary base to the pivot of the monetary system (we are light-years away from that now!). Under the hard money regime of the Deutsche mark the 1000 DM note was popular especially as a constituent of safe haven demand outside Germany (contributing to the partial success of the monetarist experiment). Anyhow, the ECB evidently ignored or was ignorant of the quip by the Bundesbanker who said that trying to tackle crime by cancelling large denomination notes was like banning Mercedes cars because they are popular with criminals.

References

Fabius, L. (1995). *Les Blessures doe la Verite*. Flammarion.
Simonnot, P. (1998). *39 lecons d'economie contemporaine*. Gallimard.

12

The Great Crisis of 2008

Question 15

Simonnot: Let's tackle now the great crisis of 2008. One has forgotten (above all in France) that the first sign of the cataclysm came from BNP Paribas. On 9 August 2007, the biggest French bank, a giant as you know, forbade investors to pull money out of three of its investment funds backed by sub-prime US mortgage loans, explaining that it could not determine the value of the funds because of the "complete evaporation of liquidity" in the market for this paper. This one announcement from BNP brought about immediately a contraction of these same markets.

I am a client of XXX, a bank of the same type as BNP, of which I withhold the name for obvious reasons. I went to see the person who is responsible for my account at the branch in the neighbourhood where I live and I asked him whether this bank XXX also had in its portfolios papers backed by these famous sub-prime mortgages. This person swore to me, hand on heart, that this was not the case; that XXX was well managed and did not take such financial risks. Now, as came out later, the accounts of XXX were in fact totally infected by such toxic assets. The person in charge of my portfolio at XXX had thus lied to me. From this we see a classic problem of asymmetric information between client and bank. Certainly the bank does not know everything about the client. But most of the time it knows more than the client about itself. Can the market deal with this problem of asymmetry? Apparently not, since all sorts of rules in the bank profession try to resolve it. But they fail in that purpose as we have seen. So what is to be done?

Brown: The issue of asymmetric information plagues in various degrees all asset markets—in credit the borrower knows more than the lender, in real estate markets the present owner (or constructor) knows more usually about the building and its plot of land than the potential buyer. At least in some of these cases the buyer can make exhaustive enquiries and demand information before proceeding. In the case of a bank depositor or money market fund holder (of units) an individual request for authoritative information, answerable on pain of considerable legal jeopardy, is not possible; the holder/buyer must largely make do with available public information and this is often hardly transparent. Perhaps, compliance penalties can increase the buyer's (depositor's) grounds for confidence in statutory information. But it may well be the case that even the chief executives of big financial institutions hardly know the true span of risks which the organization under their command has assumed. This ignorance may be due to stupidity, carelessness, lack of insight/imagination, or sheer failure of information channels; yet the same chief executive may have a flare for dancing when the music is on and enjoy the share-price run from which they score large personal gain, perhaps related to options.

So, what can the ordinary saver do amidst this jungle? In the preferred world of no deposit insurance and markets enforcing discipline, the saver has to rely on information that enters the public sphere and the enforcement of its quality by independent market watchdogs (if institutions do not allow these to function that would certainly be grounds for suspicion). The role of the financial press, including investigative journalists, is also crucial—and this left much to be desired in the run-up to the 2007/8 crisis. It is not clear that an oligopolist media extracting main revenues from the financial sector (for advertising or whatever) could feasibly mount an in-depth examination of possible dangers there—let alone obtain authoritative input for this purpose.

Question 16

Simonnot: In a manual written for economics students, the following statement is made about the sub-prime crisis: "The intensification of competition which resulted from the deregulation of the financial markets and from the fact that certain entities henceforth switched to financing themselves in the markets direct led banks to re-develop the products they offered—they sought to expand their deposits and loans amongst entities (individuals and businesses) which did not have access to the financial markets". And in a footnote, the authors push the nail in: "the development of sub-prime loans in the US followed in large part from this logic—to grow the customer base the banks were no longer content with lending to households classified as prime (the best risks), but lent notably in the mortgage market to clients offering less guarantees" (Beitone and Rodrigues 2017). One could cite tens of other texts of the same view: the sub-prime crisis which provoked the greatest global crisis since 1929 came from deregulation of financial markets and the greed of bankers for profits cost what it may. The market, one time again, was to blame. No mention of the fact that the same American bankers were obliged, under penalty of fines, to grant sub-prime loans to certain social classes. Surely this error of analysis, very largely shared by our élites, explains the manner in which they subsequently sought to administer remedies in the wake of the 2008 crisis?

Brown: There are two big points to make in response.

First, the sub-prime US mortgages were just one part of a global credit bubble. Alongside and driven by the same forces (essentially monetary, as explained in the second point below) were Spanish mortgages, UK mortgages, weak sovereign bonds in Europe (from Greece and Portugal to Spain and Italy), yen and Swiss franc borrowing in the so-called carry trade, covenant lite loans to corporations, and much else including massive off-balance sheet operations (lending and borrowing) of banks in the US and Europe via their special purpose vehicles.

Second, the high speculative temperature which built up in credit markets (and beyond), reflecting widespread irrational behaviour in various forms (in particular investors dropping their normal caution and scepticism) stemmed from monetary inflation. Central banks pursuing their 2% inflation targets (in the case of Japan the target was lower until 2013 but from a situation where prices were stable or falling slightly) at a time when the natural rhythm of prices was downwards (due to the rapid progress of globalization and technological change) steered interest rates to abnormally low levels through 2002–4/5 in the aftermath of the Nasdaq crash and subsequent "recession" (2000–2). In fact, we should consider the virulent asset inflation in the early and mid-2000s as a continuation phase of the great monetary inflation dating back to the previous decade. In hindsight, with all the subsequent data revisions which have occurred, it is dubious whether there really was a recession at the start of the 2000s, even in the US. Already from the mid-1990s the Greenspan Fed was following a quasi 2% inflation standard and that was at a time of a strong natural rhythm of prices downwards (explained by the IT productivity boom). This monetary inflation spawned asset inflation. When eventually a big climb in energy prices accompanied a late-cycle run-up of reported consumer price inflation in the US through 2005–2006, the Fed engaged in monetary overkill keeping rates on a high plateau through 2006–2007, including the first stage of the credit bubble bursting.

The abnormally low rates during the early and middle years of the renewed cyclical expansion from 2002 fuelled a "hunt for yield". Income famine investors became unusually ready to accept speculative narratives which emerged at this time (and some which had been already around for some time). Examples included the hypothesis that European financial integration as spawned by European Monetary Union meant Greek bonds were almost as safe as German; European banks in the new world of the euro and financial integration were on the road to Eldorado; home prices could never fall and in the new age of home ownership for all supported by the government mortgage credit risks were small. There was widespread misplaced confidence in new types of debt securities buoyed by the ratings as awarded by credit agencies. Turning to the popular currency carry trades, borrowing Swiss francs or yen to leverage up investments in Europe (including real estate and private equity), how could this go wrong—the trend should continue as your friend (a version of the momentum trading which is popular under conditions of asset inflation).

Question 17

Simonnot: Now I would like to shed light on a point of history. The attention of observers has been focused on the bankruptcy of Lehman Brothers September 15, 2008 as the trigger to the cataclysm which struck the global economy. And a whole literature has developed alongside on TBTF (too big to fail) or TITF (too interconnected to fail). But isn't it the case that an agreement with Barclays was about to be concluded which would have avoided the bankruptcy of Lehmans and wasn't it the British authorities (the Chancellor of the Exchequer and the Financial Services Authority) who in scuttling this at the last moment were really responsible for the catastrophe? Recall the observation of Alan Greenspan, the once celebrity president of the Federal Reserve: "the real issue is not that an institution is too big or too interconnected to fail but that it is too big or too interconnected to liquidate quickly".

Brown: We are now discussing what the central banks, governments, and regulators could have done to reduce the severity of the financial crisis once this was "upon them", leaving completely to one side their varying culpabilities for the vast monetary inflation of which the crisis and ensuing great recession was the result, supplemented by their varying responsibility for a bizarre tightness of monetary policy in the very late stage of the cyclical expansion. "Vast monetary inflation" does not just refer to the years say, 2002–4/5 but also the mid and late year of the previous decade, when the Greenspan Fed was leading the way with its policy of holding inflation low and stable during a productivity boom, thus generating tremendous asset inflation. The mild (and perhaps non-existent recession of 2001) could not possibly on its own have restored the corrupted price-signalling mechanisms in the asset markets back to health, given the extent to which these had been corrupted (e.g. over-receptiveness to speculative narrative telling and to positive feedback loops from capital gains to expectations); a long period of sound money would have been required for that.

Even if the US government or foreign banks and their respective governments had rescued Lehman, the crash and crisis would still have been very severe—though not all concentrated perhaps in those weeks. Lehman and its immediate aftermath triggered heavy US government support for a whole range of financial and non-financial institutions (one thinks of TARP—the government sponsored re-capitalization of large US banks). Without the Lehman bankruptcy there may have been a harsher crisis elsewhere in the global financial system in the absence of those US government interventions.

Let's come back to the specifics of Lehman. If indeed the UK authorities had given the go-ahead for Barclays to buy out Lehman, within a few weeks one could well imagine a fantastic run on that British bank. After all the big UK banks did succumb to the global crisis that autumn. Barclays did not require government support as it concluded a capital-raising deal with Qatar, later the subject of criminal proceedings (finally dropped in 2018) relating to bribery and corruption and private legal complaint (still live).

Suppose simultaneously a US banking crisis had been unfolding and markets realized the extent to which Barclays had become overstretched with its Lehman acquisition one could imagine Barclays having gone the same way as Royal Bank of Scotland and Lloyds Banking Group (in effect becoming nationalized). Ultimately, the UK taxpayer would have been on the hook for an intervention to "save Lehman"; and alongside the European banking crisis could have already been much more severe at that time with obvious negative global economic consequences.

Question 18

Simonnot: Under these circumstances, it seems all the same strange that Barclays declared itself as interested in the purchase of Lehmans? Could it not have anticipated the subsequent run which you have mentioned? Or did it assume that in any event the authorities would come to its aid?

Brown: The big question is what did the shareholders and bond holders of Barclays know?

To take one step back, think of that great merger in late summer 2007—ABN/AMRO, RBS and Fortis. There had already been an early credit and money market quake a few weeks before. Yet the shareholders of all three banks almost entirely voted in favour of the merger. How could they be so irrational, one might ask? Perhaps they were still living in the land of fantastic speculative narratives—even those now confronting a harsh reality.

And so forward to Barclays. Perhaps management knew some of the concerns mentioned above. But they presumably judged that the shareholders if Barclays would respond positively to the news of their bank picking up Lehmans for "nothing". We don't know whether that would have been the case. There are grounds for doubting it. Even so, given the collapse of bank shares that was to continue in the rest of that autumn (2018), clearly equity investors on the eve of Lehman's closure were grossly over-optimistic.

Should Barclays management, even if convinced that their shares would rise on the news of buying Lehman, have been cautious given their greater inside knowledge about the real conditions in the banking industry? Yes. And they should have been where possible issuing equity to redeem bonds (reducing leverage) rather than doing the opposite. Incidentally, Alex Pollock (R Institute Washington) finds that the amount of funds that the large US banks spent buying back their equity (and increasing leverage) in the years 2003–2007 far exceeded the amount of capital injected into them subsequently under the TARP program.

Question 19

Simonnot: The argument often used by Bernanke and his fellow-travellers in coming to the support of banks was that to invoke "moral hazard" in the midst of a financial crisis would be "dangerous and misadvised". Example: my neighbour smokes in bed. He sets fire to his house which is made of wood. Out of grounds of moral hazard I do not call the fire brigade. To rescue the drowsy smoker would only encourage him to continue in his ill ways and encourage other smokers to do likewise. But if my house is also made of wood and is just next door wouldn't I dash to the telephone to call the emergency services? (Note in California according to their own statements private sector fire extinguishing services only come to the aid of neighbours if a fire there would threaten the house of the customer who called them.)

Brown: You raise the fascinating question of moral hazard, and for purposes of exposition we should assume that we are talking about a fire which did not threaten to cause physical harm to individuals (say all unoccupied for sure). We should start with Chair Bernanke's re-nomination hearing in the Senate in autumn 2009 (President Obama chose to stick with this Bush appointee not least because he embraced mammoth new financial regulation as being designed in the Democrat-controlled Congress). Senator Bunning famously told Bernanke "you are the moral hazard" (criticizing him for having generated the bubble and bust via monetary policy—including the over-severity of the tightness in the late stage of the business cycle expansion phase).

There is surely no justification for bailing out bond holders and equity holders in a failing bank. Ideally, though, there should be a mechanism for orderly liquidation. And in principle deposit holders get paid back first, before bond holders can obtain any funds in a liquidation process. If there is a moral hazard it is banks dubiously marketing liabilities as if these are always redeemable at par. Deposits in a fractional reserve banking system are repayable in cash on demand, unless illiquidity means that there must be a temporary suspension, in which case they are converted into roll-over deposits. That should be the warning on the packet when clients (including companies) buy bank deposits. Yes, there could be different categories of deposits—insured (where the bank pays the insurance fee on behalf of the customer), non-insured in banks with high equity ratios and high cash holdings, and so on, and the client should be free to choose.

The actual banking world in 2007 was very far from that ideal. There was huge ambiguity about which deposits and other liabilities were always repayable at par. A lot of false promises were implicitly on the wrapping paper. It might not have been the best time to let people suffer who had been fooled by the ambiguity—or if not fooled had been counting on government support during a financial crisis. It is a judgement call, but surely the bond holders in banks could have been made to suffer greater loss, whilst preventing financial

Armageddon. Prevention did not mean rewarding the shareholders with the bestowing of vast new effective monopoly power (in part a product of regulations) and monopoly rents to match for a few banking behemoths.

Reference

Beitone, A., & Rodrigues, C. (2017). *Economie Monetaire*. Paris: Armand Colin.

13

American Capitalism Versus European Capitalism

Question 20

Simonnot: Before considering the way in which the euro-zone resolved the crisis of 2008, it seems necessary to underscore a fundamental difference between the US and Europe as regards banking. Conversely, American enterprises borrowed more intensively than European in the financial markets. The share of bank loans in the financing of enterprises is much more important in the euro-zone than in the US. From when dates this difference? How can we explain it? Which is the best mix for enterprises? And for the banks? What are the implications one can foresee for the next crisis? How does Great Britain fit into this picture?

Brown: How can we explain changes over time and differences between countries in the pattern of corporate financing—whether via bank finance or placement of notes (bonds, notes, commercial paper) directly with non-bank investors?

As a first point we should highlight credit paper issuance, and the fact that this is a much less significant source of corporate finance in Europe relative to the US. But it may be the case that much of the credit paper is held by banks or by financial subsidiaries of the banks (including in the last cycle the notorious special purpose vehicles). So, in the US investment banks in the last cycle were large holders of a range of paper issued by both corporates and the household sector.

Everything else the same, if the cost of intermediation via banks increases relative to capital market or money market issuance, then one would expect a higher ratio of credit to pass outside the banking system, directly from lenders to borrowers. And one might imagine that the increased costs of regulation since the crisis have had such an effect. Most plausibly that has been the case with respect to investment grade debt. On the other hand, the credit crash of 2007–2009 most likely induced some greater cautiousness of investors with respect to non-bank paper, especially given perceptions that banks would always be bailed out (as regards depositors). The opposing influence has been the hunt for yield as driven by radical monetary policies; investors desperate for income might well take on more paper into their portfolios rather than lower yielding bank deposits.

Does disintermediation—the channelling of credit outside the banking system—make the risk of bank crisis greater in some respects? That is the case if it is especially prime borrowers who migrate away from the banks. And that has been the case. Large prime borrowers have growingly been able to tap credit markets at rates with which banks (given internal cost structures including compliance with regulations) could not compete. And so, the direct loan portfolios of banks would tend to become higher risk in content. Banks could have bolstered their equity capital base so as to keep bank deposit risk low. That patently did not happen in the last cycle—as we have seen banks were buying back equity and raising their leverage ratios. It may have been happening (re-capitalization) in the present cycle at least in the context of the US where bank equity valuations in some cases have come to reflect huge monopoly rents.

The hunt for yield—and the associated speculative fever in high-risk (including junk) bond markets—has put downward pressure on credit spreads which banks can get on their lending to commercial customers. In principle that should have meant some shrinkage of banks overall. Bank management, however, in many cases has sought to keep business expansion going by cutting margins on lending to high-risk borrowers. Perhaps the chickens will come home to roost in this in the next cycle.

Why is credit intermediation outside the banking system so much smaller in Europe than in the US? One explanation is the size distribution of firms. The US has a much larger (relative to economic size) supply of corporations whose capitalization is big enough to support a market for their debt which would be fairly liquid. It also seems to be the case that European banks are undercharging on credit in many cases—able to sustain large overall balance sheets and quash potential competition of non-bank credit markets because equity market investors are more tolerant (than in the US) of such sub-optimal behaviour (with respect to profit maximization) by bank management. All possible explanations—I can't claim to know which one to choose with any great confidence. And I am not knowledgeable sufficiently about the UK data and banking industry to explain the particular differences there.

Question 20, Part 2

Simonnot: Are not the right of shareholders better respected in the US than in Europe?

Brown: Yes, shareholders in US are better respected in some senses (over-respected some would say). A case in point: compulsory nationalization of tottering banks such as stripped shareholders of rights to explore better options (e.g. through capital reconstruction including debt–equity swaps) would have been more difficult (in US). In some ways one can argue that the US government was far too generous to US shareholders in the bail-out programs. For example, the Federal government guaranteed new issuance of bank debt during and immediately after the crisis before first calling for new equity capital which would have diluted outstanding amounts (which would have caused greater financial suffering for present shareholders). Another case to consider: the market for direct control (takeovers) is a crucial aspect of how shareholders can exert a disciplinary effect on management and for a multitude of reasons that may function less well in Europe than in the US.

Question 20, Part 3

Simonnot: Patrick Artus, chief economist of the Bank Natixis, maintained recently (Le Monde, 28 January 2019) that American enterprises are more fragile than European: "American enterprises are financed two thirds by the issuance of debt and one third by bank loans—a very different situation from European enterprises which are financed essentially by banks. The rise in cost of capital market debt led American enterprises to reduce their issuance of debt in the second half of 2018 to less than $20 bn per quarter. US corporate issuance of high-yield debt has completely disappeared since the end of 2018. This quasi-stop has translated into a fall of capital expenditure starting in the third quarter of 2018". To that we should add some powerful wealth effects from a decline in stock market prices leading to a fall in private consumption which in turn feeds back to weaker capital spending. Artus infers from all this a particular financial vulnerability of the US economy the US responding more severely to swings in financial market conditions than the European. What do you think of this diagnosis?

Brown: I don't agree that US enterprises making greater use of bond markets (especially junk bonds) than European (who borrow much more from banks) means the former (US enterprises) are especially fragile. If there is a seize-up in junk bond market issuance most enterprises have unused lines of credit with banks. And in any case any rational finance officer would build into calculations that the new issue market in corporate debt, especially junk, is not always open—adopting strategies such as over-issuance and extending maturities of paper during the good times whilst building up a reserve of liquid short-maturity assets, securing credit lines then, and taking advantage of favourable opportunities to issue equity. If the debt markets remained shut for long time, then yes there could be problems; but the US credit industry (private equity included) is very agile at drawing up liability restructuring programs—including debt for equity swaps.

It is not obvious that at the level of the US economy as a whole, capital spending was reined back because of debt issue market drought in the period mentioned. The key weak element was shale oil and gas spending which had had a mini peak early in the year. Yes, the shale oil and gas sector is highly leveraged and very dependent on high-yield debt markets. Arguably, if there had not been asset inflation with its feature of overpriced high-yield debt, the shale oil and gas industry would have made greater use of equity capital and there would have been less investment overall (probably the rational outcome; there has most likely been over-investment and malinvestment in the energy sector in consequence of the credit bubble; so yes, when this burst, it could have dampening influence on investment in this sector).

The credit bubble especially in high-yield debt has meant over-leverage and some malinvestment/overinvestment in the US and other parts of the globe (including emerging markets). Has Europe been less exposed this time than the US to the bad influences of credit market asset inflation? That is not at all clear. European investors to escape negative rates have participated in carry trade into US assets and emerging markets—depressing the level of the euro and leading to a bloated export sector in euro-zone economies. All this malinvestment will add to the burden in the next downturn.

Question 20, Part 4

Simonnot: Perhaps there has been malinvestment or overinvestment in the US shale oil sector. Yet all the same that has permitted the US to again become the number one produce of oil in the world and thereby reduce our dependence (not just the US) on Saudi Arabia, which has used and abused its power since 1973. Now the benchmark oil price ($50–60 per barrel) is American not Saudi. There is no longer the risk of the price climbing through $100. On September 14, 2019, it sufficed only a few drones, wherever they came from, to paralyse a half of Saudi oil production. Five years earlier this would have propelled the price to the stratosphere. This time it hardly moved after the attack. The value of this result across all the oil-consuming nations is surely considerable. So this leads on to a more general question—how should we define overinvestment and malinvestment?

Brown: Malinvestment can create gains for consumers, absolutely. The bigger point though is that there would have been greater prosperity overall if the malinvestment had not taken place and instead the invisible hands had efficiently guided capital spending.

For example, many consumers gained from the over-building of railroads which occurred in the various booms and busts in mid-nineteenth-century US history, even though the losses of investors (whether in bonds or equity) reflected an overall partially wasteful process. Yet in the bigger picture, Fogel and Engerman ("Railroads and American Economic Growth" in *Essays in Economic History* [Johns Hopkins University Press 1970], author, Robert W. Fogel) found that prosperity gains overall were remarkably small when compared with the hypothetical evolution which would have occurred if the canal network had been extended and utilized in the absence of railroad construction.

Monetary inflation at the time of the railroad "craze", in the 1880s and early 1890s (up to the crash of 1893) came in the context of the dollar on the gold standard (gold convertibility of the dollar had been re-established in 1879, this time without silver, after a long interlude during the civil war and its aftermath). Monetary inflation had its source on the demand side for gold spurred by the regulatory regime in the US put in place by the National Banking Act (passed during the Civil War). By the 1880s, this regime had become the catalyst to "fractional reserve" innovation far in excess of rational bounds, due to prevailing illusions that deposits were always as good as cash.

The "economization" in demand for monetary base drove overall monetary inflation. Gold did not drain out of the US (which would have checked monetary inflation) as foreign demand for investments in the booming US economy was so strong. Rapid productivity growth and globalization camouflaged monetary inflation in the goods markets, where prices were gently falling (more slowly than in previous decade when they also came under downward pressure from the monetary steps towards resumption of convertibility). The description of the US in the 1880s as in a monetary inflation jars of course with the folklore of a long Great Deflation from the mid-1870s to mid-1890s—a diagnosis which rests simply on studying price indices.

Moving forward in time from the railroad boom and bubble, in the case of shale oil and gas there has been the big advantage for consumers of security, in comparison with uncertain delivery from the Middle East. Yet in principle this is something with which well-functioning markets should cope. Consumers of energy globally would pay a premium price in long-term contracts for North American supplies. This premium would in turn incentivize investment and production accordingly. Perhaps there is a case to argue that long-term contracting has exhibited some market failure (as a non-expert I cannot make this case). If so, then there would have been an argument for governments in consuming nations in the rest of the world to give tax breaks which would have incentivized such long-term purchases or investment, and similarly in the US.

The energy price crash and widespread bankruptcies in the shale oil and gas sector through 2014–16 is at least superficial evidence of underlying malinvestment during preceding years.

How to define malinvestment?

In the "classical" Austrian school literature the concept is intimately related to monetary inflation (see Sechrest 2006). Artificially low interest rates artificially stimulate demand for capital goods—and more generally production processes which are "time intensive" (long gestation). But there is no fundamental rationale for the economy to switch resources into capital goods from consumer goods and so a growing underlying imbalance forms which eventually manifests in a business recession plus related crisis. That is the essence of the Austrian business cycle theory.

The concept of malinvestment now widely transcends these origins though they are still the guiding principle. The asset inflation element (twin of goods and services inflation) in overall monetary inflations goes along with much irrationality and this spawns malinvestment in various forms. Irrationality may take the form of "hunger for yield" or of "positive feedback loops". Both involve investors dropping their normal scepticism towards speculative narratives, encouraged to do so either by desperation for yield or by a string of capital gains, both of which stem from monetary inflation. These asset inflations spawn a boom in the credit carry trade—where investors move into risky bonds and become less sceptical than usual towards the promise of higher returns on these. They are especially keen on risky bonds which seem to be backed by cash flow streams.

The result is that the cost of capital is driven down especially in sectors of the economy where there are such powerful narratives forming and where these sought-after types of debt security are available. In the present long cyclical expansion since 2009, examples include debt issuance related to popular types of real estate investment (newly constructed apartment blocks secured by rental income or state-of-the-art warehouses promising income from the online commerce boom); and there have been the debt issues of shale oil and gas firms which were especially popular in the years 2009–13, when the narrative of high energy prices forever and looming US supremacy in this industry were enticing investors at a time of powerful monetary inflation (with the Federal Reserve engaged in radical monetary experimentation during the long aftermath of the 2007–2009 recession).

The diagnosis and measurement of malinvestment is not at all simple, not least in view of the considerable counterfactual historical analysis and controversial monetary analysis involved. Malinvestment is generally more detectable through the rear-view mirror, once the business cycle boom is over, than in actual real time. Even so, what can we say about where the malinvestment finds itself in the present expansion (beyond the example of shale oil and gas which has already suffered correction)? One suggestion is the intensity of the digitalization revolution. In retrospect, we might find this has some similarity with the earlier railroad example.

Evidently there has been much downside to digitalization—operating costs, internet flaws, viruses, cyber-attacks, undermining of democratic processes, invasion of privacy rights, and crucially, empowerment of monopoly capital. Yield chasing under conditions of monetary inflation, meaning capital market prices which reflect highly speculative narratives without normal rational weighting of downside risks related to the new technology, mean over-rapid and dangerously excessive journeys into the forest of the unknown at ultimate costs—both economic and political (see the introduction to this dialogue). Within the tech sector, it seems that monopolization is intrinsic to the digitalization process—the winner takes all. In the broader economy, the technological advances seem to be implemented in a way which is firm specific and which can shut-out competitors. Hence, the star firms in each industrial sector seize the advantages of digitalization; but unlike in previous technological revolutions the seeping out of these to competitors is remarkably slow if it takes place at all (it is not just a question of the would-be competitor buying available equipment or poaching talented workers and executives from the lead firm). The star firm's elevated profits are reflected in wage gains for its workers on average falling behind their productivity performance. (Prices of the star firm's output fall nonetheless reflecting stellar efficiency performance and the strategy of gaining market share.)

Amidst desperation for yield and positive feedback loops investors have poured funds into exchange traded funds (ETFs) concentrated on large capitalization stocks. This in turn has tended to lower the cost of capital for actual or potential monopolists.

Would-be monopolists, whose potential monopoly future is well-judged in the marketplace, can amply afford to cut prices in the present (perhaps on a predatory basis), and this is one way in which the digitalization revolution proceeds speedily. Moreover, in the climate of expectations where digitalization has much buzz, firms which out of scepticism adopted change slowly, could find their equity prices slumping; and never mind long-run potential costs of the technology, they must scramble now for fear of being overtaken by a potential star firm which would then seize monopoly advantage.

It is not the fault of monetary conditions that digitalization carries serious dangers of monopolization which could fatally undermine a free market capitalist order and economic liberalism. But monetary inflation has increased these dangers. The narrative of actual and potential monopoly power has been especially powerful in exciting equity investors in the inflationary environment. Huge gains in financial power for the monopolists or monopolists-to-be helped to numb political responses which may have sounded the alert on the dangers of monopoly capitalism related to the digitalization revolution. Vigorous and ever-watchful anti-trust enforcement in the US would have been a circuit breaker to the cycle of malinvestment in digitalization.

The judgement ultimately for economic historians focused on malinvestment will depend on their counterfactual analysis of how the US economy would have evolved under sound money—how much less digitalization, how much more investment in other sectors, how much less monopoly, how much more freedom.

Postscript: Should we consider the benefits of digitalization in the pandemic (facilitating work at home and online shopping for example) as a mitigating factor in the diagnosis of mal-investment? The case for doing so is not strong. With less intensive (but still widespread) digitalization governments might have been more cautious in pressing the lock-down button, facilitating instead market forces in their role of increasing the supply of infection-free services and making work (and transport) less subect to infection risk. Given the monopolization of much of the technology industry, the pandemic set off supply responses which were far from optimal as detailed in the epilogue to this dialogue (Chap. 23). In particular infection-free services in many cases depended on labour input which was exploited—unable to earn the safety premiums against infection risk which would have been obtained in a competitive markets—leading in consequence to an excessive curtailment of bricks and mortar alternatives which could have adapted to producing lower infection risk output. And in the darkness of the pandemic, surely many consumers would have preferred more choice in their purchasing of goods and services than what the great monopolists or duopolists promoted by a long and virulent asset inflation had to offer them? Finally, the pandemic may have increased the potential for monopoly abuse by big tech into the post-pandemic era, with potential competition enfeebled.

Reference

Fogel, R. (1970). Railroads and American Economic Growth. In R. Fogel (Ed.), *Essays in Economic History* (pp. 157–203). Baltimore: Johns Hopkins University Press.

Sechrest, L. J. (2006). Explaining malinvestment and overinvestment. *The Quarterly Journal of Austrian Economics*, 9(4).

14

The Submission of the Euro to the 2% Inflation Standard

Question 21

Simonnot: Let's come now to the manner in which the euro-zone reacted to the crisis. Recall that according to the Maastricht Treaty, the ECB was assigned only one objective "the stability of prices" in contrast to the Federal Reserve which must also aim for full employment. At the time, this was viewed by some as a triumph for monetarists (German) over Keynesians (French). Some suspected that Trichet as President of the ECB (from 2003) submitted himself too willingly to the German diktat. This suspicion was all the more justified as we know from the document he wrote at the French Treasury at the start of the 1990s, where he harboured great ambitions for the French franc. We will return further ahead to the role of Trichet at the ECB. For the moment, just one question: the euro, as constructed, was surely better defended against what we have described as deflation phobia than the US dollar?

Brown: As you say there is no dual mandate for the ECB and in consequence one might have thought that the absolute priority given to stable prices would have meant the euro should have been harder than the dollar. But that is not how matters have turned out. Why not?

A key first point is that right from the start the ECB embraced the emerging 2% inflation standard. When Professor Issing's committee drew up the framework for monetary policy in late 1998, it essentially put Europe on that standard—and at the same time abandoned the monetary base or a broader monetary aggregate as pivot to the monetary system as had been the case for the Deutsche mark, opting instead for the "corridor system" of interest rate control. There was the sop to the remaining monetarists at the Bundesbank of the so-called "second pillar"—meaning that the policy makers at the ECB would monitor the growth of M3 (thereby undertaking monetary analysis); the first pillar consisted of econometric-based inflation (and broader economic) forecasts founded on neo-Keynesian principles and an array of tentative judgements (based on estimations) about such magnitudes as the neutral interest rate and the natural rate of unemployment. The monetary pillar had no real substance in terms of input into ECB policy making.

So why did Professor Issing take that course when he was under less pressure than his counterparts at the Fed to pursue a framework which would ostensibly achieve aims in the labour market (and attainment of higher employment on average over the cycle if you believe the neo-Keynesian doctrines). This is a puzzle. A tentative answer would be that this framework seemed to provide more possibility for a softer monetary policy than otherwise, and this was deemed as essential to keeping the new monetary union intact. There was a strong view as published in ECB material that a positive rate of inflation would make it easier to have internal devaluations in the form say of Italian wages falling in relative terms to German without there being any need for absolute nominal wage cuts.

Professor Issing went even further down the road to inflation targeting in early 2003 when he announced that undershoots of the 2% inflation target would be viewed as seriously as overshoots. The cynic would say that this announcement, coincidental with the Federal Reserve proclaiming that it was now "breathing back inflation which had fallen too low", was designed to limit any potential rise of the euro against the dollar.

Could all of this have been different? Yes. Professor Issing's founding committee in late 1998 could have decided that stable prices meant zero inflation in the long run (on average). It could have made the monetary base pivotal and rejected the interest rate corridor system. But what then would the ECB have done if and when a future crisis emerged in the form of markets speculating that one or more country would have to leave the union? In an ultimate sense, the soft money framework postponed and perhaps blunted that question. Backdoor lending from the ECB to sustain the union might well not be possible under a hard money union. This is not to claim in any way that Professor Issing foretold the future monetary and debt crises within EMU— but perhaps such ideas were there at an intuitive level.

Question 22

Simonnot: Jean-Claude Trichet has been widely criticized for having raised the policy rates of the ECB in summer 2011 (just a few months before the end of his mandate), whilst up until this date he had followed the fall of interest rates in the wake of Lehman's bankruptcy. Indeed, some attribute to this rise of rates the recession which followed in Europe whilst in the US growth of GDP continued. Why do you think Trichet took this decision and was it responsible for the "second recession" which cost Europe so dearly?

Brown: The mini-tightening of monetary policy by M. Trichet in 2011 (as measured by the size of rate move) is a small detail compared to the huge error in the opposite direction (excess ease—in fact rampant monetary inflation) in the years 2003–2005, which should be seen in the context of monetary inflation extending back into the last years of the DM-zone and the start of EMU (say 1993–2000). That early period was the first part of the great monetary inflation under Chair Greenspan. If the Bundesbank or the ECB at the start had defied the inflation in the US monetary hegemon (albeit showing up more starkly in asset markets than goods markets given the camouflage of rapid productivity growth led by the IT revolution) then the DM and later the euro would have spiralled upwards against the US dollar (as had occurred in the early 1970s or in the mid-1980s, when the Bundesbank had defied the Fed's lead); but this time the Bundesbank in its dying days under Chief Tietmeyer (a Kohl appointee) was committed to not having any run-up of the DM (which could sink the prospect of monetary union) and at its start the euro plunged against the dollar as the ECB continued with essentially a policy of monetary inflation. Then came the bout of further monetary inflation under Trichet (already launched by Otmar Issing a few months before he became Chair). All of this monetary inflation, where asset inflation continued as more virulent than goods inflation, was the dominant cause of the European sovereign debt crisis and second recession.

In the first few years of Trichet's mandate, the focus of this ECB Chief focus was on the "unsustainability of the US current account deficit (in the balance of payments)" and the related (according to his view) troublesome weakness of the US dollar. That was a total misreading of the situation, albeit that Trichet grounded this view on analytical input from top officials in the French Treasury now seconded to his "inner cabinet" at the ECB; he should have seen dollar weakness as a symptom of inflationary US monetary policy primarily (as conducted by the Bernanke/Greenspan Fed and driven by President Bush's ambition to win the November 2004 election) and have been determined (as the great Bundesbankers of the 1970s) to defy this even if the consequence were a transitory powerful rise of the dollar/euro exchange rate—who knows, into the 1.70s and 1.80s. His failure to follow the illustrious lead of Dr. Emminger's Bundesbank, on top of the similar failure of his immediate predecessors, meant that Europe got immersed in the same powerful asset inflation as the US and indeed the global economy (in fact one can argue that asset inflation was at its most virulent in Europe). One aspect of that asset inflation was the European lending mania into weak sovereigns and mortgage asset markets together with a bubble in European financial equities—all of which set the stage for the subsequent crisis.

Then there was the huge mistake of 2007, once the credit quakes started to rumble, M. Trichet continued with a belated tightening of monetary policy, rather than promptly easing monetary conditions sharply and fostering a sharp fall of rates. Exactly as for the Bernanke Fed at that time, M. Trichet appeared transfixed by the 2% inflation target (with inflation then above that level) and so insisted on an entirely sterilized monetary operation to relieve illiquidity.

Fast forward to 2011. Perhaps by then M. Trichet was having some remorse about slavishly following soft US monetary policies. And it is remarkable that he was ready to pursue two tiny rate hikes in the first half of that year despite a strong euro against the dollar. His motivation from published texts and statements appears not to have been second thoughts about the 2% inflation standard but misguided forecasts that a strong economic recovery was underway which could go along with inflation rising above target within two years. In any event, the chickens were coming home to roost from the asset inflation which he had fanned in the earlier period (2003–2005). The already erupted sovereign debt crisis of Greece and Portugal and Ireland was about to spread to the big ones—Italy and Spain. If M. Trichet had not tightened monetary policy in 2011 would this second stage of the sovereign debt crisis still have occurred? Almost certainly yes.

Question 23

Simonnot: At Deauville, Monday 18 October 2010, Angela Merkel and Nicolas Sarkozy demanded an amendment of the Treaties with two objectives. The suspension of voting rights within the EU for any country in grave violation of the pact (budgetary) and the creation of a permanent rescue mechanism. This device, if one believed media accounts, did hardly anything to modify or suppress the clauses (in the Maastricht Treaty) about no bail-outs of member states in the euro-zone. How can we explain the immediate market reaction—an acute crisis of market confidence and a dizzy climb of long-term interest rates?

Brown: The aspect of the Deauville summit meeting (October 2010) between Chancellor Merkel and President Sarkozy which most upset markets (for weak European sovereign debts) was the suggestion that from 2013 there would be a requirement that private sector lenders (to the weak sovereign) participated (via debt re-arrangement, in effect reduction) in overall resolutions of debt crises which involved official EU support. This had not happened so far; especially in the Greek crisis EU (ECB) funds had been deployed without making private creditors of the Greek sovereign suffer write-offs or freezes. So, it was understandable that private creditors, for example of Italy and Spain, would suddenly take fright.

Ultimately, if a flight of capital was to form out of a member country's sovereign debt and banks there were three stark alternative outcomes, one involving exit from EMU even though such a possibility gets no mention in the Treaties. First, the country (bank and sovereign) could default at least in part, whilst staying in EMU; second the country could get access to EU support, staving off (or indefinitely postponing) default and exit; or it could promptly exit EMU. The second alternative was the one followed in all cases so far. At Deauville, the hint was that the second alternative would involve also the first (though there was the risk here that capital flight could develop to such a degree as to overpower any potential EU support); the third alternative is "out there" but has not happened yet.

15

Draghi: "Whatever It Takes"

Question 24

Simonnot: In a speech in London, July 26, 2012, Mario Draghi, the new president of the ECB, declared "in accordance with its mandate the ECB is ready to do whatever it takes to save the euro. And believe me that will be sufficient". These few words sufficed to calm the markets and to bring down interest rates. How can we explain that this was considered then and still today as a sort of miracle accomplished by the Italian magician? Is this not additional proof of what Greenspan described as the "irrational exuberance" of markets—a phrase continuously seized upon by advocates of market regulation?

Brown: When Sig. Draghi talked of "saving the euro", the euro as a possible hard money or as a European "Deutsche Mark", within the status quo institutional and legal arrangements (as set by the Maastricht Treaties), was already beyond salvaging. The monetary inflation which the ECB created during its first decade (following the inflationary years before under the dying sovereign Bundesbank) had culminated in a fantastic bust. The choices ahead were: first, starting anew on designing a sound euro and related institutional structures without all the revealed flaws of the old, in effect terminating the Maastricht euro experiment; second, simply returning to national currencies with no journey into a new improved monetary union; or third, continuing with the status quo of a rotten soft euro, but now firmly held together by the ECB engaging in permanent manipulations, monetary engineering, vast largely camouflaged taxation and monetary repression. In London, Sig. Draghi in effect claimed that he had secured the third route for the future of European Monetary Union, boasting about the ECB's role in accomplishing that "feat".

If Sig. Draghi had made this boast without any "understanding" first with Berlin, it would hardly have been meaningful. Perhaps on the day of the statement there would have been some closing of short positions (in weak euro sovereigns and the euro), reflecting the possibly diminished "danger" of a euro break-up. But that is all. Chief Draghi would not have had the authority on his own, to carry out "whatever it takes policies". If Berlin were opposed to the implementation of these, Draghi would have had to walk back from his bold talk. A top German government official had only to air the view that the Bundesbank did not have the constitutional authority to cooperate with Draghi's boldness, whilst alongside indications emerged that the German Parliament (Bundestag) could not pass the necessary legislation for the Federal Republic to participate in European "bail-out" institutions, for Draghi's talk to turn to ridicule.

The reasonable assumption is markets understood Chief Draghi's speech hinted strongly that he had consummated a deal with Berlin. Indeed, shortly afterwards details of the OMT program (outright monetary transactions) emerged. This would in effect allow considerable monetization of short-run debts of weak sovereigns. Berlin did not make any challenge. The Merkel–Draghi "axis" was visible to all.

Question 24, Part 2

Simonnot: Let's accept your explanation, but we must still say why Frau Merkel gave her consent to Sig. Draghi? Under what pressure? According to what reasoning? For what end? What roles did the French play in this abdication? And why did the Bundesbank accept the de facto situation?

Brown: Why were markets so sure that Chief Draghi had already consummated a deal (to do whatever it takes) with Chancellor Merkel and that the Bundesbank would not mount effective opposition?

Chancellor Merkel had already embarked on the train of "doing whatever it takes" the previous year (2011)—specifically at the May 2011 EU summit; she had blinked first. There French President Sarkozy had made an empty threat of "pull out" of EMU if Germany did not agree to Greek bail-out. If only she had said, okay, go, we can speculate that Sarkozy would have been back in no time to accept her terms for EMU continuation. At that time, the Bundesbank under the leadership of Axel Weber had showed some discomfort. His resignation followed, but this lacked demonstration effect as there were many cynics in the marketplace who attributed it to Weber's chance to become Chair of UBS. Chancellor Merkel appointed Jens Weidmann in his place. As her chief economic adviser and former IMF economist, he was viewed as non-ideologue at least half-sympathetic to prevailing neo-Keynesian dogma in the central bankers club if not the most enthusiastic—hardly the person who would wage war for a hard currency, though he might make some "song and dance".

In summer 2012, the clouds over Italy and Spanish debt had darkened. The OMT program effectively provided for monetization of short-term debts in those countries subject to their signing up to an EFSF bail-out program with all its conditionality. Chancellor Merkel had already taken the decision to back the status quo in EMU even if that meant a soft euro and vast contingent liabilities for German taxpayers. There was so much scope to hide the future potential tax bomb and also present taxation in the form of growing interest rate repression. Selected by Chancellor Kohl for fast lane promotion after her emergence within the Christian Democratic Party in East Germany following unification, she had demonstrated total loyalty to his policies including Europe. After stabbing him in the back and becoming leader of the CDU in 2000 (and Chancellor from November 2005 onwards), she showed no inclination to truck with elements of euro-dissent within her party. True there was the potential opposition from Finance Minister Schauble to bail-outs of weak EMU members; but there were cynics who saw the apparent conflict between the Chancellor and her Finance Minister as a case of a "good cop, bad cop" play. Ultimately, the finance minister was not a serious threat: and in any case he had been a full perpetrator of EMU as number two to Chancellor Kohl during the key founding years.

We should also recognize the absolutely key influence of the Obama Administration in laying the ground for Chief Draghi's "do whatever it takes" boast. Treasury Secretary Geithner was a busy diplomat, well connected to the movers and shakers in the drama of the failing European Monetary Union. As the senior official in the Treasury below Secretary Summers in the late years of the Clinton Administration charged with consummating the IMF loans during the Asian and emerging market/Russian debt crises of 1997–98, subsequently a US-appointed director at the IMF, and then as New York Fed President, he knew who to call, whether in Paris, Brussels, or Frankfurt. He also became welcome eventually in Berlin given the presents he was bringing to overcome resistance there to rescue plans for monetary union.

Amongst the motives of the Obama Administration (additional to its general pro-France and pro-EU leanings) in pressing for a continuation of the

EMU status quo was concern that a radical change in direction could be another Lehman moment—something it desperately sought to avoid not least given the approaching November 2012 US presidential and congressional elections. Geithner was ready (as empowered by President Obama) to offer US assent to huge loans from the IMF to the weak European sovereigns far in excess of normal legal limits (especially relative to size of quotas)—loans which on some definitions would eventually "bankrupt" that institution and in any case were of dubious validity (in terms of the IMF statutes) given that they were not for conventional balance of payments financing.

The claim that IMF funding on the massive scale approved by the Obama Administration (which had already agreed to big increases in IMF quotas in 2010) was the essential condition for the monetary Metternichs in Berlin and Paris to triumph is not an exaggeration. It would have been wholly possible for the US Administration to use its effective veto power in the IMF to halt those loans. That was not going to happen given the top economic policy officials (including Larry Summers as Chief Economic Advisor) which President Obama had selected and evidence of their past and present conviction that vast IMF loans in international debt crises were the way to stop a repeat of the 1930s. There was no inclination amongst these officials to consider unsound money as the culprit for crisis and sound money as the cure. Moreover, the cronies of the Administration on Wall Street (see Durden 2015) linked in to top Obama Administration officials in various ways, not just via Secretary of State Hillary Clinton and the Clinton Foundation but much more broadly, had no truck with such heresy which was so much at odds with self-interest. The Big US Banks had been all-in the euro-integration bubble of the previous decade with hugely capital-intensive networks built on the premise that monetary union was here to stay and flourish. The Crash had revealed their massive lending into the European banking system. When ECB President Draghi delivered his speech in London, the real news was that he knew the Obama Administration was behind "whatever it takes". As vice chairman of Goldman Sachs International between 2002 and 2005, he surely had fine intuition regarding the total landscape of Wall Street and its links with Washington, knowing when a deal was a deal.

Let's return to the role of Bundesbank Chief Weidmann. Media reports suggest that he did offer his resignation in response to Draghi's "do whatever it takes" speech and its effective endorsement by Merkel. But he subsequently withdrew his resignation, deciding that staying on was the best way to safeguard the independence of the ECB and also to continue the defence of hard money principles. This tale does not make much sense. Germany had the potential to set the terms of EMU's evolution from this point. Political forces though would have to bring pressure for this potential to be realized. Weidmann in tamely remaining at his Bundesbank and ECB desk would not help stimulate that political process. The nickname of Weidmann is "weichmann" (softy). In subsequent EMU history he has repeatedly justified this nickname, as for example when he gave a speech in 2017 defending ECB independence against German critics who were lambasting the QE program. Yes, in 2012 summer markets could have expected that he would challenge in some token way the ECB's authority to pursue OMT program or other "do whatever it takes" policies of balance sheet expansion in the German Constitutional Court. But Merkel knew, and markets knew, that this would surely be a lengthy process, likely to get nowhere. It was just self-serving show/charade for the decaying one-time hard money citadel of the Bundesbank under President Weidmann.

Question 25

Simonnot: In their BIS paper (2012) "Central bank balance sheets as policy tools", the economists Durre and Pill cite data and graphics which show that the ECB has monopolized a considerable part of bank intermediation. Do you agree with this? And if so, what are the effects of this monopolization? Should one not see there a sort of "sovietization" of the European banking system? Is the same phenomenon evident in Great Britain?

Brown: The thesis is that the ECB took over the broken-down interbank intermediation within the European Monetary Union—replacing loans from Bank A to Bank B (most likely A in Germany and B in Italy) with a loan from A to the ECB and from the ECB to B. And things have remained like that since or even got larger (in terms of the turntable role of the ECB).

Let's go back to square one. In the monetary boom years 2003–2007, banks inside EMU were engaging in interbank lending to an extent which could not be justified by sober rationality. The climate was one of bubble in European financial (and bank) equities with widespread and strong belief in the new era of European monetary integration. The first shock was when this interbank market seized-up in summer 2007.

Bank management and bank shareholders should have known better. They should have realized the large net loan exposures to banks and countries beyond prudent limit, especially given uncertainties as to whether there was a lender of last resort within EMU, and the possibility (not talked about) that in principle EMU could blow up. There should have been an awareness that banks were highly leveraged and high risk in many cases.

So, what to do when reality pierced through fiction? One option would have been to have a standstill on interbank repayments related to those banking institutions paralysed by illiquidity, followed by an agreed plan on refunding the respective interbank debts with equity or loan capital. Some banks would have taken large haircuts on interbank loans and panic might have erupted. The alternative was to insert ECB as intermediary—but at what price? How much would the hard-pressed weak banks (their shareholders and bondholders) have to pay for that favour, and how much would the imprudent banks who had got into this situation have to pay for some degree of protection?

A main critique of the ECB's huge intervention into the intermediation process is that it failed to impose serious charges as outlined. This ignored Bagehot's principle that lending in such circumstances should be at a penal rate. Weak banks, and especially in Italy, with growing access to very cheap funding via the ECB, just became zombies rolling over their balance sheets and in turn rolling over loans to zombie borrowers. The pain of restructuring was delayed or postponed indefinitely. Zombie borrowers, whether corporate or personal or state, got new leases of life. The alternative scenario of a big shake-out and restructuring would have led to a big and rapid shrinkage of the European banking industry and a growing role for non-bank intermediation in the US. And maybe there would have been new entrants into the banking industry without the legacy problems and thereby with a competitive advantage. None of this happened to any substantial degree.

Question 25, Part 2

Simonnot: But this installation of the ECB as "intermediary of last resort" in addition to its role as "lender of last resort", won't that induce a systemic ankylosis for an indefinite period? Is it the same in the US and Great Britain? And how will one exit? Follow-on question: this supplementary role for the ECB, isn't it contrary to the European Treaties?

Brown: In effect, the ECB has become a huge permanent lender to weak banks; and an absolutely core component of this operation is the flow of surplus funds from banks in Germany into the Italian banking system. In the books all of this appears as short-term money market operations. But the economic reality is long-term lending to (and in effect capitalization of) the weak banks at subsidized rates with the ultimate default risk parked in the ECB. As you say, this whole operation. Hence high-powered money (equivalently monetary base) is totally dislodged from the pivot of the European monetary system. (By construction it was already dislodged but not totally already at the start of EMU when the architects abandoned any plans for Bundesbank-style reserve requirements and adopted a corridor system of interest rate manipulation.)

Is this pattern of financing sustainable in the long run? The biggest question here is whether German savers (whether individual or corporate) will continue to tolerate the zero or negative returns on bank deposits (in Germany) or whether at some stage there will start to be a drain of funds into alternative forms of credit intermediation. In effect, the deposit base of German banks would shrink—and those one-time deposits would flow instead into credit paper issued by German and other European borrowers. In this way, the implicit intermediation tax would be avoided. The big overhang of excess reserves would get even bigger (relative to a shrunken demand for reserves by German banks). This would bring even more downward pressure on German bond yields (more into sub-zero territory)—and so German banks would be holding even more reserves as a share of their total assets. It is implausible that they could find a profitable business model in these circumstances; perhaps they would switch to more charges on deposits and bigger fees on lending, but this would accelerate their overall decline. And at the margin, the German public would switch increasingly to holding cash rather than bank deposits. Increasingly, banknotes held by the German public would be the counterpart to the huge ECB stock of interbank lending.

Is this consistent with the Maastricht Treaty? I am not a legal expert; and lawyers are a very weak reed on which to base sound money (Markus Kerber excepted!). I would have thought that huge ECB creation of reserves to lend into weak banking system filled up with weak sovereign debt was against the "spirit" of the founding documents—but so what? The guardrails against unsound money practices which were in the Maastricht Treaty according to its architects have long since collapsed or been exposed as phantom.

Does a similar situation exist in the UK or US? No. The central bank balance sheets there have not been filled up with interbank loans. The nearest comparison is the filling up of the Fed's balance sheet with mortgage loans (mainly issued with guarantee of housing corporations). But there is path to shrinking these—not re-investing maturing proceeds and selling off in the marketplace.

References

Durden, T. (2015). *Untouchables: Obama Cronies Protected Wall Street's Most Criminal from Prosecution*. Zero Hedge.

Durre, A., & Pill, H. (2012). *Central Bank Balance Sheets as Policy Tools*. Bank for International Settlements.

16

The Greek Crisis

Question 26

Simonnot: Let's come now to the "Greek crisis" and first of all the question of Greece's entry into the European Monetary Union. At the time there was the suspicion that Goldman Sachs, as advisory bank to the Hellenic authorities, had "massaged" the presentation of Greek economic statistics so as to facilitate Greece's entry into the union. In your book, *Euro Crash*, you maintain that the real state of the Greek economy was masked voluntarily by the Frenchman, Christian Noyer, then the ECB vice-president (who afterwards became the Governor of the Bank of France) for strategic reasons (e.g. Greece had just been invited to become a member of the International Organization of the francophone countries) and also business (Greece a customer of French armaments industry). How was it that other members of the monetary union, notably Germany, didn't notice this deception, and that if were allowed to take place, that it would put in danger the euro itself and would cost so dearly not just Greece but also those countries that came to its support?

Brown: The issue is whether Greece made it into the euro-zone due to the artful financial services of Goldman Sachs or to the grand aims of the Quai d'Orsay (as advanced by Noyer, previously the top official at the French Treasury, successor Trichet there) with none of the key players in the drama fooled by the Goldman data.

The direct answer is some combination of the two, but those fooled were unusually reckless about dispensing with safeguards against such trickery. Yet trickery and French policy aims on their own would not be sufficient to get across the required hurdles to the finishing line of EMU membership. That required a Franco-German deal. Germany was set on expansion of the EU to the East. France was not keen on that project. So, what was the trade-off? Germany accommodated France in some respects in matters regarding European Monetary Union including Greek membership.

And, in all the years since, I have found no evidence that Berlin realized in advance the full extent of dangers ahead regarding a potential European sovereign debt crisis. More likely in the sunny days of the great monetary inflation of 2002–2007, which came remarkably soon after the brief storm of 2000–1/2 (prior to which there had been the monetary boom of 1995–99 which overlapped the creation of EMU), German officials like most market participants were lulled by the sirens of the new "Great Moderation".

These were the years of tremendous optimism about financial integration in Europe—a lead speculative narrative of the asset inflation. Along with this, sovereign debt spreads were compressed to tiny amounts even when possible future scenarios were ugly if anyone cared to think about them. In my book, *Euro on Trial*, published in 2004, I had a chapter on how the euro could break up, but when I spoke about this topic most audiences regarded any such idea as wildly away from the mainstream.

German officials were influenced by market circumstances as described and it is doubtful that they ever drew up scenarios of how Greek entry (or early Italian entry at the start) could influence outcomes in an explosive fashion. The monetary chapters of the Maastricht Treaty were written for a permanent monetary union with no exits; anything else was heresy.

Yes, Germany in the lead-up to EMU had been very concerned to set fiscal limits. And an overriding concern here was that foreign countries should not take advantage of German savings to fund their own profligacy. But Greece is a very small economy: how could it really have serious influence on Germany? Yes, there was some realization about the danger of banking crisis in small countries and how this could have magnified impacts via contagion; that was one factor in the initial rejection of the Baltic candidates (subsequently reversed); several years after the EU and ECB approved Greek entry, those two institutions blocked a Lithuanian entry request (which on geo-political grounds Berlin would have been supporting surely), whilst Paris would have been unenthusiastic (given its lack of enthusiasm about EU expansion to the East).

Question 26, Part 2

Simonnot: All that said, once the Greek crisis had erupted, wouldn't it have been better to let Greece exit the monetary union? Given the tiny size of its economy, which you underline, a such "Grexit" could surely have been easily supported by other members of the union? Isn't that what Germany wanted? Why was France opposed? And if Germany was inclined towards an exit for Greece, why didn't the German view prevail?

Brown: Here are some explanations, some overlapping, and not mutually exclusive.

Once a Greek exit takes place, the myth that EMU is forever and dissoluble becomes shattered. If Greece goes, why not Spain, Ireland, Italy in the future? The Maastricht Treaty had promoted this myth—no mention anywhere of possible exits. The "euro-elites" might have considered that it was worth their co-citizens paying upfront to keep this myth alive, rather than suffer a crisis of contagion and a related spreading of the realization that there is existential risk in the euro. (In any case "paying upfront" could be camouflaged in many ways from attracting voter attention). If existential risk became established, then there would be no one unified money market anymore; rate differentials would emerge reflecting risk of each member country leaving at some point.

Banks and non-bank financial institutions had large sums lent to Greece or vulnerable to big loss on a Greek exit from euro. The creditors (which included US financial institutions with loans to European banks vulnerable to Greek default), by prevailing on governments and central banks to go softly on Greece, to take their time, and only discuss debt haircuts after much delay, had much time to rescue as much as they could—pulling funds out and having these replaced by effectively official financing. Crony capitalism lives on! German banks and financial institutions, amongst others, had a direct interest in this state of affairs. As we have discussed (question 24, part 2), the Obama Administration was dead-scared that Europe could trigger a Lehman crisis under its watch, with 2012 elections on the horizon, and played a key part in the diplomatic dealing to prevent a Greek exit.

The big exporters who are a key constituency of the CDU party in Germany have great fear of a euro break-up and of a return to cheap currencies especially for Italy. No doubt this had an influence on Chancellor Merkel's decision making, at least as a background factor. Greek exit, on this view, could have become a catalyst to an Italian exit.

If Greece had left the euro, and a Greek euro (let's call it drachma) had re-emerged, there is every reason to think this would have collapsed without external support. Greece would have faced hyperinflation. Quite soon the rest of the EU (and possibly the US) would have had to join in a multilateral financing package for Greece to end financial monetary chaos along with a humanitarian crisis (which eventually could mean a return of Greek military dictatorship and departure from NATO: Russia and China could score geo-political advantage). Perhaps both Berlin and Paris and ultimately Washington believed that a botched and stage-by-stage bail-out operation upfront under which Greece remained in EMU was better and indeed less expensive than this hyperinflation and eventual response alternative. Yes, on the other side of hyperinflation there might have been a bright future for Greece; but which politician anywhere would be plotting that course? Better to keep kicking the can down the road.

Question 26, Part 3

Simonnot: Was the Greek crisis perfectly forecastable? Or was it at least predictable for those who knew the reality underneath its accounts? But if it was so easy to predict by those in the know, did they in fact make the prediction in good time? The question follows, if many lost, who gained?

Brown: This is a perennial question in different forms across many episodes of market mania/irrationality; can the sober rationalist using skill gain from the manic behaviour of the ultimate losers? Timing is always a big problem, and the cost of shorting can also be high. Presumably, the wise who had a good idea about what was coming did not invest in Greek bonds during the irrational phase (say 2003–2007 when funds were flowing into the "high coupon" European sovereign debt markets chasing ever-smaller yield margins on the dubious hypothesis that monetary integration justified their slightness and also possibly their eventual fading away). But going short was not so easy; and in any case profits could be long in coming if at all due to bail-outs, which were also foreseeable to some extent. Who wants to be on the wrong side of a multi €100 bn bail-out by the euro-establishment (underpinned by German taxpayer and indeed ultimately the US taxpayer)? So who were the gainers?

Some Greeks were big gainers—those who got their funds and money out of Greece during the heyday into Germany and the US. That would never have been possible on such favourable terms and on such a scale in aggregate during the days of the drachma. We should also consider as gainers those making profit and enjoying income bonus during the heyday (a whole list here including corrupt officials, unionized workers in state sector, those enjoying effectively superfluous jobs in public enterprise and government, businesses gaining from inflated state expenditure and much more)—when Greece was living far above its means with huge budget and current account deficits apparently financed without friction and at little cost. No doubt many of these realized that good times could not roll on forever and acted accordingly in the management of their finances.

17

Banking Union

Question 27

Simonnot: Let's come now to what is called the project of Banking Union as launched in 2012. The principle argument used by the advocates of this new European institution is that "banking nationalism" (to use their terminology) has been an aggravating factor in the financial crisis. This situation, they claim, translates into a one-to-one relationship between the financial situation of each State and that of the banks under its authority. A fragile banking system makes fragile the state on which it is dependent, and reciprocally, a state in financial difficulty puts in danger banks which are under its sovereignty. Hence, a banking union would seek to break these vicious circles—circles which they claim we do not see in the US where banks are not tied to one or other of the states in the federation. On top of these considerations there is a sociological analysis according to which there has been a perverse "concubinage" between the states and the banks at a national level in the sense that the same social classes make up the cabinets of government and the boards of the banks. For example, in France the graduates of the same well-known star "polytechnics" occupy the top posts in the Treasury, Bank of France, and the banks. What do you think of these analyses and the Banking Union project which follows from them?

Brown: The starting premise of a banking union in Europe is that banks need support, most explicitly in the form of deposit insurance, but also in terms of potential emergency access to public finances in situation of financial crisis. The opposite premise is that deposit insurance has been a curse—as has been contingency access to public funds in crisis. If neither were available, then banks whose business model involved the marketing of high-quality deposits to the public, which in virtually no circumstance would become irredeemable (temporarily or beyond), would pursue low-risk strategies (including high-equity capital, low or zero leverage) so as to build credibility. Banking union under such circumstances is an irrelevance.

How can we get from here to there? As of now Europe is plagued by a weak banking industry. Specifically, how could Italian banks be rebooted into free market banks no longer dependent on public support? A radical proposal would include widespread bankruptcy and restructuring together with removing impediments to new entry into the banking industry whether from inside Italy or outside. As a matter of social equity, "legacy" deposits would be protected. In sum, the road to competitive free market banking has many political hurdles along the way. In practice, as in so many other areas, the short-term solution has been to kick the can down the road. Crucially, the ECB has ensured (in conjunction with the German chancellery) that a huge flow of negative interest rate money continues into the Italian banks. The ultimate provider or guarantor is the German taxpayer.

There is no idealism in this kicking down the road or in proposals for banking union (though as you mention some proponents buttress their claims with cosmetic idealistic views). The raw facts are that European citizens are paying for the continuing bail-out, implicit or explicit, of weak banks. And without banking union to date the German contribution to the bail-out is very large. Is it imaginable that Berlin could formulate proposals which would mean the flow of money from Germany into Italy and other weak sovereign debt/banking countries would diminish; the cost of supporting a type of "banking union" with all its contingent tax liabilities in Germany could be less than for the present status quo. That is possible, though doubtful, and it would be a hard sell in the German political arena.

Some supporters of a banking union would reject the premise that in any case a free market banking system without contingent public support including deposit insurance is the ideal to be pursuing. They would nurture a state-protected euro-wide banking system. Federalist Europeans would argue that the financing of this protection should be federal as indeed is the case in the US. In this model, however, the federal authorities would be able to impose strict effective limits on the individual states' scope to run-up contingent liabilities. There would be federal-wide regulation to match. And state governments would be highly limited in their scope to run up deficits. These conditions are far away from the present situation in Europe.

Question 28

Simonnot: Jean Pisanni-Ferry wrote in *Le Monde* (26, May 2019): "The perverse interaction between insolvency of the banks and insolvency of the states has not been cut (by banking union). Attenuated by the passage of the large banks under the direct control of the ECB it has not disappeared as the outbreak of Italian fever in autumn 2018 illustrated". This sober reflection of one promotor of the banking union project, 7 years after its launch, is surely significant?

Brown: Proponents of banking union may claim a little success, though recent market events such as you mention raise doubts. Objectively, in any case, reduction in the circumference of the vicious circle in so far as it has occurred is due mostly to the vast QE and other radical monetary measures of the ECB. For example, Italian banks have disposed of significant shares of their one-time holdings of Italian government bonds to the Banca d'Italia. At the same time Italian banks have suffered continued loss of deposits (some created by non-bank Italian sales of government debt as the counterpart to QE operations) which have been transferred net to Germany. Banks there which in general have large surplus funds re-lend these amounts into the ECB (via the Bundesbank), and they get transferred back to Italian banks through the support operations in place. In sum, Italian banks are now less exposed to the Italian sovereign than say 10 years ago; but their deposit base has shrunk also, so there is still an infernal circle in place.

What is the prospect of the infernal circle coming to an end at some point? One way in which this could occur is in an Italian exit from European Monetary Union. A period of high inflation would bring a fall in the real value of debt outstanding. There would be a new source of demand for bank deposits in Italy in nominal terms (as expressed in say Italian euros). And if the exit were to bring an economic miracle, banks would be able to obtain new capital on the basis of improved business prospects.

Question 29

Simonnot: Why does the European Commission go to such trouble to convince the Italian government to return to its claimed path of budgetary rectitude, threatening it more or less openly with sanctions which would be viewed very badly and which would reinforce populism in Italy? Last time, several months ago, the brutal climb of the Italian spread (spread of Italian government bond yields above German) convinced the government in Rome to present a budget plan less jarring from the viewpoint of Brussels? Why not wait for the next similar market crisis?

Brown: If the Italian state were borrowing in international capital and credit markets without any promise (implicit or explicit) of support from EU (including ECB), then yes, the market could take care of the Italian fiscal situation without the EU Commission getting involved. If the market did not like the Italian budget arithmetic, the new issue market for Italian state loans would dry up. And a crisis in the market for outstanding debt could force Rome into remedial action. But we are a long way from that situation. Most important, there is the incessant gravy train (or drug train) of negative interest rate funding from Frankfurt, which starts at the ECB back door. The cost of this train delivery is borne first and foremost by German taxpayers. But these costs are on a contingent basis (evident only when eventually Italy rearranges its debts or leaves the monetary union). So long as this train runs, the credit markets are pricing in its continuation; that is the most important credit assessment ingredient, not the state of Italian finances. Berlin, in an effort to contain these eventual costs, must depend on the Commission to do its work. Of course, Berlin could stop the train and force Italy into a market-determined path of budget improvement. But that would be in conflict with the Merkel–Draghi pact to save the euro status quo, meaning keeping failed Italian state and banking entities on perpetual life support.

Question 29, Part 2

Simonnot: Why and how is the cost of this gravy train (butter plate in French) supported first and foremost by the German taxpayer? Don't taxpayers in other countries make a contribution? And why would they not?

Brown: As a practical matter, most of the flight of deposits out of the Italian banking system has gone into the German banking system. The counterpart to this is a huge creditor position of the Bundesbank (which receives the excess deposits from the banks in the form of reserves) with the Target 2 system of the ECB. Ultimately, these funds are re-lent (via the ECB and Banca d 'Italia) into the Italian banking system (LTROs, repos and all the other artificial lending props).

If Italy were to exit EMU at some stage, these Target 2 loans from Germany would surely suffer large loss in terms of the euro (without Italy) or of a new German euro. That is the present contingent liability for German taxpayers—adding potentially to German public sector debt.

More widely, the ability of European institutions (such as the EFSF) to raise funds in capital markets at fine rates for the purpose of lending into Italy and other weaker sovereigns depends on the fact that there is effectively a German guarantee. Yes, there are also co-guarantees from France, etc. But in terms of market perception the German backing is critical.

Question 29, Part 3

Simonnot: Are there statistics on the subject of transfers of Italian deposits, and why is there this tropism of Italian deposits for German banks? Doesn't German banking have its own difficulties? Shouldn't French or Belgian or Dutch or Luxembourg banks serve also as refuge for Italian depositors? This displacement of deposits, isn't it an involuntary tribute to the banking union project, the clients of Italian banks voting with their feet, in effect?

Brown: We know that the credit balance of the Bundesbank with the Target 2 system of the ECB and the debit balance of the Banca d 'Italia with the same has increased in step with the QE operations (Italian central bank buying government bonds). The debit balance of Italy with the ECB Target-2 upped from around €208 bn to €480 bn in the period end 2014 to end 2018 (incidentally similar increase in debit balance for Spain). The Spain and Italy increase in debit balance pretty well equals the increase in German credit balance over the same time interval. There is no data to demonstrate a transfer of deposits, but divergence of deposit growth between these countries is in line with this occurring. And we should not, of course, assume that it is just domestic deposits which may have been moving into Germany, but also foreign (including foreign bank) deposits from Italy and Spain. Evidently German banks have many problems also, but the reasonable assumption would be that the value/effectiveness of the virtual government guarantee of deposits is much stronger in Germany (the Federal Government there with top international credit rating) than in Italy (or Spain), or for that matter in France or Belgium, especially taking account of ultimate currency risk were Italy to leave EMU and Germany to launch a new Deutsche mark.

Question 29, Part 4

Simonnot: If the euro did not exist, would Italian depositors be able to transfer their deposits into Germany without converting their liras into Deutsche marks, thus bringing about a devaluation of their money? Isn't it therefore thanks to the euro that the Italians can find refuge in German or other banks? Isn't there a point of leverage there to bring pressure on the Italian government?

Brown: Absolutely; if there had been a floating exchange rate between the Italian and German monies, then the desired transfer of funds into Germany would have driven up the DM and down the lira to an extent which would discourage this from occurring (implicit here would be an overshooting of the lira's fall against the DM matched by some expectations of an eventual recovery). Surely though the Italian government and the Italian bankers would welcome in some sense the fact that their citizens could not so easily escape their ailing condition so cheaply? Maybe the Italian government less so because it would no longer be raising finance at the ultra-cheap rates resulting from ECB transfer operations and monetary manipulations; yes, it could levy inflation tax instead but that is politically unpopular.

Question 30

Simonnot: How can we explain that financial integration in the euro-zone is inferior to what it was before the crisis according to the ECB's own calculations?

Brown: According to the main indices of financial integration, this has begun to rise again in recent years inside the euro-zone but has not approached the level on the eve of the 2007–2008 crisis. My problem in answering this question is a total lack of confidence in the indices as prepared by the ECB. Without being an expert in these, what I have read about them suggests that they treat narrowing spreads between sovereign debt markets as a positive reading for integration, and similarly for spreads between bank debts. One of the indices treats the degree of co-movement of asset markets between countries as a positive indicator. Yet I would maintain that in a well-integrated financial market across the EU, the opposite would be the case. Integration should not mean pricing given categories (government bonds, bank bonds, equity) of assets at the same level across national frontiers irrespective of different risk or other key characteristics; rather integration means that these frontiers should not be the source of differential pricing for assets of the same characteristics in terms of risk, return and liquidity.

For example, the fact that spreads between sovereign bond yields came down to virtually zero in 2006 (including Greece, or Italy, vs. Germany) should not have been read as a sign of grown financial integration (Fed Chief Bernanke in an infamous speech praising the euro at the time did just that—see Bernanke 2004)—but as a sign of sick integration. Efficient markets would have reckoned with the higher default risks and the possibility that no bail-out clauses in the Maastricht Treaty could mean under certain circumstances debt write-downs. Similarly, efficient markets would have taken note of the grown and dangerous leverage in the banking industry in all European countries and what this meant for differential risk, given dependence on sovereigns for aid.

A further episode of global asset inflation since the crises of 2010–12, featuring this time huge actual and potential interventions from the ECB, has brought spreads back down to low levels. That is an indicator of sickness not health.

What would be better components of financial integration? Some suggestions are: divergences in credit spreads across the euro-zone for bank credits of similar risk; new entry of foreign euro-zone financial institutions into domestic markets; divergences in indicators of financial institutional competition across the member countries (including life insurance).

18

The Underperformance of Europe

Question 31

Simonnot: How was it that Europe suffered a second recession after the great recession of 2008 in contrast to the US? In consequence there has been an overall underperformance by the European economy of the US. Is it because the ECB delayed so long in implementing non-conventional monetary policy as adopted by the Federal Reserve? Or is it because of the budgetary and fiscal policies of Obama, then Trump?

Brown: The fact that unlike the US, the euro-zone suffered a second recession, from September 2011 to December 2012, was absolutely not due to tardiness of the ECB in adopting QE and other measures of monetary radicalism (which the Fed implemented earlier).

First, we should recall that in fact the US economy did experience a significant growth cycle downturn from June 2010 to September 2012. Part of the explanation for this was knock-on effects from the sovereign debt crisis in Europe.

Second, the 2011/12 recession in the euro-zone stemmed directly from the outbreak of the sovereign debt crisis and related banking crisis which had no counterpart in the US. This outbreak should be seen as a belated outcome of the monetary inflation in the euro-zone from 2003 to 2005, which had spawned a virulent asset inflation including sovereign debt, credit (e.g. mortgages in Spain and Italy) and financial equities, in particular. In the US, there was no counterpart to this delayed asset deflation—everything had fallen together in late 2008. (A historical precedent was the delayed bankruptcy of

Germany in summer 1931, well after the start of the global recession and initial crisis.)

Third, there is absolutely no evidence that the Obama fiscal reflation and Fed QE did any good in stimulating the US economic expansion; in fact, there is much evidence to the contrary. This was the weakest ever upturn following the Great Recession ever recorded in the US. (Before this, the so-called Zarnowitz rule always applied; the stronger the downturn the sharper the subsequent economic recovery.)

Fourth, if the ECB had fully implemented Bernanke-style monetary radicalism at the start (say in 2009–2011) that would have meant a much weaker euro—thereby challenging a key element of the US reflation policy, dollar devaluation. The bad feelings which would have resulted between the euro-elites (in Frankfurt, Paris, Berlin) and the Obama Administration regarding responsibility for launching currency war would have jeopardized the cooperation which played such an essential role in later salvaging European Monetary Union (see answer to question 24).

Question 32

Simonnot: Did this underperformance make the euro-zone more fragile than the US when addressing the next cyclical downturn?

Brown: Probably—but the rationale goes far beyond comparing cumulative growth rates in recent years. Vulnerability is determined first, by the extent of accumulated malinvestment and over-leverage (much of which is camouflaged by artful financial engineering during the boom period); second, by the potential strength of economic recovery mechanisms.

Is there now more accumulated malinvestment in the euro-zone than in the US? We cannot know for sure, even though superficially it seems that European monetary policy has been even more aggressively radical than US in recent years (say from 2015). Thus, we could hypothesize that the bigger the monetary inflation (in this cycle so far more evident in asset inflation than report consumer price inflation) the bigger the distortions including malinvestment and thereby the subsequent fall. In fact, superficial assessment of relative monetary ease may be wrong and the hypothesis mentioned is not proven. In any case, we won't discover the full extent of malinvestment until after the crash (a bit like Warren Buffet's observation that we find out who is swimming naked only when the tide goes out).

We can hypothesise about mal-investment in Europe. There has been a fantastic real estate boom/bubble in Germany (commercial and residential real estate construction well above trend); and the super cheap euro created by ECB policy in recent years (aggressive QE and negative interest rates) has surely led to a bloated export sector in the euro-zone, perhaps most of all in Germany but also more generally. The export boom in Europe and especially Germany has been highly leveraged on Asia, especially China, at the epicentre of global asset inflation. Very likely over-leverage will be discovered in some areas of the European corporate sector when asset price deflation and recession set in; and of course, the excess leverage in the financial sector from the last cycle has still not been corrected. Finally, when considering excess leverage and potential financial instability one has to fear the extent to which pension funds and life insurance companies in the euro-zone have been obtaining yield (in the context of domestic negative rates) by taking huge bets on high-risk US and emerging market credits.

As against all this there is also likely to be huge malinvestment and excess leverage in the US. One just has to think about Silicon Valley including Big Tech, commercial real estate (including residential apartments, warehouses, offices and some retail), and the shale oil/gas sector. Everyone knows about the rampant leverage in the corporate sector, disguised in part by sky-high present equity valuations. The private equity bubble will burst at some point and this is concentrated in the US (though also important globally). One also has to think about the malinvestment in human capital. Bottom line: the long-run toll of asset inflation in this cycle could be very large in the US and euro-zone; we should be humble about our ability to prognosticate where worse.

By contrast, when it comes to economic recovery mechanisms, there are some grounds for greater optimism with respect to the US than Europe. This has nothing to do with the scope for monetary stimulus—which as we have seen likely did more harm than good in the present cycle (and also in many previous cycles); recoveries from recession have occurred over large spans of history without central banks administering "contra-cyclical policies", driven by the invisible hands of free markets. Rather the issue is the relative strength of these free market forces driving recovery. We should consider crucially the strength of creative destruction—the generation of new investment opportunity and the efficient removal of accumulated malinvestment. Including crucially those of creative destruction. Also relevant is the relative strength of the obstacles in the way of these free market forces generating upturn from recession. Judgement here is highly tentative. Conventionally, one would say the US is better placed than Europe in this assessment of free-market-driven recovery potential. The build-up of monopoly power in the US economy together with the entrenchment of neo-Keynesian dogma in monetary and fiscal policy making there, should mean even greater caution than usual in predicting the future will be like the past.

19

The Balance Sheet of Draghi

Question 33

Simonnot: The mandate of Mario Draghi has now come to its end; what balance sheet can one make of this? Better or worse than that of Jean-Claude Trichet?

Brown: Trichet committed the original sin of fanning monetary inflation (albeit underway for some time before he took the Chair, but approved by him in his capacity as Bank of France Governor and a key member of the ECB council) and as such deserves opprobrium especially as his appointment did not turn on his behaving in that way. Specifically, during the first two years of his tenure as ECB Chief (starting in autumn 2003) that institution stuck with a very easy monetary policy, which at the time he implicitly defended as essential to countering the unwelcome strength of the euro versus the dollar. Remember that during 2003–2004, the Bush Administration was directly pursuing a weak dollar policy (albeit not specifying this in public statements) and the Federal Reserve facilitated that by "breathing inflation back into the US economy"—all for the greater purpose of winning the November 2004 elections.

If Trichet had been a true descendent of Dr. Emminger, believing fervently that European monetary independence should mean not following US monetary inflation, he would have developed and pursued a sound money policy and allowed the euro transitorily to rise towards the sky. That was what happened to the Deutsche mark in the years 1969–78 when the Bundesbank defied the example of the Arthur Burns Fed. Trichet turned his back on that example and homed in on the unsustainability of the US current account deficit as if this was a real problem rather than a monetary symptom.

True, before Trichet took the chair, the ECB in Spring 2003 had adopted a strict version of the 2% inflation standard, its Chief Economist and ex-Bundesbanker Issing having launched this at his infamous press conference. But Trichet enjoyed the political freedom in his first two years to pilot a different path. Indeed, his past history had included indications (perhaps false!) of favouring hard money policy (see our earlier discussion in this dialogue, question 14). He chose not to do so. The result was that European sovereign and bank debt markets became the epicentre of global asset inflation—and consequently in 2007–12, Europe was afflicted with credit and banking collapse even more severe than in the US.

Even when the collapse started, it seemed Trichet had no grasp of the phenomenon of asset inflation and how it turns into asset deflation. He continued to keep monetary policy remarkably tight through 2007–2008, even raising interest rates in response to an oil price bubble which fed through to transitorily high goods and services prices. Almost certainly that action made the financial crisis and economic downturn worse.

Without Trichet there would have been no Draghi (both as ECB chairs). Mario Draghi's reputation which helped set him up for the top monetary job was as a fixer and regulator who had chaired the BIS committee on financial stabilization (proposing and implementing mega regulation) as set up after the 2008 Crash. As an economist he was a disciple of Stanley Fischer and well in tune with Bernanke-ism. There was no expectation amongst those ultimately responsible for appointing him to the top of the ECB that Mario Draghi would suddenly decide to blame unsound money for the crash and great recession and embark on the road for sound money. None of the power-brokers in his appointment wanted that. Draghi has delivered what was expected of him. On top, Draghi has demonstrated the skills of a great diplomat, knowing first and foremost how to accomplish his ends in the power centres of Berlin and Washington, working crucially with the US during the crisis—having a particularly good relationship with President Obama's financial fixer, Treasury Secretary Geithner.

Draghi was Draghi, he never pretended to be anything other than a fixer and an MIT-trained monetary engineer—whether doing what it takes to save the euro or other tasks. His academic reputation as a student of pioneering neo-Keynesian professor and subsequent monetary official Stanley Fischer helped him enormously claim the mantle of "central bank independence" and enjoy high respect within the Obama economics team. Trichet could have followed a hard euro policy in 2003–2005 and survived. Draghi could not have done so without risking the break-up of the current euro; he had no inclination anyhow to follow such a policy and his appointers knew that.

Yes, Draghi's policies have been abhorrent to political and economic liberals (in J.S. Mill sense)—whether negative interest rates, financial repression, massive back-door aid to weak banks and sovereigns, always with a special sweet spot for the onetime financial and political élites in his home country, Italy. All of this was possible due to Chancellor Merkel's acquiescence and Mario Draghi knew that only too well. He was the man for Merkel and of course the Elysee Palace. He served them well. Yes Mr. Fixer has also been a big-time Mr. Devaluationist. And that is exactly what Berlin and Paris wanted, though they would never dare say so explicitly.

Mario Draghi on 30 January 2020, visited the German President to receive that country's highest award, the Order of Merit (given also on earlier occasions to previous ECB Presidents). There was much chatter in the media about Draghi as the saviour of the euro. But as noted already in the answer to your question 24, he was no such person. He played a part (not the most important) in preventing the deeply rotten euro by 2012 from dying and securing a route along which the status quo of a flawed monetary union could survive in Europe most likely for many years to come. That meant also blocking alternative routes to a new sound euro under a reconstructed monetary regime. Draghi had undoubted talent in helping to establish in Europe the tyranny of unsound money.

Question 34

Simonnot: Let's turn to your project for reform of the euro. A question before we get started: this project is not conceivable without a profound and intimate collaboration between France and Germany. But in present circumstances is that still possible? And if one refers to the nature of that collaboration for the last 10 years wouldn't it give back to Germany a hand (position of monetary power) which it has lost since the creation of the euro?

Brown: Without France and Germany in agreement about the conditions for reform, there will be no successor to EMU-1 (the present unreformed EMU) except perhaps in the form of a narrow monetary union of Germany, Holland, Belgium, Luxembourg and Austria. Accord between Paris and Berlin is an essential condition for a reformed wide union but is no guarantee that this will escape the doom of the present union. The power of inspiration required for that hopeful outcome is hardly evident at present.

The nature and extent of Franco-German "joint leadership" in any serious reform of the European Monetary Union (EMU) depends very much on the circumstances in which this takes place.

Take first a reform drive starting in the context of a widespread public revulsion, obvious in France and Germany (and also wider afield), against the central bankers in Frankfurt (the ECB) for having brought about vast financial instability through their radical monetary policies, ending in Great Recession and Crash. The devastating consequences, including loss of savings (and pensions) for a huge number of individuals, could become the basis for an inspired cooperative push towards reform in which Paris and Berlin would set the agenda and take the key joint decisions. The reform drive would depend on strong political forces being in the ascendant in both countries which shared this diagnosis of what had gone wrong (most of all unsound money) and what had to be put right (joining the road to sound money).

By contrast, if the drive for reform comes in a situation of an already grave crisis for EMU, where this is heading towards a likely break-up under the unstoppable force of huge capital flight (most likely into Germany), then Berlin might start calling the shots on its own.

For example, Italy might have been forced out of the union (in the sense of having to suspend one-to-one convertibility between deposits in Italy and the rest of the euro area due to capital flight provoked by fears of sovereign and bank defaults, likely accompanied by speculation on an exit by Rome from EMU) and devastating forces of contagion threatening the survival of the wider union. This could occur without there being any serious idea about monetary reform guiding political leaders in either Paris or Berlin—just a mixture of improvisation and pandering to popular misconceptions.

Berlin for example could call for redoubled budget austerity and for holders of weak country debt and bank deposits to take haircuts. But this rhetoric would not be accompanied by any serious reform demands, most importantly the ending of the 2% inflation standard, the banning of negative interest rates, QE and back-door lending by the ECB.

Alternatively, the crisis may have erupted in the context of widespread suspicion that Germany is "cooling" on monetary union. Then an ultimatum based on long-developed popular criticisms (including direct or indirect German taxpayer funding of bail-outs and negative interest rates on savings) would emerge from Berlin setting conditions for a revamped union (EMU-2).

Negotiations with Paris would likely start with Berlin establishing minimum conditions for the launch of EMU-2 rather than going it alone.

French power to strike a balanced deal would not be trivial even given the starting ultimatum. Paris could play to a still widespread reluctance in

Germany to unleash dark nationalism from the past and preference for European cooperation. Paris could use the duality in the German political landscape to its advantage—albeit one should never underestimate the importance of diplomatic skill or the lack of it.

Looking to the Kohl–Mitterrand relationship is not at all helpful as a template for the creation of EMU-2. The historic Franco-German bargain which consummated EMU-1 was based on deeply erroneous prescriptions and trade-offs.

The cynic could say that if Franco-German leadership produced such a fatally flawed monetary union at such a historic moment of potential creation in Europe, there is no basis for hope about a reformed EMU-2 any time soon. A long time in the wilderness must precede the realization of the joint ideals of "sound money" and "Europe". There should be a slaying of troublesome ghosts from the past.

These have included German ordo-liberalism. That has been the basis for putting trust in so-called independent central bankers supposedly outside the political arena to do what is best. Central bank independence became the false idol of EMU-1, blinding most to the much greater importance of a set of rules and fundamental principles to be followed. Another ghost has been money as a tool of the state (national or supranational) rather than a good which should be of high quality in competition with other stores of value and mediums of exchange.

Slaying of past ghosts requires confronting history. A Cahier Noir has yet to be published, or a Parliamentary Enquiry launched, whether in France or Germany, about how checks and balances essential to a well-functioning liberal and democratic order failed to halt the journey into a deeply flawed and damaging monetary union.

It is possible that this time in the wilderness will end with spring shoots appearing first in France, not Germany. These would amount to a renaissance of sound money principle. That is not to say that this has much circulation or political influence within France actually. But nor does it have greater effective weight any more in Germany.

Speculating about the rebirth of monetary orthodoxy in either country and how this could flourish into a Franco-German drive for a reformed EMU-2 should be based on what might happen most likely many years from now rather than on the present landscape. France's past traditions and experience of monetary orthodoxy are surely as strong a root for hope as Germany's brief hard money era from the late 1960s to the early 1980s.

Question 35

Simonnot: If all the same one wants to see the good side of this history, it would be to note that the euro, by its own dynamic, as vicious as it seems to be, has escaped being taken over by the governments of the euro-zone, the honey pot of money creation remaining just outside the reach of the statist bears. After a twentieth century of great inflation caused by a complete detaching of money from any real anchor (devaluation following devaluation), according to this optimistic assessment European citizens have discovered or rediscovered that money does not have to be a "royal characteristic/good", contrary to what one teaches in our schools and universities. Indeed, must not be such if it claims to be a good money. Shouldn't this practical lesson be the starting point for construction of the new euro?

Brown: It is true that under the regime of the euro, governments have not obtained "inflation tax" revenues on anything like the scale rampant during much of the twentieth century. But instead governments have obtained vast revenues from a new alternative tax, also stemming from the process of monetary inflation, what we could describe as a "monetary repression tax" (MRT). The ECB has been an extensive levier and collector of MRT, distributing the proceeds to member governments on a very unequal basis, mainly in a way to sustain weak public finances and banks. The power to levy MRT in Europe, as in the US and Japan, stems from the combination of the 2% inflation standard with the long coincidence of a sustained downward rhythm in goods and services prices due to real non-monetary forces.

Specifically, so far throughout the lifetime of the euro, a varying combination of non-monetary disinflationary forces including digitalization, spurts in globalization and productivity growth, and emerging resource abundance has been subjecting goods and services prices to downward influence. If central banks including the ECB had been following sound money policies, prices would have been falling. Instead, by aiming for 2% inflation they have repressed interest rates to levels far below those which would have pertained under sound money. The difference between the actual repressed rates and the sound money rates can be thought of as a tax. One might imagine that the suppression of rates would go along with spending boom which would ultimately drive observed inflation much higher, meaning MRT would metamorphize into "conventional" inflation tax. But this has not happened; in large part because the continuation of the 2% regime and the huge asset inflation which has accompanied this means that there is a considerable reticence to invest especially in long-gestation projects. Everyone and their dog fear a bad outcome in the long run. Growing monopoly power (itself to a considerable degree a by-product of asset inflation—see introductory essay to this volume) and accumulating malinvestment have also weighed on new investment in general terms (and so on overall prosperity).

No precise calculation is possible of the MRT as we do not know for sure the neutral level of interest rates which would have prevailed under sound money—huge counterfactuals involved. But let's say in euro-zone, German 10-year government bond yields would have been at 2.5% rather than say −0.5%. Throughout the euro-zone space, MRT could well have been running at 3% plus. Without this the Italian government deficit would be at say 6% of GDP. Weak banks in Italy and indeed throughout the union, including Germany, gain from artificially low rates applying on their loans from the ECB, a form of disbursing the MRT revenues. The collection and disbursement of the MRT is not of course entirely at the discretion of the ECB. This institution's pursuance of manipulated low rates and its pattern of lending are all ultimately sanctioned by member governments, most importantly in the form of understandings between Berlin and Frankfurt one might say (the so-called Draghi–Merkel axis).

The tax collectors and their beneficiaries cannot count on MRT always being as high as today. The disinflationary forces mentioned will surely become less powerful at some point. Then the central banks in their pursuance of revenues for their political masters would have to switch emphasis to the historically better known inflation tax. Bottom line: the low level (compared to history) of inflation tax so far under the euro-regime is no source of cheer about the future condition of the euro.

Question 36

Simonnot: Recall that in the minds of the founders of the European money, the euro-zone should walk on two legs: a monetary leg and a budgetary/fiscal leg. The pressure of time, due to geo-political factors (the fall of the Berlin Wall and German unification—this latter was a long French nightmare) and also the German wish that the euro should be as good as the Deutsche mark (according to the expression of that time) one had to make do with walking on one leg—the monetary leg—with the setting up of the ECB. But for the founders, money was essentially an attribute of the state, money could only survive if backed by a European budget, the embryo of a Federal Europe, and thereby of a European fiscality, enhanced by a capacity to issue European bonds (backed by all member governments).

It is not impossible, besides, that in the calculation of the founders, the fatal failure of the one-legged euro in their view would be the essential catalyst to the coming about of the European state which they desired and just which many Eurocrats are trying to sell us today.

In the construction of the new euro, shouldn't one set out in bold that first, budgetary and fiscal sovereignty is perfectly legitimate, the various peoples do not have to accept that decisions about revenues and expenditure of their state are made outside their control; and second, this sovereignty should be perfectly compatible with the new euro, the financial markets playing the roles of safeguard and warden? In this way one would play upon the actual popularity of the euro and at least the equal unpopularity of the Eurocracy in all its forms.

Brown: The story that the founders of the euro believed that ultimately the euro should be the money of a European federal state and indeed could only survive as such, has been told in many places with some variations. It does not seem that all the German founders were of that mind. (I have personal recollection of a symposium in 2010 with Otmar Issing where this Bundesbank founder specifically stated that it has always been his view that European federal government was not required and that markets should constrain bad fiscal behaviour. Crucially, though, Issing did not make the point that sound money is required for markets to function well in that disciplinary function).

Belief in the need for a European state seems to have been a dominant French view (one thinks of Delors and Mitterrand). Delors is said to have aired the view widely that the Euro would be the first step towards a politically integrated Europe rather than the other way around—in the sense that euro survival would require political integration.

Historically, the Bundesbank's position in the 1980s was that political union was an essential first step before monetary union, and there were speeches in which reference was made to the political unification of Germany in 1870 preceding the issue of "one" German money. This position did not reflect any enthusiasm for political union amongst those Bundesbankers—more likely it was a talking point for moving very slowly (but in the event Chancellor Kohl managed to blow that caution apart).

Could in fact a new euro flourish if the statist view of money (and in this case its essential tie to European political integration) were abandoned?

As you say, if the markets were given the chance (free of intervention) to fully discipline member governments in their fiscal habits, then the taxpayers in the fiscally more prudent countries would not have to fear that they would be bailing out the profligate. For this discipline to be effective, there would have to be no asset inflations where hunt for yield means that weak government debt becomes overpriced (relative to fundamentals); also no back-door lending at the ECB (e.g. member central banks using special credit lines to stanch runs on their banks stemming from feared national bankruptcy); in the ultimate, the weak countries with weak banks if serious about staying in the union in a situation of sapping confidence in their credit worthiness would have to rescue their union membership by pulling on their own bootstraps (and this would involve sometimes haircuts for bond holders in the banks and in the government).

In such a union, there could be no pretence that union for all is eternal. Anyone practical would see the risk under some conditions of EMU exit for the weak (with possible re-entry later).

20

The Principles of the New Euro

Question 37

Simonnot: Let's come now to the principles of the new euro based on those of sound money. What would these be today? (We will come later to how to put them into effect.)

Brown: First, a necessary preamble: in the present global fiat currency world, no money has equal attraction everywhere. Only gold money in a world where all countries use gold as money would have such a property. In the fiat monetary world as it is, there are strong protective barriers—founded on such frictions as legal tender, transactions costs, exchange risk and distrust of foreign power abuse (the political jurisdiction issuing the given money taking advantage of foreigners who use its money). These barriers mean that even if the US dollar were a super sound money (which it has never been so far!), it would not become universal money (in the sense of gold above). Its use would be more intensive inside the US than outside.

Alternatively put, individuals are conditioned by such barriers to exercise a degree of home bias towards using the fiat money which is issued within the jurisdiction where they live. State power within each country bestows considerable advantage on the national money vis-à-vis foreign monies most obviously through legal tender laws and compulsory use in transactions with the government sector.

In this world, Europe has its own domestic money or monies. Universal money is not an option. The extent of domestic money circulation (whether one for a union or many separate sovereign monies) depends partly on the quality or otherwise of the world's number one international money, the US dollar. The more attractive is the latter (in terms of money's functions), the less would be the use of any European money (multinational or national).

Even so, super-soundness of the US dollar would not dissuade Europeans using their domestic money or monies to a considerable degree. Moreover, in the fiat money world there is no guarantee that today's super money is tomorrow's super money. It would be derelict of Europe (through its representative institutions) not to develop a monetary infrastructure, creating its own domestic alternative, even if the US currency were for now ideal. In fact, the US dollar has always fallen short of the ideal standards for the highest quality money, albeit by varying degrees. Monetary inflation and the waging of currency war have plagued the US money.

Following on from this preamble, the prime aim of creating a European money (the euro) and a monetary union of European countries within which this circulates as domestic money, should be for this to be of the highest quality (defined for the three functions of store of value, medium of exchange and unit of account). Indeed, the quality should be higher from the perspective of residents in each and every member state than what they could have obtained otherwise.

The advantages of the new euro (compared to the situation for sovereign monies without union) should extend far beyond the elimination of exchange risk within the union and of transaction costs of exchanges of monies for payments. The old euro delivered these. The core attractions of the new euro would stem from its soundness.

What are the key aspects of soundness which the new euro should be built upon?

A sound money euro would not be an instrument of state power, whether as a means of raising tax revenue in various forms (including notoriously inflation tax and monetary repression tax), or of redistributing revenues between member governments (including those institutions receiving government subsidies in various forms), or of manipulating the flow of credit towards one or several governments or countries (as occurs for example in the Target-2 system or more specifically "ECB backdoor lending operations"), or for promoting government economic policy.

Indeed, the presumption should be that so-called contracyclical monetary policies have failed and are doomed to continuing failure when assessed correctly. The degradation of monetary standards for the greater purpose of "economic policy" would not be permitted in a sound money constitution.

Under a sound money regime, on average prices of goods and services over the very long run tend to return to a constant mean, but over short and medium periods of time prices fluctuate upwards or downwards. There is no official setting of interest rates whether for short or long maturities. Rather, these are totally free of intervention or other forms of manipulation. There is no targeting of inflation or the price level.

Towards implementing these principles, the sound money has to be firmly anchored. That is indeed deeply challenging in a monetary environment where central bankers and governments (including the ECB) in recent decades have presided over a complete dis-anchoring. History and principle suggest that anchoring depends on a rules-based control of the monetary base (either automatic as under gold or quasi-constitutional as in the brief monetarist era) for which a broad and stable demand must exist, not hyper-sensitive (but elastic nonetheless) to small changes in interest rates.

There is no magic wand for anchoring a money. The founders of the new euro must establish it as work in progress mandated at the highest constitutional level; in the interim they should provide guidance on the transition (more to follow in subsequent questions and answers).

Question 37, Part 2

Simonnot: Why make complicated when one can make simple? Today, the greatest gold power in the world (only taking account of central bank reserves) is (bizarre one never hears about this) the euro-zone itself, with 10,000 tonnes, almost 2000 tonnes more than the central bank of the US. Would it not be the simplest and most efficient to found the new euro on gold?

Brown: In my original response to this question I proposed that the new euro be firmly anchored and this meant that monetary base must again become the pivot of the system. I designated this plan as "work in progress" when the new euro is launched rather than something which is settled even before the launch. I had great reservations in suggesting delay and you are right to question whether this is appropriate. Why not move immediately to gold convertibility? Yes, establishing the new euro as a gold money would be one way of anchoring. Indeed, it may be the only way if there are no grounds for confidence in constitutional rules regarding growth of a fiat monetary base.

Let's look first at the euro as a gold money in principle and then second whether it makes sense to "go for" this idea right at the start in view of the political dynamics related to launching a new European money. Full gold convertibility for the new euro would mean the following.

A say, 500 euro gold coin would be minted whose gold content would be fixed as so many grams (around 10 grams taking US$ price per kilogram at around 55,000 [50,000 in early 2020] and a dollar/euro rate of 1.10); the public could obtain this coin on demand in exchange for euro banknotes; for a tiny fixed fee the public could get gold bullion exchanged into gold euro coins of equivalent weight; gold coins would be received by banks on a 1:1 basis in exchange for paying out banknotes or creating deposits of the same euro amount. There would be no restrictions on melting down gold coins for bullion.

In effect this would be the same arrangement as for gold currencies before 1914 and for the US dollar right up until March 1933. There was a key difference, however, between these two regimes.

Under the pre-1914 system, above-ground global gold supplies and the monetary base of the global money supply (for all countries on gold) were highly overlapping. Under the US gold standard of 1918–33 (with almost all other countries either not on gold or on a gold exchange or bullion standard with convertibility in practice outside the US only applying to huge quantities or via the US dollar), the monetary base of the US (as almost the only full gold country) had a much looser link to above-ground global gold supplies (in part due to the huge sales of gold in the US by France and Britain during 1915–17, see question 4, page).

In this truncated gold standard, the Federal Reserve did not leave the supply of monetary base in the US (an aggregate which became meaningful once the world gold standard had fallen apart in 1914) to be determined by gold movements in and out of the country. They at times strenuously used other tools (especially open-market operations) to influence its path.

That would be the most likely and feasible path taken by the monetary authorities under the new euro regime. The situation of large and potentially volatile shifts in demand for gold bullion in the world outside the euro-zone would encourage this resolution. These shifts might occur for example in response to geo-political developments or to a change in the outlook for inflation in the US. Investors globally would continually assess how much of their gold exposure to hold via the now gold-based euro and how much directly in the metal.

One big potential shift: holders outside Europe of bullion might decide to change radically its weight in their portfolios now that the price of gold and the euro (say, in US dollars) had become almost perfectly correlated. The authorities of the euro-zone may well not allow huge and sudden shifts in demand for gold to have a one-to-one impact on the monetary base. Rather they would boost the supply of non-metallic components of monetary base (especially deposits at the central bank) to at least partly compensate for say, an external drain of gold, thereby modifying the rise of interest rates and also of the gold and euro price (in dollars).

In order for the euro-zone authorities to have the flexibility to act in this way (with respect to the overall supply of monetary base within the zone), there must be such a surplus of gold in official reserves that convertibility of the euro does not come into doubt (as was effectively the case for the US from 1918 to 1932, even allowing for the trumped-up gold scare of 1931 to which according to Milton Friedman and Anna Schwartz the Fed over-reacted—see Friedman and Schwartz 1963). A large part of the backing for high-powered money (alternatively described as monetary base) would still be non-metallic.

This suggests that ideally the legal gold equivalent of the euro should be set at a level such as this surplus was assured. At today's euro–dollar exchange rate (say 1.10) that could mean a gold price substantially above the $50,000 per kilogram at present (March 2020). Speculation that the new euro would be based on gold and that monetary use for gold (largely as gold coin) in the euro-zone would correspondingly add to global demand for the yellow metal could be the spark to that further price rise; there would be a tempering influence however from the consideration that at last the world would have an international gold-based money and so the demand for safe haven against growing fiat money chaos could diminish.

This type of euro-gold system would be far from the pre-1914 global model. Yet we could well imagine that demand for monetary base across the member countries (of gold-based European Monetary Union) should be much larger and more stable than in recent decades. A fillip to this occurring would come from an assault on anti-competitive practices which now favour payment (and credit) card settlement in retail trade rather than cash. The components of monetary base (gold, gold coin, deposits at the central bank) would be highly distinctive with no close substitutes unlike the case for a wholly fiat regime featuring in addition extensive deposit insurance and non-penal access to. Hence anchoring of the monetary system should be possible to attain, albeit far from perfectly.

There would be new sources of danger and concern. The crucial exchange rate between the US dollar and the euro (the former still not on gold) would become influenced by demand–supply conditions in the gold bullion market. The gold price in dollars would move perfectly in step with the euro–dollar exchange rate. There would be two-way forces operating between the gold and euro markets to simultaneously determine those almost perfectly correlated prices.

The nearest historical example: the situation for the franc–dollar and gold–dollar exchange rates in the brief sub-period of European gold bloc history when the dollar was wholly inconvertible into gold (March 1933 to

January 1934). The euro-zone is much larger relative to global economy than France in the mid-1930s (or France plus Switzerland plus Belgium plus Holland—the core members of the gold bloc) so that is a point of cheer for the new regime. The historical example, though, does alert us to the danger of currency war.

For example, the US government could seek to devalue the dollar against the euro by operations in the gold market—stepping up gold purchases so as to raise the gold price in dollars.

Hence, it could be crucial that the creators of the new euro reach understandings internationally about codes of international behaviour which would fit the new regime (inhibiting currency war). On the US side there would surely be much effort to ensure that the new euro-zone regime did not facilitate money laundering globally.

Back to the start: should a gold euro be part of the launch prospectus for the new euro or listed under work in progress for the post-launch designers of the new regime? Much would depend on the circumstances of birth. If the new euro comes into existence as Paris and Berlin desperately seek to salvage monetary union from the fire destroying the old one, then implementing a gold regime in timely fashion may be all but impossible.

If, by contrast, a gentle launch is possible with the date of death for the old regime yet to be determined then gold becomes a more feasible option right from the start. Even here political dynamics may argue against losing political support for a new euro amongst potential supporters who are still cautious about a return to gold. On the other hand, the political dynamics may support gold at the start, especially if that becomes a rallying point in the German scene amongst savers long robbed and abused by the old euro-zone authorities.

Question 37, Part 3

Simonnot: You quote the gold bloc 1934–36 in your response—an experience which has not left good memories in France, which is the least that one can say about it. It ended up with three devaluations under the Front Populaire (I like very much to recall that Mitterrand also proceeded to three devaluations according to much the same timing). But aren't there lessons to be drawn from another experience, totally forgotten today: the Latin Union, which you quote yourself as a forerunner to the new euro which you describe (Euro Crash, pp. 184–85)?

Brown: For most of its existence, the Latin Monetary Union (LMU) functioned as part of a global gold standard. Most countries in the world outside the LMU were also on the gold standard (with the notable exception of China which was still on silver). And so the LMU was in effect a union between some European countries to share common gold coins. This meant that the band of possible exchange rate fluctuation between LMU currencies was even narrower than between any LMU and non-LMU currency. Exchange transaction costs would also be especially low or non-existent between LMU currencies.

By contrast, the gold bloc of 1933–36 consisted of a group of European currencies which were still to varying degrees convertible into gold, with key currencies outside the bloc (the US dollar, Sterling, and the German mark) either inconvertible or only partially convertible. (From January 1934 the dollar became convertible into gold again for non-US residents at its devalued rate). The situation for the gold bloc currencies, of which by far the largest was France, became untenable as the Roosevelt Administration in late 1933 engaged in a deliberate policy of driving up the dollar price of gold (in effect devaluing the dollar against the franc). Alongside there was a big increase in hoarding demand for gold globally; once the US fixed a new much higher gold price ($35 per ounce) in early 1934 huge capital flight occurred from the gold bloc—mainly out of France into the US, meaning huge gold shipments across the Atlantic (in west direction) as the French authorities sort to defend the franc's gold (and now effectively US dollar) parity against waves of speculation on the gold bloc disintegrating.

A gold euro as described in my answer to the previous question would not at all be in the situation of the LMU, unless the US in particular also came fully on to gold at the same time (highly implausible). On the other hand, the situation of the gold euro could be much better than of the gold bloc. That depends on there being "currency peace"; hence, the importance of the euro-2 gold launch being in the context of a US–Europe understanding. There are grounds for optimism here. After all, Europe through its radical implementation of QE and negative interest rates has been usually the currency war aggressor in recent years (since 2014/15). It would be offering to cease this aggression.

Question 38

Simonnot: "An instrument of exchange without a past is not imaginable. Nothing can take on the function of an instrument of exchange which has not already been an economic good to which people assign a value in exchange before even it is in demand as an instrument of exchange" writes Ludwig von

Mises (Human Action 2018). Our new euro, will it obey this famous theorem of the Austrian School economist?

Brown: At one level the hypothesis of Mises which you quote has been disproved by the many decades now during which purely fiat money has been the dominant, in fact virtually exclusive, form of money spanning all three functions: transactions, unit of account and store of value.

At another level, though, we could argue that an essential condition of the dollar assuming its global hegemon role has been some degree of convertibility into gold right up until 1971; since then, the continuing huge gold reserves of the US (whether in the US Treasury or Federal Reserve) and the possibility that some type of gold convertibility might be restored in the distant future have been elements (in the dollar's hegemony). When we turn to key currency countries outside the US, a far back history of convertibility in gold may well have been a pre-condition of their now wholly fiat monies enjoying such large and widespread demand; some comfort is also provided by a presumed zone of stability (not based on any treaty or other arrangement) within wide margins for these currencies against the US dollar. Specifically, these key fiat monies (e.g. in Europe or Japan), by the time they became fiat, already had huge circulations, which continue through well-known network effects even after the initial conditions (including gold convertibility) have disappeared.

The euro has been in a different situation. It has no pre-history to its present fiat money status as a gold money. The huge and immediate demand for this currency on its launch was in reality a legacy demand from the individual sovereign monies. The founders of the euro understood this, when they established a phased withdrawal and replacement of sovereign monies by the euro (in appearance) even when the former were already essentially dead.

It was far from certain that the euro would have enjoyed wide popularity, sufficient for all the network effects to flourish, under all circumstances. We could have imagined that a sceptical European public would have switched towards the dollar. In fact, the success in part depended on the cleverness of the popular slogan that the euro would be the European version of the Deutsche mark—just as hard. That claim has been fraudulent but nonetheless it was successful in allowing all the necessary thresholds to be surpassed for the euro to emerge as a highly liquid international money.

When we turn to the next euro, euro-2, which could be launched when euro-1 fails, it is not self-evident that there is a way to assure its success in capturing a huge demand both within the monetary union and outside. That is where the gold link might be essential.

Question 39

Simonnot: If the new euro at its start is not based on gold, with what would we replace the well-known automatic mechanisms of money based on metal? One of these is a general rise of prices of goods and services (this translates into a fall in the value of money) having as consequence a constriction in the supply of money; and any general fall in prices of goods and services (equivalent to a rise in the value of money) triggering a growth in the production of money and consequently the supply of money—a stabilizing mechanism which (this fact needs emphasis) requires no intervention in any form.

Brown: The automatic mechanisms are unique attractions of a full global gold standard. You cite one mechanism in particular—the one which determines how much gold is mined (the supply of new above-ground gold supplies); this mechanism plays a key role in constraining long-run swings in prices of goods on average. The supply of monetary base grows more flexibly (when considered over periods of say several years), though still at only a low rate, than under a Friedman-style monetary rule of x% per annum. This means that periods of persistent monetary shortage or excess induced by shifts in demand for monetary base—bearing down on prices or pushing them up—should be less severe. The essential conditions for these automatic mechanisms of the international gold standard to function include normal very slow increases in the overall stocks of above-ground gold (coming from new mining production), large and stable demand for gold money (and gold in any form), not hyper-sensitive but elastic with respect to changes in money market rates, and full confidence in gold convertibility of notes. We should stress this last point. Sound money based on gold requires adherence of the money issuer to the pledge of convertibility. In the case of the new euro that means no suspension of the commitment to convert money on demand into gold euro coins or to mint gold euro coins freely from gold bullion presented (in accordance with the legal weights specified).

If most of the world were on the gold standard, then indeed we could have considerable confidence that under this monetary regime prices of goods and services over the very long run would tend to "regress towards the mean", consistent with persistent rises and falls (of prices) over medium-term periods; meanwhile, the mean might gradually shift. The marginal costs of mining new gold may rise or fall relative to prices in general, though historically under the international gold standard when we consider the very long run constancy seems to have prevailed. Arguably, the fact that the real price of gold in terms of US purchasing power is now (2020) more than double what it was under the full gold standard in the decades up to the First World War reflects the tremendous demand for safe haven in the evermore frightening world of fiat money together with the fact that all the easy to get gold has now been got (with spade and shovel) out of the earth's crust. But if an international gold money were born then we could see a more normal growth in demand for gold. This would mean the real price might again become stable in terms of the very long run. A decrease in haven demand for gold could be balanced by an increase in demand for monetary purposes (specifically gold coin circulating). We should stress here the very long run and the global dominance of the gold standard.

Over the short and medium terms, sustained swings of prices on average away from the mean are possible (under a gold standard regime) due to the influence of real factors (surges in productivity growth, globalization, resource discovery, structural changes in labour markets and product markets which bring wages on average to a changed level relative to overall productivity—and whilst this is occurring the path of prices on average is pulled away from long-run mean). That would be the case under any sound money regime, gold or non-gold.

For example, a productivity surge would lower costs and prices; yes, this would stimulate gold mining production if indeed mining costs fell in step, but the reaction of gold supply and the influence on money supply throughout the gold standard world would be slow (not at all compatible with fiat money managers aiming at price level stability or inflation stability over a period of 2 years). And we should also consider here the growth of real demand for money likely during economic boom, meaning that in the peak expansion phase of the cycle, demand for gold as the base money would likely grow solidly (putting upward pressure on money market rates despite increases in gold production). Decreased unionization and the rise of the gig economy may impart a downward shift to wages and also prices to some extent; under a full gold standard this may not stimulate any increase in supply of money (newly mined gold) if mining costs (and particularly wages) were not pulled down by these labour market dynamics; but they may well be influenced to some degree.

The gold euro, euro-2, as described here, would not start life as part of an international gold standard. Rises of prices (in euros) on average for goods and services in the new euro union would not lead to a meaningful curtailment in the growth of global gold supplies in any automatic fashion such as to cause a tightening of monetary conditions. Rather, any automatic tightening of monetary conditions within the euro-zone would come from the demand side for money.

A persistent rise of prices would go along with a raised demand for money (in nominal terms), which in turn would mean an increase in demand for gold. The result could be a growing gold shortage within the union, which would have the effect of pushing up interest rates in the euro money markets. But this would induce an influx of gold from the world outside as gold holders there responded to the opportunity to earn a little more interest on a near alternative to gold bullion, the gold-based euro.

Hence, the automatic restraints on price rises via tightening of monetary conditions might be quite defective (relative to the situation under a global gold standard). It is possible, at some point, that rising prices in the euro-zone could create some doubts as to whether gold convertibility would persist. The political climate in the euro-zone would be an important factor here (e.g. politicians calling for devaluation or gold convertibility suspension as a way of restoring competitive advantage). Doubts would unleash a huge drain of gold out of the euro-zone (as holders of euros sought to get into the metal before convertibility ended), forcing a big rise of interest rates, well beyond what would be required to rein back prices.

In sum, a truncated gold standard in the euro-zone as described may well not produce fully the admirable stability features of the global gold standard. It could still be better, however, than the alternative routes we could think about towards creating a sound money regime—all of which involve some type of constitutional enforcement (dubious at best) of complex rules specifying changes to the specified growth of base money dependent on behaviour of goods and services prices or to estimates of trend economic growth.

Question 40

Simonnot: Suppose then that the new euro is not based on gold for the reasons that you mention. By what would we be able to replace the automatic disciplines (non-political) of the gold standard?

Brown: We have been discussing the handicaps of a euro based on gold when the rest of the world and especially the US is not on gold. The hypothetical "first best" comparison for demonstrating these has been a gold standard world as in the decades before the First World War. The handicaps are considerable, but the bottom line of my answer to your new question is that they do not outweigh the hazards of a purely fiat euro, even one designed to be in accordance with sound money principles. A gold euro should be the first choice even where the world outside remains a zone of wholly fiat money. Furthermore, there is the possibility that the birth of a gold euro in time would become the catalyst to political forces in the US in favour of sound money, interpreted as the dollar moving on to a gold standard. In that case, the journey which starts with a gold euro on its own could progress to the much better situation of both the US and Europe on gold. At the start of the journey, a European monetary union based on gold could take two forms.

In the first, monetary base wholly would be gold. Banknotes or reserve deposits issued by the monetary authority (and held by the banks) are 100% backed by gold. In addition, gold coin is held directly by the public and banks. Growth in the monetary base (currency, reserve deposits with the monetary authority, gold in circulation or in bank vaults), would be determined entirely by gold flows into or out of the European Monetary Union.

In the second, the monetary authority in Europe would exercise discretion in determining the extent to which its notes and other liabilities were backed by gold, all subject to maintaining adequate gold reserves or access to gold (e.g. from governments) to honour the convertibility pledge. In effect, the monetary authority would have considerable freedom to pilot a path for monetary base independent of gold flows. For example, it may increase the supply of monetary base (in the form of currency or reserves) by buying government securities. This was the situation and practice, for example, of the Federal Reserve during the period of full gold convertibility of the dollar (into gold coin) from 1919 to 1933. Convertibility sets limits to discretion in piloting the monetary base. If the public (domestic or international) becomes concerned about an inflationary bent, for example, accelerated redemptions into gold would force a change of policy.

It is this second form of euro gold standard which is the most plausible alternative to a pure fiat system designed to achieve sound money. It is hard to imagine the type of political forces which would back a rigid link between gold and high-powered money such as existed say in Great Britain under the Peel Act (from 1844 to 1914 when Sterling was on gold) especially if the US and rest of the world are not also under the same monetary regime. Nonetheless, the constraint of the convertibility pledge (euro into gold coin at fixed par) is a firmer basis for belief that principles of sound money will be respected than simply a monetary constitution in theory enforceable in the highest court. Sound money advocates could well suggest rules which should guide the monetary authorities under the second form of gold standard, during the presumed long stretches of time when they are not constrained by actual gold drains.

In the case of purely fiat money, soundness depends entirely on the force and adequacy of such rules. These rules as set out in a European monetary constitution document would be preceded by a bold statement of aim.

According to this, the currency (the euro) issued by the authority is to be of the highest quality—where quality relates to store of value, medium of exchange and unit of account.

One key aspect of quality: the given money should not be subject to the expectation its purchasing power eroding significantly over the long run. Under a sound money regime, there is some tendency for prices to revert to a mean over the very long run, albeit this mean might drift up or down (equal chance in either direction). In the short or medium-term, there are strong grounds for expecting prices on average of goods and services to sometimes trend down and other times up in accordance with changes in the rhythm of productivity growth, technological change, globalization and so on. All of this would be spelt out in the small print of the aim section of the monetary constitution.

The next section of the monetary constitution (below the first section describing aim), should be about anchoring the new money. A key challenge for establishing a sound money is fostering a monetary base for which there would be a strong and stable demand. A firm pivot position for the monetary base in the overall monetary system means that the authorities by keeping the growth of this to a very low but variable level (as was the case for gold supplies under the gold standard), allowing interest rates to be determined totally free of market intervention, can achieve their statement of aim (as above).

The trick to making monetary base pivotal is that it should consist of a distinct asset for which a large and stable demand exists; in all its forms (whether currency or reserves) it should pay zero interest and so money market rates are determined by the supply and demand of reserves. Steps towards this objective would be closing down all credit facilities for the banks from the central bank (or monetary authority). Instead of banks having access to central bank credit, they should hold large amounts of reserves with the central bank (or monetary authority). This would mean no "too big to fail" banks, no deposit insurance, and of course no target-2 clearing system with automatic overdraft at the European central bank.

Towards boosting demand for monetary base, large denomination notes would be again printed (say €1000 notes), on the basis that an expanded role for cash in the economy would go along with a more stable and larger demand for monetary base. A level playing field would be introduced vis-à-vis credit cards and payment cards (with retailers being freed from the oligopolies pressuring them not to charge premiums over cash prices for their use in payments).

The European monetary authority would not stick to a Friedman-type x% invariable rate of expansion of monetary base. Some changes could be made in line with estimates of sustained long-run changes in the real demand for monetary base. These came about endogenously in a gold standard world. In a fiat money system, supply changes have to be administered—or else the shifts in demand could lead to sustained price falls or rises over and above the normal fluctuations which occur related to the real factors mentioned above.

A third section of the monetary constitution would recite the principle that interest rates should be wholly market determined—meaning the monetary authority does not set policy rates in short-term money markets nor does it seek to manipulate long-term rates in any way at all. The creation of a well-pivoted monetary base as in the second section is a condition of success for implementing the third section.

There would be a fourth section of the monetary constitution outlining the legal provisions for how the monetary authority in the union is to be governed—meaning its actions and policies in accordance with the first three sections. Maybe in total contrast to the ECB, an effective guardrail would be very short-term periods of office for the chief officials (as in the Bank of England before 1914 when the Governor would serve only a one-year term). But we should be under no illusion: governance is a big trap for fiat money regimes even with ideal constitutions. Monetary authorities are easily corrupted in the sense of their main aim becoming the provision of finance to governments, much of it through the back door; hence the attraction of gold convertibility as a safety valve.

Question 40, Part 2

Simonnot: You say monetary base in all its forms (whether currency or reserves) should pay zero interest rates and so money market rates are determined by the demand and supply for reserves. But you don't say whether these reserves are compulsory or not. If the reserves are compulsory (as with stipulated reserve requirements), doesn't it makes sense that they pay interest (positive of course), given the sacrifice they impose on the bank? That stands out as one of the arguments used by the advocates of paying interest on reserves at the time of legislation providing for that notably in the US Congress.

Brown: Reserve requirements would not be stipulated as a legal minimum in the design of a fiat euro in accordance with sound money principle. Banks could choose whatever level of reserves that fitted their business model (as was indeed the case in say Britain under the pre-First World War gold standard). If there is no promise of government support for "too big to fail" banks and no deposit insurance and no borrowing facility for banks from the monetary authority except at penal rates in financial emergency conditions, then banks would tend to hold substantial reserves without any compulsion so as to avoid temporary illiquidity which could start a run on its deposits. This would be the case even though reserves are non-interest bearing. And note, under a gold standard regime where banks' main holding of reserves is in the form of gold coin or gold certificates, by definition these pay no interest. In these sound money regimes, the banks are not in fact being taxed on their holdings of reserves at all. The reserves are a distinct asset, for which there is no close substitute, and they provide a convenience yield consisting of liquidity and safety. Under a gold standard or a strict sound money fiat system, government bonds and bills by definition carry some default risk however small; for the government cannot simply print money to meet its bills. Hence, gold or fiat base money is safer than government bonds or bills under a sound money regime; banks would want to hold some of their assets in this safest and most liquid of assets.

Question 40, Part 3

Simonnot: The €500 note is no longer printed since the end of 2018 because of claims that it facilitated tax evasion, terrorism and money laundering. It made possible the transporting of enormous sums easily and discretely. A million euros in denominations of 500 weighs 2.2 kilograms compared to 22 kilograms for the same sum in €50 notes. With €1000 notes a million euros would weigh only one kilogram. Are these arguments not legitimate? Claims were made that these notes were hardly used in current transactions and that corresponding their suppression would not be at all inconvenient for common mortals.

Brown: The argument that large denomination banknotes should not be issued because they enable crime is not at all persuasive, though it has been advanced as you say by the ECB (in consultation with others) as grounds for its decision to freeze new issuance of €500 notes. And in the US, the argument underscores the refusal of the authorities there to increase note size beyond US$100. Yes, their disappearance (if universal, not the case at the moment given for example 1000 CHF notes) could add to the costs of some illicit activities, but the individuals and organizations pursuing these could surely find substitutes. It is possible that the payment systems which are devised as an alternative in the "shadow economy" would in fact add to the amount of black or grey activity (including those organizing the payments system) and aggravate the threat against the victims (as in the protection rackets). Even if despite all this, there were a reduction in total illicit activity however measured, that does not justify eliminating the large notes (or not producing them). For there are considerable benefits for actors in the white economy in having large denomination notes—most of all convenience in transactions (a ban on large notes adds to the incentives to use the plastic cards of the credit card oligopolists), expanded scope for privacy, as a store of value (yes, many individuals would hold large denomination notes as part of their savings even where no illegal intent, not trusting fully in banks and lawyers to dispose of these as wished at death or in family break-ups, and wary of bank costs). And in aggregate as we have seen the bolstering of demand for monetary base which large denomination notes brings (by stimulating the overall attractiveness of currency) is a positive development in the road to establishing a sound money (which must be firmly pivoted on monetary base as described); that is a large gain for a free society which far outweighs possible costs as above. Rather than closing the roads to freedom so as to raise the costs of some illicit activity, would it not make more sense to add to the crime prevention forces directly? No doubt the circulation of gold eagles in the US or gold sovereigns in Britain under the gold standard enabled some illicit activity—but that was not an argument surely for exiting early a sound money regime. One could well suspect that the ECB had another agenda—reducing the scope for individuals to avoid its monetary repression taxation and especially negative interest rates by hoarding large denomination banknotes. We should also consider in a world of crony capitalism, how far the gainers from handicapping cash, big tech (which has a voracious appetite for big data, not available from cash transactions) and big finance (credit card oligopolists) are in cahoots with big government (including the central bank).

Question 40, Part 3

Simonnot: I hear your arguments. But don't you underestimate the cost in time (time is money, do I need to remind you?) and the painfulness of payment in cash? Just this morning, at the fruit and vegetable shop, I was in a queue behind a formidable elderly lady who wanted absolutely to make exact payment (to the centime) in cash. Weighed down by her shopping bags, she sought to find at the bottom of a really deep wallet coins of 5, 2 and even 1 centime so as to pay her bill. Impatient behind her, I confess that I did not share the admirable patience of the cashier who even proposed to help the client in her task, an offer she evidently refused despite trembling hands. The whole operation took interminable minutes precious for ordinary mortals like me. It took me an eighth of a second to make the same operation by swiping my bank card on the machine. No doubt Big Brother will be able to know now and for all time to the exact centime how much I spent at what time and at which shop on carrots, turnips, and apples, but I don't care about this unveiling of a part of my privacy so that I gain time and comfort.

Brown: Is there a waste of time in the use of cash? Evidently, sometimes, as you discovered in queuing behind a shopper searching for the correct change. But let's consider the waste of time in use of cards—the taxi driver who has to pursue non-credited card payments to his account and finds himself a victim of fraud pursuance for which he is not insured (and even if so, the waste of time dealing with insurance claims). No doubt there are ways in which retailers can reduce the time waste for their clients resulting from cash payments (e.g. the use of automatic check-outs, staff training as to how to get the person with change difficulties out of the queue) and forces of competition would promote these. And if (as would occur were there no credit card oligopoly power) clients were charged extra for using cards (rather than the cost of these being borne by the retailer) then there would be greater use of cash, making adaptation by retailers so as to reduce waste of time more worthwhile in terms of their business. (An example of adaption could be one member of sales staff available to come and help with a situation such as you describe.) No longer having to pay monopoly rents to the card companies (in the form of agreeing not to pass on to customers the fee levied on the retailer by the card company for each transaction), the retailer would have some greater revenue capacity to improve the service for customers who pay by cash.

The bigger point here is that there should be a level playing field between cash and cards—and this means breaking up the credit card and bank card oligopoly and providing the big denomination notes which many customers would value for making transactions (and thereby avoiding card charges amongst other benefits). If customers get keener terms for paying in cash rather than by card (as could well be the case with level playing field as described) there would be less shopping on line (where cash cannot be used in settlement) and more in "brick and mortar stores", less big data available to Big Tech and Big Finance, less negative sum advertising (as driven by big data), less gig drivers and "slaves" in warehouses, and higher employment in stores.

Question 40, Part 4

Simonnot: If there are not mandatory reserve requirements and if interest rates are freely determined by the interplay of supply and demand in the money market, what remains for the new central bank as a tool of intervention or control, if however must intervene?

Brown: "Tool of intervention" is perhaps an anachronism under the new order of a sound money euro. The monetary authority will not be intervening to fine-tune the business cycle or more specifically to generate occasional monstrosities in the form of super-long business expansions which ultimately end up in a huge crisis and great malinvestment. Yet there is an important steering function for the monetary authority—setting the amount and growth path for the monetary base (once this has been established as the firm pivot to the new monetary system as already described). The constitution would set the guidelines (low growth in absolute terms but flexible according to certain criteria—all in accordance with the ultimate aims of the new regime). The monetary authority would have to monitor sustained changes in the path of demand for monetary base; for example, if this were to rise to a significantly higher level, there could be persistent tightness in the money market and downward pressure on prices; correspondingly, if there is a broad economic hypothesis now plausible as to why demand (for monetary base) has indeed risen to a higher level than previously imagined, the monetary authority would raise its target for monetary base expansion. If there is a gold link, then at times there will be changes in the monetary base determined by big inflows and outflows of the yellow metal. A sudden increase in demand for monetary base related to tensions in the financial system (risks of bank failures rising) would trigger the monetary authority into making additions to its supply but these would be decided upon in aggregate terms rather than in the form of specific loans to banks under stress. We should not have (in the new euro system) the monetary authority acting as the bail-out entity.

Question 41

Simonnot: Your plan for a monetary constitution, doesn't it risk reopening the door which we are trying to close, that is the possibility of discretionary intervention by the central bank? You know the question of Juvenal: *quis custodiet ipsos custodes*? If the central bank is again inducted as the guardian of the money, who will guard the guardian? Under the gold standard, gold was the guardian of the guardians. But under the fiat money system? If one finds the ideal index of money supply, isn't the automatic nature of Friedman's rule preferable to all constitutional precautions which one can imagine? From memory, according to ECB statistics, M0 tripled since 2007, whilst M3 grew by only 30%.

Brown: I am deeply sceptical like you regarding monetary constitutions. The issue is whether despite such cynicism, a purely fiat European currency, grounded in a rigorous sound money constitution would be better (in sense of delivering sound money) than a gold-based European currency in a world where the monetary hegemon, the US dollar, is not on gold. If the US and Europe were deciding on a joint monetary regime together, this dilemma would not be present. Unreservedly, the answer would be in favour of gold rather than constitution. Even if Europe is deciding on its own, then the best money would be gold-based. Until the US also adopts a gold money—and the birth of the gold euro could be a catalyst to this via the unleashing of political forces there— a monetary constitution alongside should constrict the scope of the monetary authority to veer "off the rails" despite the pledge of convertibility.

The architect of sound money constitutions for a purely fiat currency would ideally have in mind the construction of a monetary system where the demand for monetary base is stable and broadly based. Under those conditions the setting of limits on the growth of the base would be the total institutional intervention required. It would be great if it turned out that a fixed annual growth rate worked well—in the sense of achieving the ultimate aim of money not becoming what J.S. Mill describes as the "monkey wrench in the machinery of the economy". We should note, however, that under a full gold standard the growth in supply of monetary base was quite variable year to year, albeit always under a low ceiling in practice. It may be that one penalty of an ersatz gold standard regime compared to the real thing is a loss of suppleness, meaning greater scope for periods of monetary disequilibrium in its various forms. This would be consistent with the prescription just to pursue an x% annual expansion of monetary base given the jeopardy of discretionary interventions in the form of adjusting its growth rate to changed circumstances.

The attraction of monetary base as the target variable is that it is wholly under the determination of the central bank (in a fiat money regime). The central bank issues the constituents of the monetary base—banknotes and reserve deposits. Ideally, monetary base is a highly distinct asset, for which the elasticity of substitution into alternative assets (e.g. short-term bills or bonds) with respect to small changes in interest rates is not very high. Then demand for monetary base even in the short and medium-term is largely determined by growth of nominal incomes (in technical terms the income velocity of monetary base would be stable). This was the case for gold; it may also be the case for cash and reserve deposits under a fiat regime where there is broad and intensive use of cash in the economy, where banks do not have access to a lender of last resort, and deposit insurance is strictly curtailed or non-existent.

Can a wide monetary aggregate, such as M3, be a good second best for a well-pivoted monetary base as above, in the construction of a sound money regime, with a simple rule for monetary expansion, rather than a complex set of constitutional conditions? This is doubtful. Wide monetary aggregates include a range of deposits which are very close in nature to debt securities outside the particular definition of the aggregate. Demand and supply for such deposits are highly sensitive to small changes in differential rates of return between those close substitutes, as induced by changing competitive or regulatory conditions. Moreover, the supply of these deposits is in no way strictly under the control of the central bank; it may exert loose indirect control via changing the supply of monetary base if this is still the pivot of the monetary system. If, however, the latter has become un-pivoted (as for example by the payment of interest at a market rate on reserves), and the central bank relies wholly on interest rate pegging as its instrument of policy, its ability to control the supply of deposits (in a wide money aggregate) would be greatly handicapped.

The fact that M3 in the euro-zone has barely increased by say 30% since 2007 whilst the monetary base has tripled does not mean that we should re-appraise positively the potential role of this aggregate as a "monetary pillar". The tripling of a monetary base where this consists almost entirely of reserve deposits paying rates at market level—albeit now negative—as set by the central bank and where banks have access to huge credit facilities from the central bank, is virtually devoid of monetary meaning. Rather it tells us about the massive intervention of the monetary authorities in the bank and sovereign credit markets with monetary base totally dislodged from the pivot of the system. The only modest growth in M3 is consistent with overall income growth over the decade or more. But there is no means for the central bank to implement a target for this—other than the very indirect and uncertain routes of interest rate manipulation. In no way has moderate M3 growth been the cause of similarly low nominal income growth. Anyhow, perhaps falling prices throughout and somewhat lower nominal income growth would have been the sound money outcome, going along with much faster overall real income growth. Nominal income growth at a stable rate over the medium term and the elimination of business cycle fluctuations (futile in any case as success in producing a super long expansion means build-up of massive malinvestment with long-run consequences of struggling productivity growth and likelihood of crash-depressions) is not the ultimate aim of sound money construction. Rather the aim is money getting out of the way of the invisible hands in generating prosperity and not getting het up about fluctuations in prices upwards or downwards or short-run cyclical dynamics, along the way, so long as there are grounds for confidence in very long run reversion to the mean.

Question 41, Part 2

Simonnot: You write: in technical terms the income velocity of monetary base would be stable. Do you suppose that the velocity of circulation of money is stable? How can we be sure? Isn't it the most indeterminate variable in the famous monetary equation MV = PT? Moreover, isn't this velocity now at its lowest level in history, which would justify Keynesian economists claiming that we have fallen into the famous and sinister liquidity trap?

Brown: I am not sure and indeed do not expect that the income velocity of monetary base would be stable over short periods of time; but over the longer term the velocity should be well-bounded from above and below. Think back to the pre-1914 international gold standard where above-ground gold supplies were in effect the monetary base. There was evidently no short-run stability; but in the long run, monetary base grew by a low annual amount (within a 0–2% per annum range), nominal incomes in aggregate grew a little faster, and income velocity was thereby somewhat stable. Looking at the equation MV=PT, P (prices) has its own rhythm—up or downwards under the real influences we have discussed, whether productivity surges or natural resource scarcities or digitalization or globalization; prices (P) to some extent are undetermined over the short run or even medium term by the monetary developments (within bounds). V fluctuates around to reflect this indeterminacy. (Equivalently demand for monetary base is not continuously in line with an estimated long-run demand function; there is considerable variance possible which reflects the fact that individuals—and other entities—are not always re-balancing their portfolios in line with some ideal optimization formula). And even in the long run, we should not pretend that money is the all and total determinant of prices although it can be the largest or the dominant one when money is out of control. As the Austrian school tells us, we should be very cautious with the notion of "price level". For monetary base to have its pivotal role with respect to the long-run evolution of prices, there has to be a total revamp of this compared to the present situation; the revamp would induce a large and broad demand for monetary base, meaning V is well bounded from below and above over the long run.

Reference

von Mises, L. (2018). *Human Action*. New Haven: Yale University Press.

21

The Launch of the New Euro

Question 42

Simonnot: Let's suppose now that the launch of the new euro is successful. Isn't there a risk that due to its very success the European money would be driven towards the sky in the foreign exchange markets—as happened to the DM in the 1970s? Germany tolerated well that rise due to J-curve effects. But will this be the case for a new euro? More generally, would the new ECB have a currency policy?

Brown: Yes, if the new euro is successful (in terms of starting to deliver on the promise of being a sound money) it will climb accordingly in the foreign exchange markets against other currencies including the US dollar in so far as they remain unsound. The nominal climb in the exchange value of the new euro would be less though than its real climb, given the likelihood that prices would fall for at first in the euro-zone under these conditions. Moreover, the highly valued euro would spur capital outflow from the euro-zone as residents there saw a great opportunity to buy foreign assets cheaply, expecting that in the long run the euro would fall back from its new heights to reflect adjustments which would take place in the balance of payments (of the euro-zone), including greater imports. In effect, some part of the increase in global monetary demand for the euro (as reflected in capital inflow) would be offset by euro-zone capital outflows, lessening its exchange rate appreciation.

We should also note that a popular new hard money attracts international borrowers as well as investors. Borrowers like a low-interest hard money which now has a wide global circulation. Think back to the huge foreign borrowing which took place in the hard Deutsche mark or hard Swiss franc in the 1970s. The real interest cost of borrowing in the high inflation high nominal interest rate dollar was highly unpredictable. That borrowing demand mitigates upward pressure on the hard currency.

Further, we should not regard some loss of competitiveness for the traded goods sector (exports) in the euro-zone (or more generally in a hard money country) as a bad thing for economic prosperity overall, albeit there are losers and gainers. The lower cost of capital, which goes along with strong international demand for the new euro, would foster greater capital spending—including in those parts of the traded goods sector where capital intensity in production (including human capital) is high. It is the low capital intensity parts of the traded goods sector which would suffer from a strong euro. In general, the cheapening in the supply of capital is prosperity-generating (where cheapness is based on availability of savings not monetary manipulations). Also, in the big picture, we should include the gain in European prosperity that would come from the countries in the new euro-zone being spared at least part of the monetary instability (including asset/credit bubbles and bust) which they experienced in the old euro-zone where the ECB tamely imported and even magnified US monetary inflation. Less malinvestment and less intense busts are benefits—though we should not ignore the remaining exposure of the new euro-zone to inflation in the US monetary hegemon, especially in the form of violent exchange rate fluctuation (vis-à-vis the dollar) and related hardships for the European export sector (which nonetheless has considerable scope for hedging action).

We should also consider the likelihood that the US and other countries in response to success for the new euro would move away from their previous unsound policies. For example, a US Administration turning to inflationary monetary policy to win an election would find itself on a much shorter global leash than previously; the slump of the dollar against the euro would be a catalyst to inflation expectations inside the US and any stimulus would be shallower and shorter-lived before the Fed had to reverse course. This move to sounder policies outside the euro-zone would in turn limit the appreciation of the euro. (As a historical footnote, it is plausible that the dollar's plunge against the hard DM in 1978 and its influence in fanning inflation in the US persuaded the Carter Administration to bring Paul Volcker into the chair of the Fed to pursue a monetarist policy.)

It is unclear that the "Snake" and then the "EMS" ever sheltered Germany very much from an appreciating currency. Parities were adjusted frequently. The only way of sheltering would have been for the Bundesbank to run softer policies than otherwise—but in the decade of 1973–83 at least, and perhaps for a further few years, the hard money principle remained intact in Germany until it finally came under assault from Chancellor Kohl (largely through his nominations to the Bundesbank and from the steps towards first German, then European monetary integration).

Would there have to be an exchange rate policy for the new euro (so as to cope with upward potential in a world of otherwise soft monies)? The arguments here suggest not. Further if the new euro is based on gold, then the choice of par when launched could be instrumental in preventing an initial big overshoot (the lower the gold content the lower the dollar value of the new euro). This point though is less compelling than at first sight, given that the euro's appeal as an international money could become the chief factor in determining the dollar price of gold.

Question 42, Part 2

Simonnot: What would be the gold value of the new euro in the case where it would be based on the yellow metal?

Brown: The founders of the new euro, in the case of it being fully convertible into gold coin, would have to determine its gold content. Specifically, the say €500 gold coin, how many grams of fine gold would this contain? One important factor in their choice would be to avoid inflaming trade relations with the US by in effect devaluing the new euro compared to the old one.

Hence, though some partisans of the new euro gold standard might like the idea of setting a low gold content in that this would mean such an abundance of gold in the euro-zone (official reserves and private holdings) that monetary base could become almost totally metallic (with the government buying back bonds held by the central bank with gold), the implicit euro devaluation would rule this out. Anyhow, the founders of the new euro might well prefer to sustain a large non-metallic element in monetary base so that the authorities could pilot a slow growth of this in aggregate rather than it being highly sensitive to volatile gold flows in a world where the US dollar is still totally fiat.

Under the regime of the new gold euro, the dollar price of the euro and the dollar price of gold would be 100% correlated. Arithmetically, the choice of gold content for the new euro would determine the dollar euro rate for any given dollar price of gold. But the lines of causality run in both directions—from the gold market to the euro currency market and conversely. When the founders of the new euro fix its gold content, the dollar gold price of the day will imply a given euro–dollar exchange rate. This latter would continue to float but with the gold market now a big potential factor in setting its path.

In practice, the gold price in dollars is likely to rise just on news that a new euro based on gold is seriously under consideration—the presumption being that the monetary demand for the yellow metal (as reserve backing for the new currency and as circulating coin) will increase. Yes, it is possible that a hard euro would eventually mean less global hedge demand for gold than at present (most of all as a haven against inflation) but markets most likely would not jump to that conclusion at the start.

As illustration we could imagine that in the run-up to the new euro's launch, the dollar price of gold would get a boost, say to $65 per gram from around $50 in early 2020. If the founders were to aim for a starting level of $1.30 per euro (stronger than end-2019 to reflect its new soundness) that would mean €50 per gram (a €500 coin would consist of 10 gms). We don't know how much gold bullion is already hoarded by citizens within the eurozone and doubtless some of this would flow into the new gold coins (under gold standard there is free coinage).

Government (including central bank) holdings of gold and private holdings across the monetary union when aggregated together would be at a level relative to narrow money supply aggregates where the convertibility pledge (euro notes into gold coin) would be highly credible.

Question 43

Simonnot: Let's come to the practical aspects, how to install the new euro. In *Euro Crash* (p. 181), you raise the possibility of a monetary coup d'etat organized jointly by the French President and the German Chancellor in the greatest secrecy—a coup which would give birth to a new monetary constitution conforming to the principles which we have raised all through our dialogue. Three points: (a) would other members of the monetary union be willing to accept such a French–German diktat? (b) To justify this jump you evoke the protective shadow of the Adenauer–de Gaulle couple. But hardly had the Treaty of the Elysee been signed (1963) than the same de Gaulle emptied it of part of its content by an attempted sabotage of NATO and an entente with "eternal Russia". President Macron is taking the same road, re-linking with the old French yearning for a "reverse alliance" with Moscow, whilst describing NATO as brain dead and the rule (within EMU) of a 3% limit to budget deficits as obsolete: (c) from the other side, what could re-ignite the Franco-German motor could be indeed the threat that Germany would found a good euro with the countries in its hinterland, casting France into a Club

Med with its Latin sisters. Isn't this perspective more plausible than the Franco-German coup diktat?

Brown: A spontaneous coup in which France and Germany together would announce agreement on a new euro (which other members of present EMU would take or leave) seems a distant prospect in the actual environment (2020) of Franco-German relations. Even so, it is not impossible that a huge crisis centred on say Italy, triggering massive further ECB loans into Italy (for which Northern European taxpayers could ultimately fund the bill), might bring an emergency resolution dictated by Berlin and Paris—especially as this time (unlike in 2010–12) Washington is unlikely to be coming to the aid of the euro status quo (then by agreeing to massive IMF loans). Germany would wish to avoid handing out a unilateral ultimatum (we leave EMU if the ECB continues to lend into Italy) and Paris would have a keen interest in a Franco-German declaration which could pre-empt contagion spreading from the Italy to France.

This French–German deal in the midst of an Italian crisis would not focus on creating a new sound euro but most likely curtail the ECB's present and future lending—eliminating many of the loose ends in the original Maastricht constitution which allowed that institution to effectively become a massive transfer agent between taxpayers, on the one hand (including payment of the monetary repression tax), and weak banks together with weak sovereigns, on the other hand.

Beyond the scenario of a French–German coup in an emergency, the prospects for Paris and Berlin joining together to launch a new sound euro to replace the present rotten unsound euro—including all the conditions of soundness as highlighted in our dialogue—would likely depend on sound money forces coming into the political ascendancy in both countries. That is nowhere to be seen at present. In the right wing of the CDU and in the AfD, we can find elements of opinion which resent the soft money policies (especially negative interest rates and the massive transfers into Italy and Spain and Greece) of the ECB, but they do not seem to be close to power. That could change.

It is more plausible at present that Germany will move into an era of government by alternating coalitions of centre and Greens or Left and Greens. The ascendant force is the Green Party. The latter may be favourable to ECB radical money policies if these are used towards financing environmental projects especially in Germany. ECB Chief Lagarde might well be attuned to deal-making here. One might have imagined that reducing the use of plastic cards (credit and payment) and the role of vast computer power in processing retail payments whilst increasing the role of gold might have had some attraction to environmentalists, but we could suspect that the attractions of access to ECB money printing for their hugely expensive projects will have greater appeal.

Perhaps the best situation for sound money forces to gain the ascendancy in France and Germany would be the outbreak of high inflation in goods and services markets in Europe. That situation could go along with (and might be caused by) a flight of capital from the euro causing that currency to plunge. The spark to all this could be a step too far—the ECB going ever further down the road of radical monetary policies such as to finance weak sovereigns and banks whilst meanwhile the long natural downward rhythm of prices (stemming from digitalization and globalization and abundance of commodities) goes into reverse.

Another situation in which sound money forces could gain strength in both France and Germany is in a wipe-out of asset values in say the next Crash and Great Recession. Many households would find their wealth including pension assets crushed. The ECB could become correctly the target for public hatred. Paris and Berlin could join in presenting a plan for a new monetary institution and a new money. The problem here is that asset deflations and recessions produce a whole host of alternative targets for public vitriol—the private equity barons, the real estate promotors, the securities firms, the monopolists (justifiably)—easier to comprehend than the ultimate cause, unsound money. The central bankers and more generally the neo-Keynesian establishment could yet again survive and prosper, offering up new vast programs for reflation.

Finally, we should consider how US policy could be a catalyst to a Franco-German coup with respect to European Monetary Union.

One possibility is that Washington would demand an end to the soft euro under the threat of launching a tariff war. Quite simply, the US would intimate that radical QE and negative interest rates for example are unacceptable tools of monetary policy as they amount to currency manipulation. In this situation, success of European diplomacy would require speed and unity—potentially delivered by Paris and Berlin resolving on a joint approach, including promised reforms of the euro (even if this meant the forced exit of Italy and possibly Spain).

Another possibility is that the US itself embarks on the path to sound money (not in prospect at present given constellation of political forces). If Europe failed to follow suit, then the euro could collapse (a version of the case above, precipitating a resolution for reform driven by Paris and Berlin). Alternatively, Washington might demand that Europe follows the US lead or face trade penalties, setting the stage for international monetary negotiations between Washington, Berlin and Paris (the latter two representing Europe for expediency). A sound money regime in the US would in any case help sound money gain political momentum also in France and Germany, as citizens there questioned why they should not enjoy the same quality of money as across the Atlantic.

Question 44

Simonnot: Let's suppose the coup has succeeded. What would be the first measures to take for launching the new euro?

Brown: The implementation of the new euro requires a radical change in monetary regimes and institutions. This cannot be achieved in an overnight coup.

So how to progress?

The coup organizers have to agree on a blueprint of fundamental principles—for example, soundness of the new money, no lending to banks or sovereigns by the new monetary institution, the likely role (or not) of gold.

An immediate invitation would go out to all present member countries to join the new monetary union based on these principles.

Very likely markets will conclude immediately on the news of initial steps that some countries will not decide to join, or even if they decide positively, that they will not succeed in remaining members for long. And so we could expect intense flight of capital out of those likely drop-outs.

The coup organizers should have decided in advance how to deal with this situation—otherwise there could be colossal further loans from Northern Europe via the ECB into the South and East. Most plausibly the organizers would agree on a procedure for suspending membership of the present union with immediate effect for countries subject to such capital flight—and on day 1.

Quite simply, the ECB and its clearing system would cease effecting transfers into and out of these countries to the rest of the union, in effect giving forced birth say to an Italian euro or Spanish euro which would have a variable exchange rate against the original euro. Euro banknotes held in these countries would continue to be fully interchangeable with the original euro at par and so would be at a premium to the Italian or Spanish euro.

After these emergency suspensions it would be down to work for the government officials of the remaining members. Again, plausibly, Paris and Berlin would together take the lead in these.

Key issues would include how to liquidate the European Central Bank and create a new monetary authority responsible for the issuance of currency (gold backed if that is agreed).

In principle, the ECB would be turned into the EMU-1 legacy fund. On the asset side, this would include all the present loans and investments of the ECB. On the liability side, there would be the present euro-note issuance and reserve deposits of the banks. The latter would be converted into debt paper.

How to run down and eventually wind up the legacy fund?

Past and present members of the monetary union in Europe would have to agree on a plan for returning some assets direct to the individual members. There would also have to be prioritization of the liabilities—for example, do banknotes have first claim, or one-time reserve deposits?

In the liquidation and wind down there will be huge losses incurred compared to par values and again there would have to be agreement on how these losses are to be distributed between past and present members.

It could be that the new European Monetary Authority (EMA) will have loans outstanding to the legacy fund, with these jointly and to some degree severally guaranteed by the governments in the newly constructed union. There would also have to be agreement between the members of the new union as to how to compensate citizens (of the union)—if at all—for losses incurred on euro-banknotes in exchanging these ultimately into the new euro currency.

All of this is a huge task and one which should be overseen by individuals who are fully committed to the ideals of the new union. This is not a job for the Central Bankers Club (as occurred in the drawing up of the plans for the first union)!

Annex: A Little Note on Gold

Simonnot: One gram (of gold) for €50 is not at all extravagant if one makes reference to the present gold price. It is interesting to make comparison with the "franc germinal" instituted by Napoleon in 1803, of which the gold content did not change until the bankruptcy of August 1914 on the outbreak of war.

A gram of gold then was worth one-third of the franc germinal, which would make this worth €17 today.

The smallest gold coin issued under Napoleon was 20 grams. That would be worth today around €1000—much more than the notes of 500 which have been suppressed.

There existed also coins of 40 grams, of which each would be worth €2000 today.

With 25 coins of 40 grams, weighing a kilo, one would be able to walk with the nice sum of €50,000.

Part III

Conclusion

22

At the Heart of the World

It is not difficult to anticipate the criticisms which will be made of our dialogue. To promote a version of the gold standard in this first-third of the twenty-first century will be considered as at best reactionary, at worst totally unrealistic and dangerous. In advance, the reply is that such criticism has a myopic vision of history. The proposal here is not a return to a bygone past but the closure of the disastrous experience of the twentieth century which resulted for humanity in millions of deaths and destruction, the opposite of "creative destruction" dear to Schumpeter.

In terms of our dialogue, we surely all realize that it is not sufficient to explain the chaos of the present global monetary system by just going back to the mega crisis of autumn 2008. Those who have the shortest memories will make a link between the crisis which we suffer today and the decision of Richard Nixon to close the gold window on 15 August 1971, opening up at the same time the door to floating exchange rates. Still, so as to understand the stakes then, it would be necessary to link the fatal Nixon coup to the implicit obligations which the US President repudiated, those which the Treasury had subscribed to following the Bretton Woods Accords of 1944. The traveller through time, though, should not stop then if he really wanted to satisfy his curiosity, not even at the Genoa Conference of 1922, which tried to build a new world order on the lame principles of the Gold Exchange Standard. It is in that fatal European month of August 1914 where the traveller would finally get to the bottom of the search for explanations: in a few days, in a few hours, the convertibility of paper money was abandoned. "Provisionally" it was claimed, as there was absolute certainty that despite the fury of war which took over all minds, this general convertibility would be re-established, sooner or later, conforming to the solemn engagements which had been taken by banking institutions towards their depositors.

That all happened in the heart of Europe which in that era was the heart of the world.

We know now that this convertibility would never be re-established.

Certainly, the three most artificial political entities formed as a result of or following the European then World War of 1914–18, the Soviet Union, Yugoslavia, and Czechoslovakia, finished by disappearing from the map. One could have seen in their "abolition" the clearing of the road ahead to make way for good consequences. Certainly the construction of the European Union was founded on the "never again that" oath, intoned by the peoples of Europe after the First World War, and there was a widespread belief after the Second World War that the oath had been honoured.

Certainly, the euro itself seemed like a landmark on the monetary plain for the closure of a calamitous century. But one had forgotten that a society, such as it was, cannot build on the moving sands of false money. And it is not fortuitous that in the memorial fanfare for the 100th anniversary of the Great War, the advent of monetary inconvertibility in August 1914 totally passed in silence.

It remains the case that the world economy stays haunted by the phantom of gold money, which is periodically evoked as the remedy for the crisis. Recently, this repression into collective subconsciousness emerged back into the real world in an unexpected form—unimaginable without the formidable power which computers have attained—the Bitcoin and numerous incarnations which appeared in its wake. Much history surrounds the birth of this cryptocurrency, but it is remarkable that it was born in 2008, the fatal year when the global banking system was shaken by an eruption like one has not seen since the mega crisis of 1929. It is no chance happening that Bitcoin has a devotion to the language of mining. A great part of its success comes from the strict limit on the quantity that can be issued. No authority in the system, no emblem, no printing of bitcoins, as central banks have done since they came into existence. Therefore, no quantitative easing possible, the modern form of money printing.

In fact, if we had to summarize all monetary history in one phrase in contemporary language, one would say that banking institutions have the role of "trusted third parties"—intermediaries between commercial or financial partners. Now it is just these trusted third parties, less and less credible, which inventors and then practitioners of Bitcoin wanted and want to do without in peer-to-peer relations (P2P) (that is to say no intermediaries). One understands better the snarling against this money by those who govern us through the central bankers. The Bitcoin allows us theoretically to do without them. The Blockchain is in effect a gigantic account book, unfalsifiable in its actual numerical state, auto controlled, where the smallest operation is registered and verified, each bitcoin being impossible to duplicate. Thus, the Blockchain permits a reply to the old question of Juvenal, how and why trust in third parties who have obtained the consent/agreement of the two parties (to act for them)? One can always post a watcher/guardian to watch the third party. But who will check this watcher and so on? *Quis custodiet ipsos custodes?*

The least one can ask, as this dialogue amply demonstrates, is who watches over the central banks?

This question is particularly pertinent in Europe where the Frankfurt institution is supposed to be independent. We have tried here to find a reply by nearing as close as possible the disciples of the gold standard. As Europe is most responsible for monetary chaos due to its ransacking of the gold money order amidst its descent into barbarism in 1914, it doesn't seem incongruous that Europe should try to initiate an authentic reform of its money which will inevitably have good effect on the whole international monetary system.

To the support of this effort, we can call on the authority of the person who is still widely acclaimed as the greatest twentieth-century economist.

On the edge of the Genoa Conference of 1922, whose calamitous results have been discussed in our dialogue, John Maynard Keynes, in the articles which he wrote in the British press on the occasion of this event, showed himself favourable to the gold standard. To fix the new parities of money with gold, he advanced the seeming wisdom—smacking of good sense but not common sense at that time and indeed flawed by complacency about inflation—that account should be taken of the phenomenal rise of prices which had taken place during the Great War 1914–18 (Hession 1985). The official gold price ought to be raised to base the new gold standard on solid and thereby durable basis. We know that his advice was not taken and the world turned towards a Gold Exchange Standard.

At the time, Keynes criticized the US for its disobedience of the elementary rules of the gold standard—a hypothesis which we have highlighted but disagreed with in our dialogue. A point at issue is that during and after the war, the US Treasury accumulated the yellow metal without issuing the corresponding amount of money. The English economist described this as the building of a golden calf skyscraper which threatened the economic equilibrium in the world. Trying to melt it down by heating up an already virulent monetary inflation in the US, though, (in the 1920s mainly evident in asset inflation) was surely not a safe procedure for the world economy—an issue to which Keynes was apparently blind. He was silent on the history of the calf's construction—which mostly occurred during the period of US neutrality (1915 to March 1917) when the authorities there were trying to prevent massive gold sales by Britain and France (to pay for war materials) spilling over into still higher US inflation which would mean a bigger inflation tax levied on US citizens to pay in effect for the Entente's war effort.

The question which one has to ask in terms of our dialogue is not why Keynes burst in several days (many years later) what he adored (his attachment to the gold standard), even though his advised path of return to gold as above can be seen to contain the germs of his future inflationism, so as to build an abracadabra economic theory of which the falseness is demonstrated. Rather the question is why this repudiation by Keynes of the fundamentals of good money has been so much celebrated. The answer is found in the tragedy of 1914–18. We should apply to Keynes the phrase which has been his success; the fame of this British economist is "a consequence of the Great War". In effect, Keynes acquired thanks to his pamphlet against the Treaty of Versailles, *The Economic Consequences of the Peace*, very quickly a global celebrity status which no economist had enjoyed before him. By 1924, remarked his colleague William Beveridge (1924), who became the author of the Welfare State, the book had been read according to a very conservative estimation by half a million people who until then had never opened an economics book and probably would never again do so. At that date, the first bestseller ever published in economics had been translated into 11 languages.

It has been shown (Simonnot 2018) that this famous book rested in effect on a political analysis. The Allies, according to the author, should have betrayed engagements which they had entered into before the armistice. The economic analysis was false, claiming that the payment of reparations as demanded by the Treaty of Versailles from Germany was an "economic impossibility". But Keynes would pass later as an extra-lucid prophet because in effect Germany would pay only a feeble part of these reparations as he had foreseen. This default on payment, however, was due to political reasons (disagreement amongst the Allies) and not to the economic causes advanced by Keynes in his pamphlet. Besides, it is at the political level that "Economic Consequences of the Peace Treaty" would have its biggest influence, justifying the tactics of appeasement towards Hitler. A Conservative Member of Parliament, Bob Boothby, opposed to this policy, which led to the Munich Accords and the Second World War could say of Keynes's book that it was the "bible of the Nazi movement" (Bouverie 2019) in that it served as the justification of the critique of the Versailles "diktat".

It was from this position of world star that the presumed champion of economic foresight was able to announce in 1935 that he had renounced the doctrine in which he had believed until then and which he himself had taught. He had become converted, he proclaimed, to a new "General Theory of Employment, Interest and Money". This totally new economic gospel was announced to "the town and to the world" to take up the phrase used knowingly by the Popes at the start of the encyclics.

This theory in reality is only new in appearance. It takes an inflationist doctrine which runs through the centuries. As example, Count Mirabeau, called "the orator of the people" gave a speech before the National Assembly to defend with all his eloquence the issue of a new paper money, the Assignats, now of grim memory (Mirabeau 1972): "Why? Is it necessary to spell it out everything about the new money? We speak here of business desperate for sales, yet we provide no means to buy! We want business to exit stagnation. Yet we seem ignorant of the fact that with nothing (no monetary means) one does nothing; we seem not to realize that there must be a principle of life to stir us, to act and to reproduce… . It is the unit of money which creates the means of payment: it is this motivation of industry by new money which brings abundance… . Throw therefore to society the germ of life which we lack; and you will see to the dazzling extent of prosperity and splendour which in a little time will lift you up". We know to what terrible misery this "helicopter money" led ahead of time.

We could cite hundreds of examples of this monetary demagoguery and its harmful effects. *Errare humanium est, sed perserverare diabolicum*. Where is therefore the devil?

Ludwig von Mises replied to this question (von Mises 1998) and it is a pleasure to recall here his response which should close the debate: "the popularity of inflationism is to a great extent rooted in the deep hate of creditors. Inflation is considered as just because it favours debtors to the detriment of creditors".

In the first row of these debtors who stand to gain from inflation is the state. The inflationist demagogues are directly or indirectly in the service of the state whether or not they are on its payroll.

Our dialogue is nonetheless founded on the hope that the worst is not always sure and that it has happened several times that peoples drugged by inflation engage once again in the search for a good money. The crisis of the euro is an opportunity to create a new European money worthy of its name, founded on the constitutional rules which we have set down and on gold, not on a European state, improbable but desired consciously or unconsciously by the founders of the European Monetary Union, haunted as they were by the (erroneous) concept of money as a "royal privilege".

Such a euro could even find a place for itself by virtue of its quality in the heart of the world, not in order to regain the faded finery of yesteryear imperialism, but as the instrument and assurance of free exchange between peoples. Then the disastrous twentieth century will at last have closure and have passed away.

References

Beveridge, W. (1924). Mr. Keynes's Evidence for Over-Population. *Economica, 1*, 1–20.

Bouverie, T. (2019). *Appeasing Hitler: Chamberlain, Churchill, and the Road to War.* London: Bodley Head.

Hession, C. H. (1985). *Johan Maynard Keynes: A Personal Biography*. New York: Macmillan.

Mirabeau. (1972). Collection complète des travaux de M. Marabeau l'ainéee à l'assemblée nationale, l.4, Paris.

Simonnot, P. (2018). Nouvelles *Leçons* d'économie contemporaine. Gallimard.

von Mises, L. (1998). *Human Action*. Auburn: Ludwig von Mises Institute.

23

Epilogue: From Pandemic to High Inflation

Question 1

Simonnot: At the moment of writing this epilogue to our dialogue, the economy of the planet is suddenly ravaged by a global pandemic. The last great world pandemic (the so-called Spanish Flu) claimed the lives of millions. Indeed, those terrible effects were aggravated by the fact that the front-line population attacked by the virus had been weakened during four years of a war which had surpassed all previous records of atrocity. Should one not fear the economic and financial consequences of the present pandemic will be magnified due to our governments having beaten all records in recent years for bad monetary management as we have shown in this book?

Brown: The COVID-19 pandemic and the Crash of March 2020 (from mid-February to mid-March the S&P 500 fell by one third) are intimately connected events. Coincidence and sequencing, however, do not establish causality in any ultimate sense. Rather, we should view the Crash as originating in the preceding years of radical monetary inflation (starting say in 2012/13), which spawned a long and virulent asset inflation.

Asset inflation transitioning into a bust phase (one symptom of this process is stock market crash interpreted to include the phenomenon of two or more crashes say within a year or 18 months with strong rebounds in-between) under the impact of supply shock, in this case pandemic, would have historical parallel. The OPEC Oil Embargo of Autumn 1973 played a starkly visible role in the bursting of the great asset inflation dating back to 1962. (There had been an earlier mini-burst, not fatal to that great asset inflation, in 1969.) The bursting was symptomized by multiple crashes through until winter 1974–75.

The searcher for fundamental causality would look back to the great monetary inflation from the early-mid 60s onwards and the severe tightening of US monetary policy which had started in the spring (1973) in response to a sudden surge of reported goods and services inflation.

Many contemporary observers of global asset inflation in recent years have suggested that a sudden rise of goods inflation and the Federal Reserve's hypothesized late but tough reaction to this would again be the trigger to burst this time. Another mainstream scenario has been that the narratives which had built up and fuelled hot speculative temperatures would fade amidst accumulating earnings disappointment stemming most likely from over-investment or malinvestment.

History sometimes short-circuits and so it might be with the Great Asset Inflation of 2012/13–20. A massive supply shock—the COVID-19 pandemic—not a spike in goods inflation and the Fed's response, nor an endogenous fading of narratives, turned up as a powerful potential catalyst to asset inflation transitioning into its burst phase. Income-famine investors chasing thin and highly leveraged returns on risky credit products, comforting themselves by listening to highly speculative narratives about why good fortune would continue indefinitely, suddenly woke up in fright.

The extent of wake-up and of a related burst in asset inflation is still in doubt at the time of this book going to press. A huge known unknown is the length and severity of the pandemic itself. It might still be the case that only harsh monetary tightening will finally burst the Great Asset Inflation. Perhaps that end will come after many years of high goods (and services) inflation in the aftermath of the pandemic. In any case, by mid-July 2020 massive central bank money printing led by the Fed and buttressed by its announcement of vast asset purchase programs in the credit markets had, according to contemporary reports, stimulated considerable new inflows into high-yield debt funds whilst the S&P 500 had recouped almost all of its earlier losses. Large price gains for "pandemic stocks" (businesses making higher profits due to the health emergency—for example big tech firms servicing the "stay at home" economy—or likely gaining further ahead from increased monopoly power) offset stock losses in hard hit sectors.

Amidst concerns about high inflation in the aftermath of the pandemic, a strong precautionary demand for some types of real asset which could not be debased by government (through money printing) would be fully understandable. Most obvious here could be the equity of big tech monopolists (two of these were suffering from a serious decrease in business spending on adverts during the pandemic, but their share of the shrinking pie climbed abruptly) and of the number one on-line retailer also dominant in cloud computing.

23 Epilogue: From Pandemic to High Inflation

Speculative narratives about present and visible potential future monopolists "inheriting the earth" were alive and thriving, not fading.

Speculative frenzy in a recession is not a new phenomenon. In the small sample sizes available from the laboratory of history one could look at the 50 per cent bounce of US stocks from November 1929 to March 1930 or the bubble in oil and commodities during Spring and Summer 2008. No doubt the Fed's radical response to the pandemic fanned the frenzy in this case. It also produced a remarkable compacency about the danger of global credit crisis which would mean a difficult journey to full economic recovery. After all, collateral for mountains of debt have already been exposed as including huge expanses of malinvestment effected during the past quarter century or more of asset inflation. Think here of the shale oil sector, the airline industry, shopping malls, the auto industry and the huge capital investment of the past quarter-century into global supply chains.

Financial engineers had enjoyed boomtime during the asset inflation. They could thank the weakening of rational scepticism amongst investors due to desperation for yield and an impairment of judgement by strong feedback loops (capital gains enhancing confidence in dubious speculative narratives). They found innovative ways to increase leverage—often camouflaged—and so enable the equity owners to score in a marketplace mesmerized by momentum.

The private equity "industry" was at the forefront of the financial engineering boom. Its basic strategy was buying up companies, revving up their leverage by issuing high-yield debt at sky-high prices, and expecting to re-sell the companies into the public market at substantial capital gain in an ever trending-up equity market. Alongside, the private equity firms promoted to investors credit funds stuffed with high-yield corporate debt. They also became notorious for their network of cronyism in Washington (including revolving doors to top positions and targeted election campaign contributions) and other power centres. No wonder then that in early April 2020, the Fed and Treasury launched a massive corporate debt purchase program which shored up the price of high-yield corporate bonds.

The Fed programs for buying corporate debt became the subject of a powerful speculative narrative, lifting the price of both this and equity. According to the story-tellers the Fed would be holding down the cost of corporate credit into the long run and extinguishing bankruptcy risk over large parts of the US business landscape. In rational mode, investors would have been sceptical, viewing the Fed as a price taker rather than maker in the context of huge global credit and equity markets. The corporate debt in the Fed's balance sheets would surely not become gifts, rolled over in perpetuity at artificially low credit cost to the borrower. In a bankruptcy, the Fed would try to salvage what it could alongside other creditors (albeit that the Treasury in its role as limited partial insurer of the Fed with respect to corporate paper holdings would be an active party in such proceedings).

More generally, in a sober-rational marketplace, firms (especially those in sectors greatly exposed to the business cycle) would not find themselves piling on new debt to an already highly leveraged capital structure in the midst of a pandemic. They would have bolstered the share of equity in their capital structure during the good times (and well beyond the superficial rise of the equity–debt ratio, as calculated on the basis of market prices, brought about by hot speculative temperatures during the asset inflation).

If COVID 19 had struck the global economy under a sound money regime, rather than the current actual highly unsound one, there would still have been economic costs alongside human suffering. The economic system, however, would have had great potential to absorb shock. Instead, asset inflation had caused serious mis-signalling by capital market prices over many years and this had curtailed any shock-absorption capacity. Financial fragility had grown in line with rapidly accumulating malinvestment and swollen leverage.

The corollary of severely damaged shock absorbers: big government with its massive money printing apparatus responded to the pandemic in spring 2020 by orchestrating an emergency explosion of public and private debt, declaring there was no alternative way to avoid national calamity. Common sense seemed to rule out any alternative course. Anyhow, the money printers had just been absolved of any possible blame for burst, crash, or recession in the present; it was all the fault of COVID-19, stupid!

Citizens beware: did Adam Smith not say "there is a lot of ruin in a nation" (meaning that in a wealthy free market economy the scope for recovery from adverse shock is huge; Smith was admonishing a student for declaring that the loss of the American colonies would spell ruin for Britain); and do we not know from history that the political force of debtors (both private and public sector) standing to benefit from high inflation to cut the real value of their liabilities can destroy even the most powerful of fiat monies?

The business sector with a normal thick cushion of equity capital (as under sound money) could have borne in general the brunt of supply shock, in this case pandemic. According to the implicit "social contract" of capitalism, equity shareholders (business owners) earn a risk premium which in part reflects the fact that when adverse events occur they are in the front line (rather than the wage earners or secured bond holders).

Under a sound money regime, yes, the supply shock would deplete equity cushions. The rational response across many firms would be to make these good by issuing more equity in exchange for debt. If the equity owners are not at bankruptcy's door (which for the main part they would not be in the hypothetical situation of having raised plenty of equity capital during the good times), they should be able to reach a cooperative agreement with debt holders on a strategy (of which key component is debt–equity swap) whereby both share the gains from a strengthening of the corporate balance sheet (thereby reducing the danger of bankruptcy and its deadweight costs for all). The financially restructured firm would be in a better position to raise capital as might be required during the continuation of the pandemic and its aftermath. Much of that capital would be in the form of equity rather than debt.

Equity markets under sound money would price in the loss of corporate earnings during the duration of the supply shock. Tapping the equity market for new funds under those circumstances would be a fully sensible and feasible strategy for many businesses.

By contrast, if the supply shock were to coincide at some stage with an implosion of speculative narratives and bubble bursting (notwithstanding massive money printing), the loss of market value (debt plus equity) across the business sector might well go far beyond any actuarial appraisal of cumulative earnings loss. Many highly leveraged businesses (note that at market value the leverage ratio rises as equity prices fall) would find themselves at bankruptcy's door.

In the context of crash and speculative liquidation, only a feeble supply of new capital (from private sources) would come into the enterprise sector to bolster firms' preparedness (including balance sheet repair) to meet the rebound in economic activity likely to follow the supply shock and to bridge transitory losses during the pandemic. Hence, the state enters the stage as the lender "of last resort" to salvage the system, presiding over a fantastic growth in borrowing backed by the central bank (usually on condition that the finance ministry or treasury is providing a backstop up to a given date, including at least a limited insurance of the central bank against loss on extended credit). By reducing the real value of those loans, high inflation can make feasible an eventual return of the borrower to private capital markets without government (also the central bank) help. In effect, high inflation reduces leverage of firms which have revenues and assets which rise with prices of goods and services on average, so long as nominal interest rates remain far below the current inflation rate.

Question 2

Simonnot: On March 12, 2020, Christine Lagarde, president of the ECB, at a press conference, uttered this phrase, immediately judged by markets as dangerous: "It is not the job of the ECB to tighten the *spread*" (the difference between the yield on government bonds, viewed as the safest paper, and that on the bonds of other member countries). The Italian spread jumped, moving in a few days from 1.6% to 2.6%. Mme Lagarde seemed to be taking an opposite position to her predecessor, Sig. Draghi. This panic response in the markets where one envisaged already a dislocation of the euro-zone forced Mme Lagarde to change her tune. Two days later she launched a record asset purchase programme amounting to €750 billion. Didn't that violate the founding treaties of the European Monetary Union and without any voice of protest? And where will this course of action now lead us?

Brown: Perhaps the best way to interpret Mme. Lagarde's initial statement is as part of a continuing game-plan to build Berlin's trust in her. Surely, she intended to draw on that reservoir later to progress a "European" agenda as favoured of course in Paris. Consistent with that hypothesis, at the same press conference she also ruled out a cut of the deposit rate at the ECB further into negative territory—knowing full well that negative rates are especially unpopular in Germany. But this publicly aired confidence-building exercise by Chief Lagarde did not go down well in the marketplace where many were unconvinced that this was just a diplomatic sweetener without any real content.

In justifying previous support operations for weak members, the line from the ECB had been that the operation of a common monetary policy for the whole euro-zone meant the suppression of any "country premium" emerging on money market rates within the union (e.g. Italian banks paying a higher wholesale money rate than banks elsewhere). Mme. Lagarde was surely not questioning that line. Anyhow, given the market jitters, she followed up with the aggressive asset purchase program. The Machiavellian analyst could argue even that she took a gamble with testing the market at the press conference with the purpose of demonstrating to Berlin that a bold asset purchase program, presumably growing in spurt going forward, was essential to monetary union holding together.

Why no protest? The battle against the ECB conducting huge operations involving implicit transfers from strong to weak members had long since been lost. There was surely no chance of the few constitutionalists and hard money advocates left (essentially in Germany) in launching a successful new offensive in the midst of pandemic. The German Constitutional Court did rule in

May 2020 that an earlier asset purchase program by the ECB seemed to have "disproportional" broad effects outside its stated purpose of achieving the inflation target. The German government should put this concern to the ECB and do a better job of getting justifications, if any. Surely, however, Angela Merkel, now riding high in the opinion polls due to her perceived successes in dealing with the pandemic, would sort this difficulty out with Christine Lagarde. The Chancellor, after all, had consented to the now disputed program in a direct meeting with the previous ECB Chief, Mario Draghi. Chancellor Merkel could still pander to voters on the anti-euro right, standing firm against coronavirus bonds whilst cynically acknowledging in quiet that the amount of funds exiting the ECB back door to the weak nations exceeded many times over any amount from such open operations. In the midst of pandemic, Chancellor Merkel could even support further quantitative easing operations in the ECB bought large amounts of weak sovereign debt (along with the strong in due proportion) as essential to "combatting deflation and depression").

Yes, it seems that EMU is headed down a new express journey of vast transfers via the ECB to the weak nations—most of all Italy and followed by Spain. One can even imagine France being drawn into the weak category given the severity of the pandemic there and the high exposure of its banks to Italian risk amongst other issues. Indeed, it seems that France will be in the same semi-weak category with respect to the China-style stimulus plan for pandemic-struck regions of the EU as proposed by Chancellor Merkel and President Macron in May and approved by a special summit in Brussels at end-July (2020). Poland and Hungary are due to be the biggest recipients of aid per capita with Italy receiving a net cumulative amount for approved projects of around 6% of its GDP, whilst its government debt to GDP ratio was set to exceed 150% in 2021. The agreement was for an EU-wide total of €390bn of gifts and €360bn of concessionary loans to be disbursed over seven years from a fund financed by bonds issued in the name of the EU and repaid by budget contributions from all EU members in treaty-set proportions.

The potential ultimate brake on all of this: a swing in the German political pendulum away from eurocentrism to hard money principles, with populists stirring justifiable fears about German taxpayers eventually bailing out the ECB or the ECB resorting to high inflation to remain solvent. The origins of this high inflation would be the ECB powerless to "normalize" policy when the post-pandemic boom eventually arrives, given that its balance sheet is full of junk. The ECB would realize that huge losses consequent to "normalization", whether derived from disposals of junk or from the spread widening between what this institution pays on deposits and what it could collect from its loans, could inflame German populist anger.

Question 3

Simonnot: In the US during the night of 24–25 March, 2020, the Congressional leaders of the Republicans and Democrats agreed on a $2000 billion "stimulus" plan. This plan, beating all previous records (including Roosevelt), includes a direct distribution of $500 billion to individuals. Helicopter money had taken off for good purpose—could one have done anything differently under such circumstances? And what will be the result?

Brown: The distribution of helicopter money under these circumstances is an absurdity. This cannot ameliorate or reverse what is fundamentally a supply shock (pandemic). The essence of this supply shock is that suddenly safe and infection-free services (e.g. travel, eating out, shopping in brick-and-mortar stores, concerts, sport events) become unavailable across a broad span of the global economy. Instead, these services in established form now carry serious virus risk; demand may be so weak as to prompt widespread stoppage and shutdown. Potentially, suppliers could modify services to become less subject to virus risk (e.g. airlines keeping half their seats empty, stores limiting number of customers inside at any time); in the midst of the pandemic, those modified services might enjoy demand such that the supplier could charge premium prices (relative to the pre-pandemic prices) or otherwise limit access by the imposing of time-waste (in line-ups for example). In practice, governments step in and impose rationing and shutdowns.

Also, in the pandemic, many forms of labour become vulnerable to infection (one can think here of the worker in on-line distribution warehouses). Employers could reduce that infection risk—for example, keeping bigger distance between workers or in meat-packing plants; that would mean less output, less efficiency and thereby higher unit costs (some of which might be passed on to customers, depending on specific market conditions, including present shortages). How far they move in that direction depends on the bargaining power of labour (e.g. to demand big supplements to their wages for bearing infection risk, buttressed by ability to demand compensation and re-employment rights when electing to withdraw from employment during the pandemic) and on emergency regulations to protect worker safety.

For government, there are three broad economic policy responses to the pandemic supply shock, transcending the detailed enforcement of rights as described, which would be consistent with free markets and sound money—and indeed we could imagine these as hypothetically taking place under a gold standard regime.

First, there would be an expansion of social insurance to alleviate the situation of pandemic victims (including those who become unemployed—whether through lay-off or withdrawal from the workplace due to especially high vulnerability to the virus whether on account of age or medical conditions—and small businesses which lose the bulk if not all of their revenues and never had the potential like larger public companies to build equity cushions by new issuance during the good times). Alongside the big prospective rise in public sector outstanding debt related to funding expanded social insurance, the government would announce a long-run plan for post-pandemic fiscal normalization, including items such as a 10-year solidarity tax heavily focused on monopoly rents.

The details might not be legislated until the pandemic were over. But the knowledge that such fiscal action lay ahead would sustain confidence in the long-run continuation of the sound-money regime and avert a possible slump in the government bond market (provoked by anxiety about permanently vast funding requirements or in the context of say a gold standard by a feared suspension of convertibility). Alongside this social security funding, there is the question of a big bulge in government deficits (federal, local and state) due to fall in tax revenues as the economy shrinks under the supply shock. Long-term fiscal plans should illuminate how tax revenues in a post-pandemic boom would be used towards retiring debt raised during the pandemic. Under a sound money regime (including gold), confidence in such planning would be essential to allaying fears that the exit from public debt explosion will be currency debasement.

Second, the government would help provide an obstacle-free setting where debt–equity swaps could take off to a huge extent towards reversing damage to corporate financial structures including the banking sector as outlined in the answer to question one. Limited and selective debt moratoriums, which could be lifted on application by the creditor, if offering to negotiate (with the debtor) a prescribed loan modification including debt–equity swaps, could be part of that process.

Third, the central bank would boost its supply of high-powered money to meet an increase in demand for this (currency and deposits at the central bank). This surge would be due to multiple factors—including widespread distrust of banks, as depositors worried that credit impairment especially in sectors of the economy most hit by supply shock could mean bank failures. (In the context of a competitive and well-capitalized banking system, not plagued by potential malinvestment and over-leverage from asset inflation, these worries should be subdued.)

Some banks might find they are suddenly obliged to honour lines of credit to now weak borrowers and that they have problems with raising funds in the deposit markets (including from other banks) to cope with this; so they have to be able to liquidate other assets in exchange for high-powered money. This increase in high-powered money supply occurred even under the context of the gold standard, where according to Bagehot's principles, the central bank increased temporarily its supply of banknotes and deposits (with itself) in a crisis, but crucially coupling this with an absolute commitment to withdraw the extra high-powered money once the crisis is over.

Back to the US package of March 24/25. This was totally different in concept from the above. First, there was the helicopter money distribution to a very large majority of taxpayers irrespective of insurance need. Second there were massive bail-outs to particular hard-hit industries (including airplanes)— in effect sparing present shareholders from greater loss, never mind that their companies had not raised equity during the good times (and in many cases bought this back thereby increasing effective leverage). Also, the Treasury was to spend up to $500 billion on insuring the Federal Reserve against losses on its holdings of corporate debt as a backstop so that the central bank could buy much larger quantities of such paper consistent with its legal mandate. Finally, the infinite QE and zero rate policy announced by the Fed alongside had no time limit and absolutely no promise of reversal when the crisis was over.

A widespread view that the exit strategy from massive increases in government debt (and some contemporary projections put the 2-year increase in Federal debt at 35% of GDP) would be a vast levying of inflation tax is fully understandable. Indeed stripped of the ability to levy this tax (as would be the case under a sound money regime), or its variant of monetary repression tax, big government may have given much more painstaking consideration (perhaps in the midst of a tumbling market for its debt) to alternative strategies for coping with the medical emergency which would not impose the vast costs of a command-economy "lockdown".

We can think of a wartime analogy, though not complete. Large sections of enterprise and labour becoming economically inactive during the pandemic has similarity to large parts of civilian industry and employment becoming redundant during war and re-directed (either by market forces or conscription) to military combat and munitions production. The "emigres" from peacetime economic sectors (production of butter) get pay instead for producing and using munitions (guns). Supply restraints during the pandemic or war (intensified by mandatory rationing or shutdowns) go along with elevated savings. Some economists describe these as "forced saving"—an appropriate label where rationing or other obstacles to consumption are widespread during the emergency, but less so where households are responding to high prices in the immediate reflecting supply shortages in the expectation that lower prices for these items will prevail later. These high savings flow directly or indirectly into vast government bond issuance whilst investment in the peacetime or non-health-sector related economy collapses. In the aftermath of war or pandemic, these forced savings become an element in pent-up demand.

During the supply shock itself, whether war or pandemic, big government assumes emergency powers which impede markets responding freely and efficiently to scarcity, all amidst much deference to "fairness" and "social cohesion". Big business out of self-interest may well visibly respect this deference. Why risk incurring political backlash against "price gouging" when doing very well from the authorities turning a blind eye to their monopolistic abuses and meanwhile winning the prizes of cronyism?

The supply shortages during war are more acute than in pandemic because the non-civilian economy, the military sector (including defense forces and munition factories) is bidding for labor and commodities. In the pandemic, analogous shortages emanate from demand for resources by the health sector, the pharmaceutical industry, the manufacturers of protective clothing and sanitizers, equipment and chemicals, and constructors of partition systems for social distancing. In broad terms we can compare the big price rises for "war stocks" with those of the "pandemic stocks".

During war, rationing is instituted on the claim that allowing steep price rises for certain staples, especially food, would stimulate social divisiveness rather than national cohesion. During a pandemic, premium prices which would allow some consumers to enjoy special low infection-risk services, without any indirect rationing in the form of waiting in line or spending hours online, are branded "socially unacceptable". In many countries, choice in health care including access to premium services is totally suspended, with all medical resources relevant to the pandemic requisitioned by the national health provider. These types of restrictions fade once the emergency is over as and when determined by government.

The end of war or pandemic brings about a vigorous economic expansion (specifically in the non-military or non-health sectors) from a sunken level. (Peace or end of pandemic should be distinguished from armed truces or pauses in the conflict with further offensives still probable in the near term; sometimes the distinction relates mainly to "state of mind", as conflict and illness can be eternal). Supply and demand bounce upwards; business non-military or non-health capital spending is a key swing variable, rising from its depressed level during the war or pandemic. But there will be severe restraints on supply during the re-bound; in the case of war these restraints take the form of physical destruction (plant, equipment, infrastructure), accumulated obsolescence and some financial crippling; in the case of pandemic serious financial crippling, also accompanied by evidence of destruction in the sense of revealed malinvestment from previous asset inflation.

In both cases, given its huge indebtedness, government is keen to have its central bank suppress its cost of borrowing whether by monetary repression or inflation taxation. The combination of emerging capital shortage (explained by previous capital stock destruction or obsolescence matched by the growth of new investment opportunity) and curtailed supply of savings (households now have so much additional personal wealth in government debt and money issued during the war or pandemic to finance "transfers"—whether salaries in the military sector or stay-at-home supplements—that they now opt for a savings holiday) causes interest rates to come under upward pressure. The central bank resists this and so starts the journey to high inflation. In effect, high inflation is a windfall tax on capital invested directly or indirectly in loans to government and it may induce an increase in savings as households try to rebuild their wealth.

The exact path of post-pandemic high inflation including its starting date is unknowable in advance. Much depends on the extent of supply-side impairment, monopoly pricing power of the financial fit and related impairment of competition, weakening of non-monetary disinflation (including globalization) and pent-up demand.

Government actions during the Covid-19 pandemic have tended to enhance monopoly power, already well entrenched due to preceding asset inflation. For example, there was the heavy-handed closing down of brick-and-mortar stores coupled with a lack of safety regulation or market power for labour (together with legal steps to impede virus spread) in the warehouse distribution systems vital to online shopping. Separately, "cooperation" between the big tech monopolists in tracking virus spread was welcomed by Big Government rather than setting off an alarm in anti-trust enforcement offices (admittedly this alarm had long been dysfunctional). The monopolists and oligopolists claimed that their goods and services were essential to sustaining economic life during the pandemic; but 5 Apples, 5 Amazons, 5 Microsofts, 5 Facebooks, and 5 Googles, and so on could surely have done this in a more consumer and liberty-friendly way. Virulent asset inflation, however, in the decades before had smothered that potential.

In the post-pandemic economy high unemployment and high inflation could co-exist, explained by the heterogeneity in the labour market, and sudden obsolescence of human capital in occupations allied to now exposed malinvestment from the last cycle. Tightness could develop in broad sub-sectors, even with high unemployment persistent elsewhere.

What we do know in advance is that governments of several large economies with projected outstanding debt in 2021 totalling some 30–35 percentage points higher relative to GDP than on the eve of the pandemic, private sector borrowers lamed by crushingly high leverage, and pension funds massively invested in vulnerable high-yield corporate debt matched at least partly by their own fixed nominal pay-out streams, are well-disposed to inflation. They would cheer (at least in silence) the central bank seizing any opportunity presented by a rise of inflation momentum to press down hard on the monetary accelerator by vetoing any rise in nominal interest rates. In the interim, before the outbreak of high inflation, they will also be partisans of monetary repression—meaning interest rates manipulated downwards in the context of inflation obstinately low due to the operation of non-monetary disinflationary forces (including business cycle weakness, plentiful availability of commodity resources, for example).

Doesn't Japanese history, though, suggest that huge public sector indebtedness on its own is not a sufficient condition for a transition to high inflation? The concise answer is no. In Japan, virtually a one-party democracy, a highly distorted electoral system gives disproportional power to elderly conservative savers (who would have considerable clout even without distortions). In the last quarter century, there have been tremendous cumulative real income gains in Japan from that country's rapid integration with East Asia; and so there has been no groundswell of discontent focused on the critique that the huge absorption of savings by the public sector has meant the Japanese are poorer than otherwise. The corporate sector has de-leveraged in the decades since the late 1980s' bubble economy, all within the context of a huge private sector savings surplus.

Now, as real income gains from integration with East Asia (especially China) go into reverse, public finances ailing accelerates markedly, and banking sector plus pension woes related to bad investments during the great global asset inflation of the past decade and beyond materialize, the same coalition of forces in favour of high inflation could emerge in Japan as elsewhere. One-party democracy could suddenly spawn victory for a new populist party.

Question 4

Simonnot: Since the eruption of the medical crisis, the euro-zone has become more divided than ever before, notably on the eventual issue of corona-bonds.
What should we make of this new attempt to mutualize debts?

As regards the Franco-German "monetary coup", which we described earlier in this dialogue, is this aggravated disunity not an opportunity?

If yes, how to seize it?

Brown: It is wholly understandable that the governments of countries in the European Monetary Union hardest hit by the pandemic (whatever the mix of factors in that vulnerability) should play to European solidarity to get outside aid and reduce the eventual fiscal burden (including potential inflation tax burden) on their own citizens. Outside aid would be both for contributing to expanded social security and to aid firms (including banks) on verge of collapse. As a practical matter, the hardest hit member countries are also the financially weakest (Italy and Spain). Underpinning their calls for "European solidarity" has been the implicit threat that otherwise their dire situation would "bring the whole house down", meaning that an existential crisis for the European Monetary Union with its epicentre in the weak sovereigns would erupt.

We should view the whole discussion of corona-bonds within that context. The challenge for the weak (in terms of credit rating) governments pressing the case for these bonds to be issued has been at a public relations level. Their goal has been to turn sympathy for the plight of those suffering a humanitarian crisis in the South into support for European solidarity where that means huge aid directly or indirectly to Rome and Madrid. Governments joining to issue bonds whose proceeds are primarily destined for Italy and Spain but backed jointly and severally by all is a form of aid from the North to South, albeit camouflaged to a small extent.

How to turn humanitarian concern into European solidarity expressed as fiscal transfers to governments and the elites in the South? Unhelpful in this regard has been the broad knowledge about health service incompetence in the South—including flawed strategies for containment at the start (even if geneticists now trace Munich as one original source of infection into Italy), then the lack of hospital intensive care capacity and related protocols which denied COVID-19 patients hospital admission until it was often too late to administer successfully any therapeutic cure.

All this was not due to disparity of income levels between North and South but specific institutional and policy failure. So how now to politically justify solidarity with the governments and elites which had failed their peoples, even more than had been the case in the North? Surely European solidarity in the context of pandemic should mean first and foremost mutual aid in improving health sector response through close sharing of data and of specific resources (including new drugs, equipment, vaccines, human capital) or research where possible.

23 Epilogue: From Pandemic to High Inflation 199

Yet could there be anything intrinsic to monetary union in Europe which obligates the financially stronger to aid the financially weaker—also in this case the hardest hit—in times of natural disaster, in this case pandemic?

The short answer is no. In the counterfactual case of pandemic striking countries under a gold standard regime, the weak and worst hit countries would likely be forced into suspending gold convertibility. They could then resort to the money printing press to meet emergency financial requirements amidst a sharp devaluation of their now fiat currency.

By contrast, the financially strong countries under the gold standard have scope to make an emergency issuance of high-powered money in the form of banknotes and deposits at the central bank (subject to retiral after the crisis) without undermining confidence in their continued adherence to gold convertibility of their money. Their promise to take remedial fiscal action after the crisis and recession is over would be credible in the marketplace.

A gold-based regime does not rule out European or any other type of solidarity in its widest sense, if there is indeed the political backing for this. Germany and other more fortunate North European countries could decide to make mega-aid available to Italy, where the principle of European solidarity was buttressed by calculations of long-time economic and geo-political advantage. Solidarity, however, would not be built in to the "automatic rules of the gold standard".

In our earlier dialogue we discussed a new euro based on gold. If pandemic had struck this, and Italy had been in this new euro union, what would have occurred without European solidarity? Analogous to under the gold standard, the Italian state and banks would have paid out obligations as they fell due in paper Italian euros, no longer convertible into gold (or the European euro). Deposits at Italian banks would no longer have been transferable at par within the European payments system.

The Maastricht Treaty makes no provision for temporary exit from monetary union. Forced exit could nonetheless occur, but there is no ready-made protocol. Taking the legal texts at face value, whereby temporary exits are impossible, the rules of the game do indeed induce a degree of European solidarity, most directly in the form of the ECB acting as transfer agent, lending through its front and back doors into the weak countries (with little prospect of repayment) and borrowing in the strong.

In the pandemic crisis that means the ECB prints money which flows into Italy and Spain for meeting emergency financial needs of the sovereigns and banks there; but the increase in deposits which match this lending does not stay in those weak countries, instead they flow principally to Germany, where deposits are viewed as safer (in terms of default risk and currency risk, were

EMU to break up). The target 2 credit of the Bundesbank with the ECB correspondingly explodes, with counterpart debits for Italy and Spain.

Ultimately, German taxpayers could escape the intensification of long-run burden implicit in all this by the Federal Republic pulling out of EMU (and possibly launching a new euro with narrower membership) and converting only euro-denominated domestic assets (German government bonds, German bank deposits) held by German citizens (not foreigners) into the new Deutsche mark; or alternatively going along with high euro-inflation, in which case inflation tax is levied on all euro-citizens, including Italian and Spanish. High inflation would wipe out in real terms much of the indebtedness of weak sovereign and banks in Europe, so bolstering the viability of monetary union going forward subject to one big proviso. The high inflation debt cure might turn the public, especially in the North, against the whole euro-project, and bolster the yearning for a return of the Deutsche mark.

Is there any prospect that a French-German monetary coup could emerge from these profound challenges? During the height of the pandemic this seems remote. Any possibility of sound money reform is off the table for now. The Merkel government is seeking to impose some accountability and medical prioritization for aid, though this is effectively undermined by its tolerance of unrestricted backdoor lending via the ECB and its backing of EU budget expansion for a pandemic aid fund (the so-called Macron-Merkel plan). Perhaps in the aftermath of pandemic, the German electorate will shift towards supporting euro-reform in a sound direction and that could frighten the French euro-centrist establishment into new diplomacy with Berlin involving a new euro—but any sign of this is absent at this stage.

Question 5

Simonnot: Under these conditions, doesn't "dollar hegemony" as we have described it in this book risk becoming prolonged and even reinforced?

Brown: The most likely aftermath of pandemic—an era of high global inflation in which the US is leading the way with infinite QE and endless zero rate policy—would challenge dollar hegemony. Ultimately though, high inflation could set off a chain of events which would enhance dollar hegemony.

As inflation rises to a high level (say 5–10%) it also becomes more variable. No longer would there be steady-state expectations as when inflation has been running near 2% for many years. Along with the increased perceived variance of inflation both in the US and abroad nominal exchange rates of the dollar against foreign currencies would become more variable. A tendency of a rise in inflation to foster anxiety about even higher inflation could cause the dollar to fall into a downward spiral. For example, were the US to enter a period of high inflation compared to Europe the dollar could sink far in real terms; and conversely when European inflation was higher than in the US, the euro could fall into a downward spiral against the dollar.

The greater volatility of exchange rates both in nominal and real terms would mean greater insulation between the various currency areas. A big and variable exchange risk premium between the dollar and foreign currencies means greater scope for monetary independence. Businesses and individuals would become more expert at hedging exchange risk exposures; global investors would see benefits in terms of reducing exposure to inflation risks in holding a diversified portfolio of currencies, less concentrated on dollars than previously. Central banks outside the US would have a stronger rationale to aim for a radically different monetary policy—even sound money—at the cost of considerable pain for their export sector in the short run from exchange rate appreciation. By contrast, during the era of the 2% inflation standard (say mid-1990s to 2020) the benefits of sound money versus low inflation may not have justified (from the perspective of the governments ultimately responsible) a dash for monetary independence by countries outside the US.

A journey of the euro-zone into much higher inflation than the US could stop and reverse the decline of US hegemony under conditions of global high inflation. A long drawn-out existential crisis of the euro would have similar effect. The next chapter in that story could be the birth of our new euro which would challenge dollar hegemony.

Could dollar hegemony finally emerge in strengthened form from all these possible variations in the high inflation aftermath of the pandemic? That depends on whether a powerful political force forms in the US which would repudiate high inflation. If a sound money revolution were to triumph there, and sustain itself in the long run, the dollar could enter a golden century of global hegemony. That would be progress for humanity and more narrowly for Europe from the crisis-ridden century of unsound dollar hegemony which opened in the immediate aftermath of the First World War.

Appendixes

Appendix A: Original French Questions (Philippe Simonnot)

Chapitre 2. La Phobie de la Déflation

Question 1: Comment expliquer la phobie de la déflation de nos dirigeants?

Question 2: Qui ne se souvient de William J. Bryan déclarant devant la Convention démocrate le 9 juillet 1896 à Chicago: "Vous ne crucifierez pas l'humanité sur une croix en or". Le leader populiste voulait stigmatiser par cette formule la politique déflationniste menée par le gouvernement de l'époque. On était alors sous le règne de l'étalon-or. Diriez-vous néanmoins que la phobie de la déflation s'est aggravée depuis l'abandon du Gold Standard en 1914? Et pour quelle raison?

Chapitre 3. La Grande Guerre et la Fin du Gold Standard

Question 3: Peut-être Bryan avait-il tort. Mais il est devenu célèbre grâce à cette phrase évoquant la crucifixion de l'humanité sur une croix d'or. De même la formule de Keynes sur l'or comme "relique barbare" est restée dans toutes les mémoires et elle ressort encore aujourd'hui dès qu'il est question d'étalon-or. Nous devons tenir compte de la force de persuasion des démagogues.

Peu après les propos tenus par Bryan, l'humanité serait bel et bien crucifiée, mais sur des croix de bois, pour reprendre le titre du célèbre roman de Roland Dorgelès, publié en 1919. Le bronze qui servait à fabriquer des croix des cimetières avait été fondu pour faire des canons. De même l'or et l'argent avaient disparu de la circulation au sens propre (monétaire) comme au sens figuré (habituel). En effet dès le début des hostilités, les gens ont voulu récupérer l'or qu'ils avaient confié aux banques en échange de billets sur la foi d'une convertibilité immédiate et absolue. Cet engagement ne pouvait être tenu par des banques qui n'avaient pas 100% de réserves. Il a donc fallu fermer les fenêtres d'or, un geste que nous retrouverons avec Nixon en 1971 pour l'unique fenêtre du Trésor américain, mais en août 1914, il y avait encore dans beaucoup de banques des guichets où l'on pouvait échanger de l'or au prix fixé sur les billets, outre les guichets des banques centrales.

Sait-on la quantité d'or qui était encore disponible dans les banques en août 1914, en plus de ce qui était déposé dans les banques centrales? Pouvait-on éviter de fermer les guichets en Europe (même en Suisse les guichets d'or ont été fermés dès le premier jour du conflit)? La guerre aurait-elle pris un autre cours si l'on avait maintenu l'étalon-or? Fallait-il laisser flotter le cours de l'or comme vous le suggérez pour les Etats-Unis dans A Global Monetary Plague (see Brown 2016 and Brown 2011)? Cette mésaventure ne remet-elle pas en cause la pratique des réserves fractionnaires?

Observation: A la lumière de ce que vous dîtes, on comprend mieux comment tant de bons esprits de la Belle Epoque (au premier rang desquels Norman Angell, Ivan Bloch) avaient prédit au début du Vingtième Siècle que la guerre était désormais impossible pour des raisons économiques et financières. Ils avaient seulement oublié qu'il suffirait de faire sauter l'étalon-or pour que les Etats belligérants puissent financer les dépenses de guerre par le surendettement et l'inflation, bref par du papier-monnaie.

Chapitre 4. De la Naissance de L'Hégémonie du Dollar à la Crise de 1929

Question 4: L'établissement d'un Gold Exchange Standard à la Conférence de Gênes (avril-mai 1922) a-t-il joué un rôle dans la Grande Crise de 1929? Et si oui lequel?

Question 4, partie 2 et 3: Qu'entendez-vous par taux d'intérêt neutre (neutral rate)? Et par inflation des actifs (asset inflation)?

Question 4, partie 4: Ne faut-il pas tenir compte aussi de la décision de Winston Churchill, alors chancelier de l'Echiquier, de rétablir le 28 avril 1925 la livre sterling à sa parité d'avant-guerre, soit 4 dollars 86 cents? Ensuite Churchill confiera à son médecin: "Ce fut la plus grande bévue de ma vie". Et dans *The Economic Consequences of Mr. Churchill*, J.-M. Keynes posera la question: "pourquoi a-t-il fait une chose aussi stupide"? Rappelons tout de même que dans un contexte de baisse des prix en Angleterre, la livre était remontée, à la veille de la fatale décision de Churchill, jusqu'à 4 dollars 81 cents (elle était à 3 dollars 20 en février 1920). Ne pouvait-on pas profiter de cette situation pour rétablir la livre dans sa gloire d'antan (pour cinq petits cens de plus)? Et n'était-il pas louable de permettre à la Banque d'Angleterre de respecter les engagements de change qu'elle avait pris vis-à-vis des porteurs de livres sterlings?

Question 4, partie 5: Vous venez d'employer le terme d'hégémonie monétaire (monetary hegemony)? Est-ce une figure de rhétorique (la transposition d'un terme militaire ou/et politique dans notre domaine) ou bien est-ce une locution qui a son propre sens pour les économistes (comme par exemple monopole)? Et en quoi s'applique-t-elle au dollar dès cette époque?

Question 4, partie 6: Mais en quoi la puissance en question (ici les États-Unis) profite-t-elle de son hégémonie monétaire? Des déficits "sans pleurs", comme disait Jacques Rueff? Ou autres avantages? N'y a-t-il pas des inconvénients à être dans cette situation? Par exemple être obligé de tenir compte des incidences internationales de telle ou telle politique, même si un certain Conally prétendra en 1971: « le dollar est notre monnaie, mais c'est votre problème »? Ou encore souffrir d'un déficit dans la balance courante des paiements pour approvisionner le monde en dollars, aboutissant à terme à un affaiblissement du même dollar (le dit Paradoxe de Triffin)? De même que l'hégémonie géo-politique se paye en un supplément de dépenses militaires, de même l'hégémonie monétaire n'aurait-elle pas un coût qui contrebalancerait ses éventuels avantages?

Chapitre 5. Expliquer 1929

Question 5: Venons-en maintenant à la crise déclenchée en 1929. L'explication bien connue de Milton Friedman est que le Fed aurait pu éviter le cataclysme en augmentant l'offre de monnaie. Cette thèse a eu par la suite une influence immense non seulement chez les économistes mais aussi chez les décideurs qu'ils soient au gouvernement ou dans les banques centrales. Lors d'une cérémonie en l'honneur du 90ème anniversaire de Friedman, à l'université de

Chicago, en 2002, Ben Bernanke, qui n'était pas encore président du Fed, mais qui était déjà membre du conseil des gouverneurs du Fed, a déclaré: « J'aimerais dire à Milton et Anna (Anna Schwartz, co-auteur de l'Histoire monétaire des Etats-Unis): au sujet de la Grande Dépression (1929), vous avez raison, c'était notre faute. Nous sommes désolés. Mais, grâce à vous, nous ne recommencerons pas. » Et de fait, une fois président du Fed, Bernanke s'appliquera à administrer les recettes de la cuisine friedemanienne. Certes on doit reconnaître à Friedman le mérite insigne d'avoir contribué à démolir l'idole keynésienne—qui reste cependant adulée dans nombre de pays. Mais on peut se demander si on n'est pas tombé de Charybde (le keynesianisme) en Scylla (le friedmanisme). En tout état de cause, l'analyse de la Grande Dépression par Friedman ne doit-elle pas être radicalement mise en cause, au même titre que celle de Keynes, qui a eu elle aussi et a encore une grande influence?

Question 5a: Juste une précision. Qu'entendez-vous précisément par base monétaire (monetary base)?

Dans *A Global Monetary Plague* (p. 110 et 143), vous écrivez que la base monétaire ne doit rapporter aucune intérêt pour être comme une patate chaude (hot potato). Une patate chaude est une patate dont le « porteur » cherche à se débarrasser le plus vite possible parce qu'elle lui brûle les doigts. Est-ce ainsi qu'il faut comprendre la nature de la base monétaire?

Question 5b: Une suite au New Deal peu souvent mentionnée par les apologistes de Roosevelt et de sa politique « keynesienne » avant la lettre (la Théorie générale de l'emploi date de 1936), est la rechute de 1937–1938. Alfred Sauvy a été l'un des rares économistes français à le souligner. « En 1937–1938, écrit-il, les Etats-Unis ont subi une forte rechute économique; en un an, de mai 1937 à mai 1938, la production industrielle a baissé de 35%, plus vite qu'en 1929. Mais les historiens ont mis le voile sur ce désastre. » Malheureusement, il fait cette remarque judicieuse seulement dans une note en bas de page et en petits caractères (Alfred Sauvy, *De Paul Reynaud à Charles de Gaulle, un économiste face aux hommes politiques*, 1934–1967, Casterman, 1972, p. 21). Comment expliquez-vous, vous-même, rechute? Quelles en ont été ses conséquences? Et pourquoi l'a-t-on tellement occultée?

Chapitre 6. Comment l'or finança l'Allemagne Nazie

Question 6: Nous avons admis que si l'étalon-or avait subsisté en 1914, le conflit européen eût été beaucoup moins long, moins meurtrier, moins coûteux. Pourrait-on en dire autant de la guerre qui commence en 1940?

Rappelons que dans l'Allemagne hitlérienne, la détention d'or était interdite aux particuliers, comme dans l'Amérique de Roosevelt ou dans la France de John Law en 1720...

Comment: Quant à la Banque de France, comme vous le savez, elle réussit à mettre son or à l'abri.

Chapitre 7. Bretton Woods: Le Faux Gold Exchange Standard

Question 7: Venons-en maintenant aux Accords de Bretton-Woods, signés le 22 juillet 1944, alors que les combats continuent à faire rage en Europe. Les trois quarts de l'or des banques centrales sont maintenant aux mains des Etats-Unis. Pouvions-nous restaurer un vrai étalon-or, éviter d'instaurer un nouveau Gold Exchange Standard? Avons-nous échappé de peu au « bancor » de Keynes, ce dernier pourtant au sommet de sa gloire mondiale? La parité de 35 dollars l'once, imposée par Roosevelt le 30 janvier 1934, était-elle la bonne?

Question 8: L'un des "arguments" des ministres de l'OPEP lors du coup de force d'octobre 1973, en parallèle avec le déclenchement de la Guerre du Kippour, a été que le dollar perdait de sa valeur. En effet, deux ans plus tôt, en août 1971, Richard Nixon, alors président des Etats-Unis, avait fermé le "fenêtre d'or" et procédé de fait à une dévaluation de la devise américaine. Quelle était la justification d'un tel reniement de l'engagement solennel des Etats-Unis à Bretton-Woods quant à la parité-or du dollar?

Chapitre 8: Le Choix Stratégique de L'Allemagne

Question 9: Quelles ont été les conséquences du "coup d'Etat monétaire" de Nixon? Comment qualifier le régime de change qu'il a généré?

Chapitre 9. Pour ou Contre Friedman

Autrement dit, la victoire du monétarisme à la Friedman était un trompe-l'œil. Il n'en reste pas moins que ce monétarisme est devenu la théorie à la mode, Friedman prenant la place de gourou tenu jusque-là par Keynes jusqu'à sa mort, et qu'il a semblé inspirer la politique monétaire des banques centrales à partir de 1971–1972. Ces banques centrales se sont apparemment donné des objectifs conformes à la théorie quantitative de la monnaie. Par exemple, la masse monétaire devait augmenter de x% par an quelle que soit la conjoncture.

Question 10: Pouvait-on s'entendre sur une définition adéquate de la masse monétaire?

Question 11: Pouvait-on être assuré que la théorie quantitative de la monnaie de Friedman fût valide?

Question 11, partie 2: Pensez-vous vraiment que M1 (pièces et billets en circulation et dépôts à vue) pouvait être la base d'une politique monétaire saine? Une telle politique n'était-elle pas condamnée à l'échec de toutes façons?

Question 11, partie 3: Soit x (compris entre 0 et 1) la part de ses prêts qu'une banque retrouve dans ses dépôts, selon le fameux adage loans make deposits. Nous faisons abstraction ici des réserves obligatoires à la banque centrale. On démontre que, dans cette situation, le montant des prêts que cette banque peut faire à partir de ses dépôts est multiplié par un facteur $f = 1/(1 - x)$. Si $x = 1$, c'est-à-dire si la banque retrouve tous ses prêts dans ses dépôts, sa potentialité de prêts (f) est infinie. Or la révolution technologique dont vous parlez n'a-t-elle pas eu comme conséquence d'augmenter x dans des proportions considérables, le rapprochant de 1, et donc d'accroître démesurément le potentiel de prêts des banques? N'est-ce pas ce qui explique la naissance et la rapidité de cette révolution? L'introduction de réserves obligatoires est-elle vraiment en mesure d'empêcher un tel processus? Ne faudrait-il pas mieux instaurer la règle du 100% de réserves comme le voulait Murray Rothbard?

Question 11, partie 4: Dans les années 1930, en France, la doctrine dominante en matière bancaire était que le rôle des banques était seulement d'assurer la liquidité de l'économie au moyen du crédit commercial à court terme (escompte, etc.). Le financement des investissements, assurait-on, n'était pas de leur ressort, mais relevait de l'autofinancement, du marché financier ou des banques d'affaires. La création aux Etats-Unis en 1933 de la Federal Deposit Insurance Corporation était considérée par les banquiers français comme « immorale » (sic) en ce qu'elle pouvait seulement induire des mauvaises manières, dispensant les clients de chercher les banques les plus prudentes et encourageant les banques imprudentes à abuser du « multiplicateur » bancaire évoqué plus haut. Quant aux ratios de liquidité et/ou de solvabilité que se proposaient d'imposer les autorités, on jugeait que, même si ces ratios étaient correctement conçus et calculés, ils étaient inutiles pour les banques sérieuses et illusoires pour les autres qui ne feraient que du window dressing pour les satisfaire. On est loin aujourd'hui d'une telle sagesse, qui confiait à la « main invisible » le soin gérer au mieux les intérêts des banquiers et de leurs clients, tout en respectant le secret de leurs relations. Pourrait-on y revenir et comment? Je ne méconnais ni la loi des grands nombres ni les économies d'échelle. Mais n'y a-t-il pas une relation entre l'assurance des dépôts, les ratios imposés d'une part et d'autre part le *too big to fail* dont nous verrons les ravages qu'il causera par la suite?

Question 11, partie 5: *As you know, there is no free lunch.* Il n'y a pas de repas gratuits. Si le taux d'intérêt sur les dépôts à vue est nul, il faut bien admettre un système de réserves fractionnaires en sorte que le banquier puisse gagner de l'argent en faisant « travailler » les dépôts (*hot potatoes* pour reprendre votre expression). En revanche, dans un système à 100% de réserves, le banquier ne peut équilibrer ses comptes que s'il fait payer un *fee* à son client, c'est-à-dire pour ce dernier un taux d'intérêt négatif. Maintenant, quel est le meilleur régime pour les réserves des banques centrales? Si je vous ai bien compris, leur taux d'intérêt doit être impérativement nul. Mais quid du *free lunch* dans ce cas? La banque centrale se paie-t-elle en faisant travailler ces réserves obligatoires? (N. B.: nous reviendrons plus tard sur les taux d'intérêt négatifs pratiqués récemment).

Chapitre 10. Comment Naquit l'Euro

Question 12: Quant à l'Allemagne, avant la création de l'euro, ses objectifs étaient-ils seulement monétaires?

Question 13a: La création de l'euro se voulait une réponse monétaire au dollar flottant issu du coup de Nixon. Mais en même temps, n'était-elle pas issue d'un compromis géo-politique entre la France et l'Allemagne, l'abandon du DM étant le prix à payer par l'Allemagne pour l'acceptation par la France de la réunification germanique après la chute du Mur de Berlin? Rappelons que François Mitterrand, alors président de la République, appartenait, sans l'avouer jamais, à la vieille école diplomatique française, plutôt de droite (Maurras, Bainville, etc....) qui aimait tellement l'Allemagne qu'elle préférait qu'il y en eût plusieurs, et au moins deux, pour paraphraser le mot de l'écrivain François Mauriac ...

Question 13b: Ces circonstances géopolitiques ont-elles joué un rôle dans la manière technique dont l'euro a été conçu et lancé.

Question 13c: Tout de même dans *Euro Crash* (p. 196) vous rappelez que le Chancelier Schmidt avait défendu la construction du Système Monétaire Européen en 1978 devant des *Bundesbankers* réticents en mettant l'accent sur les obligations spéciales de l'Allemagne envers l'Europe in *view of its Nazi past.* Pensez-vous que Kohl était dans un état d'esprit différent quand il a négocié avec François Mitterrand? Ce passé qui, selon la formule consacrée, ne voulait pas passer serait-il enfin passé? (N B: Nous reposerons la question quand nous discuterons de la construction du nouvel euro).

Chapitre 11. Trichet Avant Trichet

Question 14: Dans une note confidentielle, datée du 13 février 1992, de Jean-Claude Trichet, alors directeur du Trésor, à Pierre Bérégovoy, ministre français des Finances, que j'ai publiée dans *39 leçons d'économie contemporaine* (Gallimard 1998), on peut lire ces trois remarques, verbatim:

« 1) La BUNDESBANK ne changera de politique monétaire que lorsqu'elle sera pleinement rassurée sur l'inflation allemande (cela ne me paraît malheureusement pas être pour demain) …

« 2) Quoi que fasse la France (SME… pas SME, Maastricht …pas Maastricht), nos taux sont liés aux taux allemands par le truchement du marché mondial des capitaux totalement indépendamment de la volonté d'indépendance de la France ou d'une éventuelle volonté de domination de l'Allemagne.

« 3) Tant que l'a Allemagne ne mérite pas (ou plus) d'être l'ancre monétaire du système (SME), notre pays doit tout faire pour convaincre les investisseurs internationaux que nous sommes nous-mêmes candidats à être l' « ancre » …, que le franc est candidat à la réévaluation contre le deutschemark …, et qu'il aura le droit un jour—aussi proche que possible—d'avoir des taux à long terme inférieurs aux taux à long terme allemands

« En refusant la concertation préalable et la coopération étroite (plus par incapacité institutionnelle que par mauvaise volonté politique à mon avis …), l'Allemagne n'offre pas d'autres choix concret à la France que de contester fermement au deutschemark son rôle d' « ancre » du système … ».

Étant donné le rôle crucial que Jean-Claude Trichet a joué d'abord dans la construction de l'euro, puis dans sa gestion de la BCE quand il en fut président, rôle que vous soulignez bien dans vos propres ouvrages, que vous inspirent ces réflexions datant, je le rappelle, de février 1992? N'indiquent-elles pas l'ambition de la haute technocratie française de supplanter dès cette date l'Allemagne dans son rôle d'étalon monétaire pour l'Europe? Ne révèlent-elles pas au moins son désir que la France soit traitée sur les marchés financiers à l'égal de la République fédérale allemande? L'exemple français ne sera-t-il pas suivi, après la création de l'euro, par d'autres pays européens encore moins dignes d'un tel traitement sur les marchés financiers? (N B: nous reviendrons plus tard sur les rôles de Trichet et Draghi après la crise de 2008).

Question 14 supplément: Juste un éclaircissement: quand vous dites: *First, monetary base had successfully operated as the pivot of the German monetary order*, pourriez-vous nous préciser pourquoi il en était ainsi en Allemagne et non en France.

Pour faire juste une incursion dans l'actualité de ce jour (5/01/2020), la décision par la BCE de ne plus émettre de billets de 500 euros, sous prétexte de lutter contre le blanchiment d'argent, ne va pas arranger les choses sur le plan de la stabilité de M1 dans la zone euro, n'est-ce pas?

Chapitre 12. La Grande Crise de 2008

Question 15: Abordons maintenant la grande crise de 2008. On a oublié (surtout en France) que le premier signe du cataclysme est venu de la BNP-Paribas. Le 9 août 2007, la première banque française, un géant comme vous le savez, a interdit aux investisseurs de retirer de l'argent de trois de ses fonds de placement comportant des titres adossés à des prêts hypothécaires subprimes américains, expliquant qu'elle ne pouvait plus déterminer la valeur de ces fonds à cause de « l'évaporation complète de la liquidité » sur les marchés de ces titres. Cette seule annonce de la BNP a entraîné immédiatement une contraction sur ces mêmes marchés.

Je suis client de la XXX, une banque du même acabit que la BNP, dont je tairai le nom pour des raisons évidentes. Je suis allé voir la personne qui s'occupe de mon compte à l'agence de mon quartier et je lui ai demandé si la XXX avait elle aussi dans son portefeuille des titres adossés à ces fameux subprimes. Elle m'a juré la main sur le cœur que, bien sûr, ce n'était pas le cas, que la XXX, elle, était bien gérée, et qu'elle ne se risquait pas, quant à elle, dans de telles aventures financières. Or, comme on l'apprit plus tard, les comptes de la XXX étaient tout autant vérolés par ces actifs toxiques. La personne en charge de mon portefeuille à la XXX m'avait donc menti. Dès lors se pose un problème classique d'asymétrie d'information entre le client et sa banque. Certes la banque ne sait pas tout de son client; mais, la plupart du temps, elle en sait plus que le client sur elle-même. Ce problème d'asymétrie peut-il être réglé par le marché? Apparemment non, puisque toutes sortes de règlements de la profession bancaire s'efforcent de le résoudre! Mais ils échouent dans cette tâche comme on vient de le voir. Alors que faire?

Question 16: Dans un manuel destiné aux étudiants de sciences économiques, on peut lire ceci à propos de la crise des subprimes: « L'intensification de la concurrence qui a résulté de la déréglementation des marchés financiers et du fait que certains agents se financent désormais sur les marchés a conduit les banques à développer leur offre ... Elles ont cherché à accroître la collecte des dépôts et l'octroi des crédits aux agents qui n'ont pas accès au marché financier ». Et en note de bas de page, on enfonce le clou: « Le développement des crédits « *subprime* » aux Etats-Unis relève dans une large mesure de cette logique. Pour accroître leur clientèle, les banques ne se sont plus contentées de prêter aux ménages classés « *primes* » (les meilleurs risques), elles ont prêté, notamment sur le marché des crédits hypothécaires, aux clients offrant des garanties moindres »). » (Alain Beitone, Christophe Rodrigues, *Economie monétaire*, Armand Colin, 2017). On pourrait citer des dizaines de textes de la même eau: La crise des subprimes, qui a provoqué la crise la plus grave que le monde ait connue depuis 1929, est venue de la déréglementation des marchés financiers et de l'avidité des banquiers à la recherche de profits coûte que coûte. Le marché, une fois encore, était coupable. On oublie au passage de rappeler que ces mêmes banquier américains étaient obligés, sous peine de pénalités, d'accorder des prêts subprimes à certaines classes sociales!

Cette erreur d'analyse, très largement partagée par nos élites, n'explique-t-elle pas la manière dont elles ont cherché ensuite à remédier à la crise de 2008?

Question 17: Maintenant, je voudrais éclaircir un point d'histoire. L'attention des observateurs a été focalisée sur la faillite de Lehman Brothers le 15 septembre 2008 comme déclencheur du cataclysme qui s'est abattu sur l'économie mondiale. Et toute une littérature s'est développée derechef à ce moment-là sur le TBTF (too big to fail) ou le TITF (too interconnected to fail). Mais un accord avec la Barclays n'était-il pas sur le point d'intervenir qui eût évité la faillite de Lehman Brothers et ne sont-ce pas les autorités britanniques (le chancelier de l'Echiquier et la Financial Services Authority) qui, en interdisant cet accord à la dernière minute, furent les vrais responsables de la catastrophe? Rappelons au passage ce mot d'Alan Greenspan, célèbre président du Fed: « *The real issue is not that an institution is too big or too interconnected to fail, but that is too big or interconnected to liquidate quickly* ».

Question 18: Dans ces conditions, il semble tout de même étrange que la Barclays se soit déclarée disponible au rachat de Lehmans, non? Ne pouvait-elle anticiper le *run* que vous évoquez? Ou prévoyait-elle-elle que de toutes façons on viendrait alors à son secours?

Question 19: L'argument souvent utilisé pour venir au secours des banques par Bernanke et consorts est qu'invoquer l'aléa moral au beau milieu d'une crise financière serait une attitude « malavisée et dangereuse ». Exemple: Mon voisin fume au lit. Il met le feu à sa maison, qui est en bois. Pour des raisons d'aléa moral je n'appelle pas les pompiers. Sauver le fumeur somnolent ne ferait que l'encourager dans ses imprudences et inciter d'autres fumeurs à en faire autant. Mais si ma maison est aussi en bois et se trouve juste à côté de la sienne, ne vais-je pas me précipiter au téléphone et appeler les urgences? Et si toute la ville est construite en bois? (En Californie, notez-le, de leur propre aveu, des pompiers privés ne viennent au secours de la maison voisine de celle de leur client que si sa destruction par le feu menace celle qu'ils sont chargés de protéger).

Chapitre 13. Capitalisme Américain Versus Capitalisme Européen

Question 20: Avant d'aborder la manière dont la zone euro a géré la crise de 2008, il semble nécessaire de souligner la différence fondamentale qui sépare les Etats-Unis de l'Europe en matière bancaire.

Comme on peut le constater dans les statistiques, la part des prêts bancaires dans le financement des entreprises est beaucoup plus importante dans la zone euro qu'aux Etats-Unis. Inversement, les entreprises américaines recourent davantage aux marchés financiers que les entreprises européennes. De quand date cette différence? Comment s'explique-t-elle? Quel est le meilleur *"mix"* pour les entreprises? pour les banques? Quelles incidences peut-on en attendre a priori en cas de crise? Comment se situe la Grande-Bretagne à ce propos?

Question 20, partie 2: Le droit des actionnaires n'est-il pas mieux respecté aux Etats-Unis qu'en Europe?

Question 20, partie 3: Patrick Artus, chef économiste de la banque Natixis, soutenait récemment (*Le Monde* du 28 janvier 2019) que les entreprises américaines étaient plus fragiles que les entreprises européennes. « Les entreprises américaines, observe-t-il, sont financées pour deux tiers en obligations et pour un tiers en crédits bancaires—une situation très différente des entreprises européennes, qui sont essentiellement financées par les banques. La hausse du coût du financement en obligations a conduit les entreprises américaines à réduire fortement leurs émissions obligataires, de 100 milliards de dollars par trimestre (pour les émissions nettes) en 2017 et début 2018, à moins de 20 milliards de dollars par trimestre au second semestre 2018. Les émissions d'entreprises *high yield*, elles, ont complètement disparu depuis fin 2018. Ce quasi-arrêt s'est traduit par une chute des investissements à partir du troisième trimestre 2018 ». A cela s'ajoute de puissants « effets de richesse », la chute des cours boursiers aboutissant à une baisse de la consommation des ménages et à une réduction supplémentaire des investissements. Artus en infère une fragilité particulière de l'économie américaine, les États-Unis réagissant plus fortement aux choix financiers que la zone euro. Que. penser de ce diagnostic?

Il y a peut-être eu surinvestissement ou mal investissement dans le *shale oil* américain, mais cela a tout de même permis aux Etats-Unis de *redevenir* le premier producteur de pétrole du monde, et donc de réduire notre dépendance (pas seulement celle des Etats-Unis) de l'Arabie saoudite, laquelle avait usé et abusé de son pouvoir depuis 1973. Le « prix directeur » du baril de pétrole brut (50–60 $) est devenu américain et non saoudien. Et l'on ne risque plus de le voir monter jusqu'au-dessus de 100 $. Le 14 septembre 2019, il a suffi de quelques drones, venant d'on ne sait où, pour paralyser la *moitié* de la production saoudienne. Cinq ans plus tôt un tel attentat aurait propulsé le cours du baril à des niveaux stratosphériques. Le cours a à peine bougé après l'attentat. Un tel résultat valable pour tous les pays consommateurs de pétrole n'est-il pas appréciable? Ce qui conduit à poser la question plus générale: comment définir le *sur investissement* ou le *malinvestment*?

Chapitre 14. Soumission de L'Euro au 2% Inflation Standard

Question 21: Venons-en à la manière dont la zone euro a réagi à la crise. Rappelons d'abord que, d'après le Traité de Maastricht, la Banque Centrale Européenne s'était vu assigner un seul objectif: la « stabilité des prix », contrairement au Système de Réserve Fédérale qui, lui, doit aussi viser le plein emploi. Dans cette limitation des tâches de la BCE, on a vu un triomphe des monétaristes (allemands) sur les keynésiens (surtout français). Et l'on a soupçonné Jean-Claude Trichet, quand il fut nommé président de la BCE, de se soumettre trop volontiers au diktat germanique. Soupçon d'autant plus légitime que nous savons, par le document du Trésor français auquel nous avons fait allusion plus haut, que Trichet, au début des années 1990, avait nourri de grandes ambitions pour le franc français. On reviendra plus loin sur le rôle de Trichet à la BCE. Pour le moment posons seulement la question: l'euro, par sa construction, n'était-il pas mieux armé que le dollar contre ce que nous avons appelé la phobie de la déflation?

Question 22: On a beaucoup reproché à Jean-Claude Trichet d'avoir augmenté les taux d'intérêt de la BCE à l'été 2011 (juste quelques mois avant la fin de son mandat), alors que jusqu'à cette date il avait suivi la baisse des taux faisant suite à la faillite de Lehman Brothers. En effet on a attribué à cette baisse de taux la récession qui a suivi en Europe alors qu'aux Etats-Unis la croissance du PIB a continué. D'après vous, pourquoi Trichet a-t-il pris cette décision et cette décision est-elle responsable de cette "deuxième récession" qui aurait coûté fort cher à l'Europe.

Question 23: A Deauville, le lundi 18 octobre 2010, Angela Merkel et Nicolas Sarkozy ont demandé d'amender les traités avec un double objectif: la suspension des droits de vote européens d'un pays en cas de "violation grave" du pacte et la création d'un mécanisme permanent de sauvetage. Ce dispositif, si l'on en croit la presse, revenait peu ou prou à supprimer, ou à modifier, la clause de non-renflouement d'un État membre de la zone euro. Comment expliquer que le résultat ait été une crise de confiance carabinée sur les marchés et une remontée spectaculaire et vertigineuse des taux?

Chapitre 15. Draghi: « Whatever It Takes »

Question 24: Dans un discours à Londres le 26 juillet 2012, Mario Draghi, le nouveau président de la Banque Centrale Européenne, a déclaré « A l'intérieur de son mandat, la BCE est prête à faire toute ce qui est nécessaire (*whatever it takes*) ... pour sauver l'euro. Et croyez-moi, ce sera suffisant. » Ces quelques mots ont suffi à calmer les marchés et à faire redescendre les taux d'intérêt (cf. graphique). Comment expliquer ce qui a été considéré et est considéré encore comme une sorte de miracle accompli par le "mage" italien? Ne peut-on y voir une preuve supplémentaire de ce que Greenspan appelait l' « exubérance irrationnelle des marchés »—formule indéfiniment ressassée par les partisans d'une régulation des marchés?

Question 24, partie 2: Acceptons votre explication, mais il faut encore nous dire pour quelles raisons Frau Merkel a donné son accord au Sig. Draghi? Sous quelle pression? Selon quel raisonnement? Dans quel but? Quels rôles ont joué les Français dans cette manière d'abdication? Et pourquoi la Bundesbank l'a-t-elle de facto acceptée?

Question 25: Dans l'article de A. Durré et H Pill, "*Central bank balance sheets as policy tools*", on trouve deux intéressants graphiques qui montrent que la BCE a accaparé une très grande partie de l'intermédiation bancaire. Validez-vous cette analyse? Et si oui, quels sont les effets de cet accaparement? N'y peut-on voir une sorte de soviétisation du système bancaire européen? Assiste-t-on au même phénomène aux Etats-Unis et en Grande-Bretagne?

Question 25 partie 2: Mais cette installation de la BCE comme « intermédiaire de dernier recours », en plus de son rôle de prêteur en dernier ressort, ne va-t-elle pas engendrer une ankylose du système pour un temps indéfini? En est-il de même aux États-Unis et en Grande-Bretagne? Et comment pourrait-on en sortir? Question adjacente; Ce rôle supplémentaire accordé à la BCE n'est-il pas contraire aux Traités européens?

Chapitre 16. La Crise Grecque

Question 26: Venons-en maintenant à la « crise grecque » et d'abord à la question de l'entrée de la Grèce dans l'Union monétaire. A l'époque, on a soupçonné Goldman Sachs, banque-conseil des autorités helléniques, d'avoir truqué les statistiques de l'économie de la Grèce pour lui faciliter cette entrée. Dans Euro-Clash, vous soutenez, quant à vous, que l'état réel de l'économie grecque a été masqué volontairement par le français Christian Noyer, à l'époque vice-président de la BCE (il sera ensuite gouverneur de la Banque de France) pour des raisons stratégiques (la Grèce allait être invitée à joindre l'Organisation internationale de la francophonie), mais aussi commerciales (elle était cliente de l'industrie française d'armement)? Comment se fait-il que les autres pays-membres de l'Union monétaire, et notamment l'Allemagne, ne se soient pas aperçus de cette supercherie, si elle a eu lieu, qui allait mettre en danger l'euro lui-même et coûté si cher non seulement aux Grecs mais aussi aux pays qui viendraient à leur secours?

Question 26, partie 2: Cela étant dit, une fois la crise grecque déclenchée, n'aurait-il pas mieux valu laisser la Grèce sortir de l'Union monétaire? Étant donné la petitesse que vous soulignez de son économie, un tel « Grexit » n'aurait-il pas pu être aisément supporté par les autres membres de l'Union? N'est-ce pas ce que voulait l'Allemagne? Pourquoi la France s'y est-elle opposé? Et si l'Allemagne penchait pour la sortie de la Grèce, pourquoi le point de vue allemand n'at-il pas prévalu?

Question 26, partie 3: La crise grecque n'était-elle parfaitement prévisible? Ou du moins prévisible pour ceux qui connaissaient la réalité de ses comptes? Mais si elle était aussi aisément prévisible par ceux qui savaient, c'est donc que ceux-là l'avaient prévue? D'où la question: Si beaucoup y ont perdu, qui y a gagné?

Chapitre 17. L'Union Bancaire

Question 27: Venons en à ce qu'on appelle le projet de l'Union Bancaire (*Banking Union*) lancé en 2012. L'argument principal des protagonistes de cette nouvelle institution européenne est que le « nationalisme bancaire », pour reprendre leurs propres termes, est un facteur aggravant de la crise financière. Ce « nationalisme », expliquent-ils, se traduirait par une relation bi-univoque entre la situation financière de chaque Etat et celle des banques situées sous son autorité. Un système bancaire fragile fragilise l'État dont il dépend, et, réciproquement, un État en difficulté met en danger les banques qui sont sous sa souveraineté. L'Union Bancaire chercherait donc à rompre ces cercles vicieux—cercles, prétendent-ils, qu'on n'observerait pas aux États-Unis où les banques ne sont pas rattachées à tel ou tel État de la Fédération. A ces considérations s'ajoute une analyse « sociologique » selon laquelle il y aurait en

Europe une sorte de concubinage pervers entre les États et les banques au plan national du fait que les mêmes couches sociales peuplent les cabinets ministériels et les conseils d'administration bancaire. Par exemple, en France le célèbre corps de l'Inspection des Finances peuple le Trésor, la Banque de France et les grandes banques. Que. penser de ces analyses et du projet d'Union bancaire qui en est issu?

Question 28: Jean Pisani-Ferry écrit dans *Le Monde* du 26/27 mai 2019: « L'interaction perverse entre insolvabilité des banques et insolvabilité des Etats n'a pas été coupée [par l'Union bancaire]. Atténuée par le passage des grandes banques sous le contrôle direct de la Banque centrale européenne (BCE), elle n'a pas disparu, comme l'a illustré l'accès de fièvre italien de l'automne 2018 ». Cette réflexion désabusée de l'un des promoteurs du projet d'Union bancaire, sept ans après son lancement n'est-elle pas significative?

Question 29: Pourquoi la Commission européenne se donne tant de mal pour convaincre le gouvernement italien à rentrer dans le prétendu droit chemin budgétaire, en le menaçant plus ou moins ouvertement de sanctions qui seraient forcément mal vues et renforceraient encore le populisme en Italie? Ne suffirait-il pas de laisser le marché « faire le boulot »? La dernière fois, il a quelques mois, la montée brutale du *spread* italien a convaincu les autorités romaines de présenter un projet de budget moins inconvenant du point de vue de Bruxelles. Pourquoi ne pas attendre la prochaine flambée?

Question 29, partie 2: Pourquoi et comment le coût de ce *gravy train* (assiette au beurre en français) serait-il d'abord et avant tout supporté par le contribuable allemand? D'autres contribuables ne sont-ils pas mis à…contribution? Et pourquoi ne le seraient-ils pas?

Question 29, partie 3: A-t-on des statistiques au sujet de ces transferts de dépôts italiens et, pourquoi ce tropisme des dépôts italiens pour les banques allemandes? Le système bancaire allemand n'a-t-il pas ses propres difficultés,? Les banques françaises ou belges ou néerlandaises ou luxembourgeoises ne devraient-elles pas, elles aussi, servir de refuges aux déposants italiens? Ce déplacement de dépôts n'est-il pas un hommage involontaire au projet d'"union bancaire", les clients des banques italiennes votant avec leurs pieds, si l'on peut dire?

Question 29, partie 4: Si l'euro n'existait pas, les déposants italiens pourraient-ils transférer leurs avoirs en Allemagne sans convertir leurs lira en DM et entraîner ainsi une dévaluation de leur monnaie? N'est-ce donc pas grâce à l'euro que les Italiens peuvent trouver refuge dans des banques allemandes ou autres? N'y a-t-il pas là un levier pour faire pression sur le gouvernement italien?

Question 30: Comment expliquer que l'intégration financière dans la zone euro soit inférieure à ce qu'elle avait été avant la crise, selon les propres calculs de la BCE?

Chapitre 18. Sous Performance de L'Europe

Question 31: Comment se fait-il que la zone euro ait souffert d'une "deuxième" récession après la "grande récession" de 2008, au contraire des Etats-Unis? Il en est résulté une sous performance européenne par rapport à la croissance économique américaine. Est-ce parce que la BCE a tardé à prendre les mesures dites "non conventionnelles" adoptées par le Système fédéral? Ou est-ce à cause de la politique budgétaire et fiscale d'Obama puis de Trump?

Question 32: Cette sous-performance rend-elle la zone euro plus fragile que les États-Unis pour aborder le prochain retournement de conjoncture?

Chapitre 19. Le Bilan de Draghi

Question 33: Le mandat de Mario Draghi venant à sa fin, quel bilan peut-on en faire? Meilleur ou pire que celui de Jean-Claude Trichet?

Question 34: Venons-en à votre projet de réforme de l'euro. Question préalable: Ce projet n'est concevable dès le début sans une profonde et intime collaboration franco-allemande. Cette dernière est-elle encore d'actualité? Et si l'on se réfère à la manière même dont vous la décrivez pour les dix dernières années, ne s'agirait-il pas en fait de redonner à l'Allemagne une main qu'elle aurait perdue depuis la création de.

Question 35: Si tout de même on veut voir le bon côté de cette histoire, ce serait de constater que l'euro, par sa propre dynamique, aussi vicieuse qu'elle puisse paraître, a échappé à une prise directe des gouvernements de la Zone Euro, le pot de miel de la création monétaire étant—un peu—écarté des pattes de l'ours étatique. Après un Vingtième Siècle de grande inflation, causée par des monnaies détachées de toute référence au réel, courant de dévaluation en dévaluation, les citoyens européens auraient, dans notre hypothèse optimiste, découvert ou redécouvert que la monnaie pouvait ne pas être un « attribut régalien », contrairement à ce qu'on enseigne dans nos écoles et universités, ou même qu'elle devrait peut-être ne pas l'être si elle prétendait au statut de bonne monnaie. N'est-ce pas de cette « leçon de choses » qu'il faut partir pour bâtir le nouvel euro?

Question 36: Rappelons que dans l'esprit des Pères fondateurs de la monnaie européenne, la Zone Euro devait marcher sur deux jambes, une jambe monétaire et une jambe budgétaire/fiscale. Le temps pressant pour des raisons géo-politiques (la chute du Mur de Berlin et la réunification germanique, cette dernière étant un vieux cauchemar français, mais aussi le souhait allemand que l'euro soit au moins aussi bon que le deutschemark, selon la formule de l'époque), on a dû se contenter de marcher sur une seule jambe, la jambe monétaire, avec l'institution de la BCE. Mais pour les Fondateurs, la monnaie étant forcément un attribut de l'État, l'euro ne pourrait survivre qu'adossé à un budget européen, embryon d'une Fédération européenne, et donc d'une fiscalité européenne, doublée d'une capacité de lancer des obligations européennes.

Il n'est pas impossible, du reste, que dans les calculs des Fondateurs, l'échec à leurs yeux fatal de l'euro unijambiste obligerait à instituer *in fine* l'État européen de leurs vœux. Et c'est bien ce que beaucoup d'Eurocrates cherchent à nous vendre aujourd'hui.

Dans la construction du nouvel euro, ne devrait-on pas afficher d'emblée 1) que la « souveraineté » budgétaire ou/et fiscale est parfaitement légitime, les peuples ne pouvant accepter que les recettes et dépenses de leur État soient décidés hors de leur contrôle, et 2) que cette souveraineté serait parfaitement compatible avec le nouvel euro, les marchés financiers jouant le rôle à la fois de garde-fous et de gardes-chiourme? On jouerait ainsi à la fois sur la popularité actuelle de l'euro et sur l'impopularité non moins actuelle de l'eurocratie sous toutes ses formes.

Chapitre 20. Les Principes de Nouvel Euro

Question 37: Venons-en maintenant aux principes du nouvel euro en tant que sound money? Quels seraient-ils aujourd'hui? (Nous verrons plus tard comment les mettre en œuvre).

Question 37, partie 2: Pourquoi faire compliqué quand on peut faire simple...? Aujourd'hui, la première puissance du monde en or (pour ne s'en tenir qu'aux réserves des banques centrales), c'est (bizarrement, on ne le dit jamais) la Zone Euro elle-même avec 10,000 tonnes, presque deux mille tonnes de plus que les réserves de la Banque centrale des États-Unis. Ne serait-il pas plus simple et plus efficient de fonder le nouvel euro sur l'or.

Question 37, partie 3: Vous citez le 'bloc or' 1934–1936 dans votre réponse, expérience qui n'a pas laissé que de bons souvenirs en France, c'est le moins que l'on puisse dire. Elle a abouti aux *trois* dévaluations du Front populaire (pour mémoire, j'aime bien rappeler que François Mitterrand, au début de son mandat à l'Élysée, a lui aussi procédé à *trois* dévaluations selon à peu près le même timing). Mais n'y a-t-il pas des enseignements à tirer d'une autre expérience, bien oubliée aujourd'hui: l'Union latine, que vous citez vous même comme un ancêtre du nouvel euro que vous préconisez (*Euro Crash* pp. 184185)?

Question 38: « Un instrument d'échange sans passé n'est pas imaginable. Rien ne peut revêtir la fonction d'instrument d'échange, qui n'ait été déjà un bien économique auquel les gens assignaient une valeur d'échange avant même qu'il ne devienne demandé en tant qu'un instrument d'échange », écrit Ludwig von Mises *(L'action humaine,* p. 447, traduit de l'américain par Raoul Audouin, PUF, p. 447). Notre nouvel euro obéira-t-il à ce fameux théorème de l'économiste autrichien?

Question 39: Si le nouvel euro à l'origine n'est pas basé sur l'or, par quoi pourrions-nous remplacer les automatismes correcteurs bien connus de toute monnaie fondée sur un métal? A savoir que toute hausse générale de prix des biens et services se traduit par une baisse de la valeur de la monnaie, et donc par une diminution de la production de monnaie, et par conséquent de l'offre de monnaie; et que toute baisse générale des prix des biens et services équivaut à une hausse de la valeur de la monnaie, et donc provoque un accroissement de la production de monnaie, et par conséquent de l'offre de monnaie— mécanisme stabilisateur qui—faut-il le souligner—ne nécessite aucune intervention d'aucune sorte?

Question 40: Supposons donc que le nouvel euro ne soit pas fondé sur l'or pour les raisons que vous invoquez. Par quoi pourrions-nous remplacer les disciplines automatiques (non-politiques) de l'étalon-or?

Question 40 partie 2: Vous dites 'monetary base in all its forms (whether currency or reserves) should pay zero interest and so money market rates are determined by the supply and demand of reserves'. Mais vous ne dites pas si ces réserves sont ou non obligatoires. Si ces réserves sont obligatoires, n'est-il pas judicieux qu'elles rapportent un intérêt, (positif évidemment), étant donné les sacrifices qu'elles imposent aux banques? C'est du reste un des arguments qui a été utilisés par les partisans de taux d'intérêt (forcément positif) sur les réserves au moment de leur instauration, notamment au Congrès des Etats-Unis.

Question 40, partie 3: Le billet de 500 euros n'est plus imprimé depuis la fin de l'année 2018 parce que, disait-on, il rendait plus faciles l'évasion fiscale, le financement de terrorisme ou encore blanchiment d'argent. Il offrait en effet la possibilité de faire transiter d'énormes sommes aisément et discrètement. Un million d'euros en coupures de 500 euros pèse 2,2 kilos, en comparaison avec les 22 kilos que pèserait la même somme en billets de 50 euros. Avec un billet de 1000 euros, le million d'euros ne pèserait plus qu'un kilo cent grammes. Ces arguments ne sont-ils pas légitimes? On prétendait aussi que le billet de 500 euros n'était guère utilisé dans les transactions courantes et que, donc, sa suppression, bénéfique pour l'ordre public, ne serait pas gênante pour le commun des mortels.

Question 40, partie 3 supplément: J'entends bien vos arguments. Mais est-ce que vous ne sous-estimez pas le coût en temps *(time is money,* dois-je vous le rappeler) et la pénibilité toute physique du paiement en numéraire. Ce matin même, à la caisse du magasin de fruits et légumes, je faisais la queue derrière une brave vieille dame qui voulait absolument faire l'appoint elle-même de ses achats, au centime près. Encombrée de ses propres paquets, elle s'est évertuée à trouver au fond d'un improbable profond porte-monnaie des pièces de 5, 2 et même de 1 centimes pour régler sa note. Piaffant derrière, j'avoue que je ne partageais pas l'admirable patience du caissier, qui s'est même proposé d'aider la cliente dans sa quête, ce qu'elle a évidemment refusé en dépit de la maladresse de ses mains tremblantes. Toute cette opération a pris plusieurs interminables minutes, précieuses pour le commun des mortels, dont je suis. Il m'a fallu un huitième de seconde pour faire la même opération, au centime près, en posant ma carte bancaire sur la machine. Sans doute *Big Brother* pourra savoir, encore et toujours au centime près, combien, ce jour-là à cette heure-là à ce magasin-là, j'ai dépensé en achat de carottes, de navets et de pommes, mais je me fiche bien de ce dévoilement d'une partie de mon intimité tellement je gagne en temps et en confort.

Question 40 partie 4: S'il n'y a pas de réserves obligatoires et si les taux d'intérêt sont librement déterminés par le jeu de l'offre et de la demande sur le marché monétaire, que reste-t-il à la nouvelle Banque centrale comme outil d'intervention ou de contrôle, si toutefois elle doit intervenir?

Question 41: Votre projet de constitution monétaire ne risque-t-il pas de rouvrir la porte que nous cherchions à fermer, c'est-à-dire la possibilité d'une intervention discrétionnaire de la Banque Centrale? Vous connaissez l'interrogation de Juvénal: quis custodiet ipsos custodes? Si la Banque centrale est de nouveau intronisée comme le gardien de la monnaie, qui gardera le gardien? En Gold Standard, l'or était le gardien des gardiens. Mais dans la fiat money system? Si l'on trouve le bon indice de masse monétaire, l'automatisme de la règle de Friedman n'est-il pas finalement préférable à toutes les précautions constitutionnelles que l'on peut imaginer? Pour mémoire, selon les statistiques de la BCE, M0 a triplé depuis 2007 alors que M3 ne s'est accru que de 30%.

Question 41 partie 2: Vous écrivez: *in technical terms the income velocity of monetary base would be stable.* Supposez-vous que la vitesse de circulation de la monnaie est stable? Comment en être sûr? N'est-ce pas l'une des inconnues les plus indéterminées de la fameuse équation monétaire M.V = P.T? Du reste, cette vitesse n'est-elle pas aujourd'hui même au plus bas niveau, ce qui donnerait raison aux économistes d'inspiration keynésienne qui prétendent que nous sommes tombés dans la fameuse et sinistre trappe à liquidités?

Chapitre 21. Lancement du Nouvel Euro

Question 42: Supposons maintenant que le lancement du nouvel euro soit réussi. N'y a-t-il pas un risque que, du fait même de cette réussite, la monnaie européenne soit poussée vers le haut sur les marchés des changes– comme le DM dans les années 1970? L'Allemagne l'avait fort bien supporté grâce aux effets de la courbe en J. Mais qu'en sera-t-il du nouvel euro? Plus généralement, la nouvelle BCE aura-t-elle une politique de change?

Question 42, partie 2: Quelle serait la valeur-or du nouvel euro au cas où il serait basé sur le métal jaune?

Question 43: Venons-en à l'aspect pratique: comment instaurer le nouvel euro? Dans *Euro Clash* (p. 181), vous évoquez la possibilité d'une sorte de coup d'Etat monétaire fomenté conjointement par le Président français et le Chancelier allemand dans le plus grand secret—coup d'État qui accoucherait d'une nouvelle constitution monétaire conforme aux principes que nous avons évoqués tout au long de ce dialogue. a) Les autres membres de l'Union monétaire pourraient-ils accepter un tel diktat franco-allemand? b) Pour justifier ce *golpe* vous évoquez l'ombre tutélaire du couple Adenauer-de Gaulle. Mais à peine le Traité de l'Elysée (1963) avait-il été signé que le même de Gaulle le vidait en partie de ses effets par une tentative de sabordage de l'OTAN et d'entente avec la « Russie éternelle ». Le Président Macron prend le même chemin, renouant avec le vieux tropisme français pour une « alliance de revers » avec Moscou, tout en décrétant que l'OTAN est en état de mort cérébrale, et que la règle du 3% du PIB[1] pour le déficit budgétaire est obsolète. A un moment où le couple franco-allemand est en état de décomposition avancée, comment peut-on espérer construire un axe monétaire Paris-Berlin?

---

[1] Rappel: C'est Valéry Giscard d'Estaing, alors président de la République française, qui, en septembre 1975, a annoncé que le déficit budgétaire serait porté jusqu'à 3% du PIB, ce qui paraissait à l'époque comme un comble d'audace. En creusant le déficit de cette manière, Giscard a en fait ouvert une porte de Pandore qui ne se refermera plus, puisqu'il faudra beaucoup d'effort à la France pour ramener son budget sous les 3% et qu'elle risque de nouveau de dépasser ce seuil!

c) D'un autre côté, ce qui pourrait pousser pour une renaissance du « moteur » franco-allemand pourrait être en effet la menace que l'Allemagne fonde un bon euro avec les pays de son hinterland, rejetant la France dans les pays du « Club Med » avec ses « sœurs latines ». Cette perspective n'est-elle pas, en fait, plus plausible que votre « coup d'État » franco-allemand?

Question 44: Supposons le *coup* réussi. Quelles seront les premières mesures à prendre pour installer le nouvel euro?

Petite Note sur L'Or

1 gramme à 50 euros n'est en effet pas extravagant si l'on se réfère au cours actuel de l'or. Il est intéressant de comparer avec le Franc Germinal institué par Napoléon en 1803 et dont la valeur-or n'a pas changé jusqu'à la banqueroute d'août 1914 pour cause de guerre.

Le gramme d'or valait environ un tiers de Franc Germinal (FG), ce qui nous met le FG à 17 €.

La plus petite pièce d'or émise sous Napoléon était de 20 grammes. Elle vaudrait donc aujourd'hui 1000 euros. Beaucoup plus que les billets de 50 et 100 euros qui ont été supprimés…. Ill existait aussi des pièces de 40 grammes, dont chacune vaudrait aujourd'hui 2000 euros.

Avec 25 pièces de 40 grammes, pesant un kilo, on pourrait donc se promener avec la coquette somme de 50,000 euros…

Appendix B: French Original of Conclusion (Philippe Simonnot)

AU COEUR DU MONDE

Il n'est pas difficile d'anticiper les critiques qui seront faites de notre dialogue. Promouvoir un ersatz d'étalon or en ce premier tiers du 21ème siècle sera considéré au mieux comme réactionnaire, au pire comme totalement irréaliste et dangereux.

Par avance, on répondra que de telles critiques auraient une vision courte de l'histoire et que ce qui est proposé ici est, non pas un retour à un passé révolu, mais la clôture de l'expérience désastreuse du Vingtième Siècle, qui s'est soldée pour l'humanité par des millions de morts et des destructions définitives, c'est-à-dire le contraire des « destructions créatrices » chères à Schumpeter.

Au terme de ce dialogue, qui ne voit qu'il n'est pas suffisant, pour expliquer le dérèglement actuel du système monétaire mondial, de remonter à la méga-crise de l'automne 2008? Ceux qui ont la mémoire la moins courte feront un rapport entre la crise dont nous souffrons aujourd'hui et la décision de Richard Nixon le 15 août de 1973 de fermer la fenêtre d'or (golden window), ouvrant en même temps la porte aux changes flottants. Encore faudrait-il, pour en bien comprendre les enjeux, relier le coup fatal de Nixon aux engagements implicites qu'il reniait, ceux qu'avaient souscrits le Trésor des Etats-Unis à la suite des Accords de Bretton-Woods en 1944. Mais le voyageur dans le temps ne pourrait s'arrêter à cette date s'il voulait satisfaire vraiment sa curiosité, ni même à la Conférence de Gênes de 1922 qui essayait déjà de bâtir un nouvel ordre mondial sur les principes boiteux du Gold Exchange Standard. Et c'est bien à ce funeste mois *européen* d'août 1914 qu'il finirait par aboutir dans sa quête d'explication: en quelques jours, en quelques heures, la convertibilité-or du papier-monnaie a été abandonnée. « Provisoirement », prétendait-on, car on ne doutait pas, malgré la furie guerrière qui s'était emparé des esprits, que cette convertibilité générale serait tôt ou tard rétablie, conformément aux engagements les plus solennels qui avaient été pris par les institutions bancaires envers les déposants.

Cela se passait au cœur de l'Europe, laquelle à l'époque était au cœur du monde.

On le sait maintenant, cette convertibilité ne serait jamais rétablie.

Certes, les trois entités politiques les plus artificielles créées à cause ou à la suite de la guerre européenne puis mondiale de 1914–1918, l'Union soviétique, la Yougoslavie, et la Tchécoslovaquie, ont fini par disparaître de la carte et l'on a pu voir dans ces abolitions les signes avant-coureurs annonçant que l'on était en train de solder pour de bon les séquelles de la Grande Guerre. Certes, la construction de l'Union européenne elle-même avait comme fondement le *plus jamais ça* entonné par les peuples après la Première Guerre mondiale, serment que l'on croyait en fait réalisé après la Seconde. Certes, l'euro lui-même semblait parachever sur le plan monétaire la clôture d'un siècle calamiteux Mais on avait oublié qu'une société, quelle qu'elle soit, ne peut se bâtir sur les sables mouvants de fausses monnaies. Et il n'est pas fortuit que, dans les flonflons mémoriels du centenaire de la Grande Guerre, l'avènement de l'inconvertibilité monétaire en août 1914 ait été totalement passé sous silence.

Il n'en reste pas moins que l'économie mondiale demeure hantée par le fantôme de la monnaie-or, laquelle est périodiquement invoquée comme remède à la crise.

Récemment, ce refoulé dans l'inconscient collectif a fait retour dans le monde réel sous une forme inattendue, et inimaginable sans la puissance formidable qu'ont acquise les ordinateurs: le Bitcoin et les nombreux avatars qui sont apparus dans son sillage.

Beaucoup de mystère entoure la naissance de cette cryptomonnaie, mais il est remarquable qu'elle soit née en 2008, l'année fatidique où l'ensemble du système bancaire mondial était secoué par une défiance que l'on n'avait pas vue depuis la méga-crise de 1929.

Ce n'est pas un hasard si le Bitcoin a une véritable dévotion pour le langage minier (mineurs, minage, etc.). Ce n'est pas non plus un hasard si une grande partie de son succès provient de ce que la quantité des bitcoins émis est à terme strictement limitée. Aucune autorité dans le système, a-t-on annoncé d'emblée, ne peut « imprimer » des bitcoins à volonté comme le font les banques centrales depuis qu'elles existent. Donc pas de *quantitative easing* possible, la forme moderne de la planche à billets.

De fait, s'il fallait résumer toute l'histoire monétaire en une seule formule dans le langage contemporain, on dira que les institutions bancaires ont joué le rôle « tiers de confiance »—des intermédiaires entre les partenaires commerciaux ou/et financiers. Or, ce sont justement ces « tiers de confiance », de moins en moins crédibles, dont les inventeurs puis les praticiens du Bitcoin ont voulu et veulent toujours se passer, partisans résolus qu'ils sont, grâce à la Blockchain, de relations pair à pair (P2P), c'est-à-dire sans intermédiaire. On comprend mieux la hargne à l'encontre de cette monnaie que nourrissent ceux qui nous gouvernent par le truchement des banques centrales. Le Bitcoin montre théoriquement l'on pourrait se passer d'eux!

La Blockchain, en effet, est un gigantesque livre de comptes, infalsifiable dans l'état actuel du savoir numérique, auto-contrôlée, où la moindre opération est enregistrée et vérifiée, chaque bitcoin étant absolument impossible à dupliquer.

Aussi bien la Blockchain permet-elle de répondre à la vieille question posée, on le sait, par Juvénal: Comment et pourquoi, en effet, faire confiance à des « tiers de confiance », même s'ils ont l'agrément des deux parties? On peut toujours leur poster des gardiens. Qui gardera les gardiens eux-mêmes? Quis custodiet ipsos custodes? Et à supposer que l'on trouve un gardien pour garder les gardiens, qui gardera ce gardien, et ainsi de suite?

Le moins que l'on puisse dire, c'est que l'on en est toujours, comme en témoigne amplement ce dialogue, à se demander qui garde la Banque centrale? Cette question est particulièrement pertinente en Europe où l'institution de Francfort est supposée indépendante. On a cherché ici à y répondre en se rapprochant le plus possible des disciples de l'étalon-or. Et comme l'Europe est la première responsable du dérèglement monétaire mondial par sa forfaiture de 1914, il ne nous semble pas tout-à-fait incongru que cette même

Europe essaie d'initier une réforme authentique de sa monnaie, qui ne pourra pas ne pas avoir d'effet sur l'ensemble du système monétaire international.

A l'appui de cette démarche nous pourrions convoquer l'autorité de celui qui passe encore aujourd'hui pour le plus grand économiste du 20ème siècle.

En marge de la Conférence de Gênes de 1922, dont on a raconté ici les résultats calamiteux, John Maynard Keynes dans les articles qu'il écrivait dans la presse britannique à l'occasion de cet événement, se montrait favorable au rétablissement de l'étalon-or. Qui plus est, pour fixer la nouvelle parité des monnaies avec l'or, il poussait la sagesse—le bon sens, en fait, mais peu commun à l'époque—jusqu'à tenir compte de la hausse pharamineuse de prix qu'avait occasionnée la Grand Guerre de 14–18.[2] Le cours officiel de l'or devait donc être rehaussé pour fonder le nouveau Gold Standard sur des bases solides et donc durables. On sait qu'il ne fut pas écouté et que l'on se tourna vers un Gold Exchange Standard. Il y avait des pistes pour la reconstruction d'un étalon-or international qui ont été explorées dans notre dialogue, mais les progrès auraient été partiels, probablement lents, et ils auraient dépendu des nouveaux partenaires qui auraient été dignes de confiance pour leur approbation des principes de la bonne monnaie. La dévaluation n'aurait pas suffi.

A cette époque, encore, Keynes critiquait les Etats-Unis pour leur désobéissance aux règles élémentaires de l'étalon-or, comme nous l'avons fait nous-même ici tout en marquant notre désaccord avec son analyse.

De fait, et ce dialogue en a fait état, pendant et après la Grand Guerre, le Trésor américain avait amassé du métal jaune sans émettre de monnaie correspondante. Cette « érection d'un veau d'or gratte-ciel »—ce fut l'expression de l'économiste anglais– menaçait l'équilibre économique du monde. Essayer de faire fondre ce veau d'or en activant une inflation monétaire déjà virulente aux États-Unis, (dans les années 20, il s'agissait principalement d'une inflation des actifs) n'était sûrement pas un procédé sans risque pour l'économie mondiale—une question pour laquelle Keynes était apparemment aveugle. Il n'a rien dit, en fait, sur l'histoire de la construction du veau d'or—qui s'est surtout produite pendant la période où les Etats-Unis avaient conservé leur neutralité vis-à-vis de la guerre européenne—jusqu'à mars 1917. A ce moment-là, les autorités américaines tentaient d'empêcher que les ventes massives d'or par la Grande-Bretagne et la France (pour payer les livraisons d'armement) se répercutent aux États-Unis par une inflation encore plus élevée, ce qui signifierait une plus grande taxe d'inflation prélevée sur les citoyens américains pour payer l'effort de guerre de ces deux pays.

---

[2] Hession (1985).

Peu connue voire oubliée, la position de Keynes en 1922, si elle était rappelée, serait une surprise complète pour nos contemporains, tant on est habitué à ranger l'économiste britannique parmi les ennemis de l'étalon-or. Ce même Keynes n'est-il pas l'inventeur de la formule célèbre (l'or, « relique barbare ») qui a tant fait pour ruiner l'idée même d'un retour au Gold Standard? Cette formule est aujourd'hui encore rappelée, proclamée, ressassée *ad nauseam* à chaque fois qu'il est question de faire jouer un rôle monétaire même minime au métal jaune.

La question que l'on ne peut pas ne pas poser au terme de notre dialogue n'est pas pourquoi Keynes a brûlé en quelques jours ce qu'il adorait pour bâtir une théorie économique abracadabrantesque, dont la fausseté est démontrée, mais pourquoi ce reniement par Keynes du fondement de la bonne monnaie a été si bien accueilli.

La réponse se trouve encore une fois dans la tragédie de 14–18. Pour appliquer à Keynes la formule qui a fait son succès, la renommée de l'économiste britannique est une *conséquence* de la Grande Guerre. En effet, Keynes a acquis, grâce à son pamphlet contre le traité de Versailles, *Les conséquences économiques de la Paix*, une renommée très vite *mondiale*, dont aucun économiste n'avait joui avant lui. Dès 1924, remarquait son collègue William Beveridge, qui sera l'inventeur du *Welfare State*,[3] le livre avait été lu, d'après une estimation très modérée, par un demi-million de personnes qui n'avaient jamais ouvert jusque-là un seul ouvrage d'économie et qui, probablement, n'en ouvriraient jamais d'autre.[4] A cette date, ce livre, le premier best-seller qu'on ait publié en économie, avait déjà été traduit en onze langues.

Il a été démontré[5] que ce livre reposait en fait sur une analyse politique: Les Alliés, selon l'auteur auraient trahi les engagements qu'ils avaient pris avant l'armistice. L'analyse économique, elle était fausse, qui prétendait que le paiement de Réparations réclamées par le Traité de Versailles à l'Allemagne était « une impossibilité économique ». Mais Keynes passera ensuite pour un prophète extra-lucide puisqu'en effet l'Allemagne ne paierait qu'une faible partie de ces mêmes Réparations, comme il l'avait prévu. Mais ce défaut de paiement était dû, lui aussi, à des raisons politiques (la discorde des Alliés), et non pas aux causes économiques avancées par Keynes dans son pamphlet. Du reste, c'est sur le plan politique que *Les conséquences économiques de la Paix* eurent le plus d'influence en justifiant la tactique de l'*appeasement* vis-à-vis de

---

[3] Que. l'on peut considérer lui aussi comme une conséquence des guerres du Vingtième siècle: il s'est agi de calmer la colère des peuples sacrifiés en masse sur les champs de bataille…Mais cet Etat-Providence est auto-destructeur, car il engendre de lui-même toujours plus d'inactifs pour toujours moins d'actifs…
[4] *Economica*, vol. 4, 1924, p. 2.
[5] Philippe Simonnot, *L'erreur économique »*, Paris, Denoel, 2004.

Hitler. Un député conservateur britannique, Bob Boothby, opposé à cette politique qui devait mener aux accords de Munich et à la Seconde Guerre Mondiale, pouvait dire du livre de Keynes qu'il était « la Bible du mouvement nazi »,[6] en ce qu'il servait de justification à la critique du « diktat » de Versailles.

C'est donc à partir de cette position de vedette planétaire que le présumé champion de la prévision économique a pu annoncer en 1935 qu'il avait renoncé à la doctrine à laquelle il croyait jusque là et qu'il avait lui-même enseignée. Il s'était converti, proclamait-il, à une nouvelle *Théorie générale de l'emploi, de l'intérêt et de la monnaie*. Ce tout neuf évangile économique était annoncé.

« à la Ville et au Monde » pour reprendre sa propre formule, empruntée sciemment aux Papes au début de leurs encycliques.

Le succès durable de cette nouvelle théorie dans les dix années qui suivirent sa publication peut s'expliquer par le statut de vedette de son auteur, mais il faut trouver une autre raison à la domination du keynésianisme jusqu'à nos jours.

Cette théorie, en réalité, n'est nouvelle qu'en apparence. Elle reprend une doctrine inflationniste qui parcourt les siècles.

Voici par exemple le comte de Mirabeau, surnommé « l'orateur du peuple », discourant devant l'Assemblée nationale pour défendre avec toute son éloquence l'émission d'une nouvelle monnaie-papier, les Assignats, de sinistre mémoire: *Quoi? Serait-il nécessaire de le dire? On parle de vendre, et l'on ne fournirait au public aucun moyen d'acheter! On veut faire sortir les affaires de la stagnation, et l'on semblerait ignorer qu'avec rien on ne fait rien; on semblerait ignorer qu'il faut un principe de vie pour se remuer, pour agir et se reproduire! […]C'est le numéraire qui crée le numéraire; c'est ce mobile de l'industrie qui amène l'abondance; […]jetez donc dans la société ce germe de vie qui lui manque; et vous verrez à quel degré de prospérité et de splendeur vous pourrez dans peu vous élever »*[7] On sait à quelle effroyable misère a conduit cet « helicopter money » avant la lettre.

On pourrait citer des centaines d'exemples de cette démagogie monétaire et de ses effets délétères. Errare humanum est, *sed perseverare diabolicum*. Où est donc le diable?

Ludwig von Mises a répondu à cette question et l'on a plaisir à rappeler ici cette réponse qui devrait clore le débat: « La popularité de l'inflationnisme est en grande partie due à la haine profondément enracinée des créanciers.

---

[6] Tim Bouverie, *Appeasing Hitler, Chamberlain, Churchill and the road to war*, The Bodley Head, 2019.
[7] Collection complète des travaux de M. Mirabeau l'aîné à l'Assemblée nationale, t. 4, Paris, 1972.

L'inflation est considérée comme juste parce qu'elle favorise les débiteurs au détriment des créanciers. »[8]

Au premier rang de ces débiteurs intéressés, se trouve l'État, comme on le sait. Et, comme par hasard, les démagogues inflationnistes sont directement ou indirectement au service de l'État, quand ils ne sont pas payés par lui.

Notre dialogue est néanmoins fondé sur l'espérance que le pire n'est pas toujours sûr et qu'il est arrivé maintes fois que des peuples drogués d'inflation se lancent derechef à la recherche d'une bonne monnaie. La crise de l'euro est une opportunité pour fonder une nouvelle monnaie européenne digne de ce nom, fondée sur les règles intangibles que nous avons définies, et non pas sur un Etat européen, improbable et pourtant désiré consciemment ou inconsciemment par les fondateurs de l'Union monétaire européenne, hantés qu'ils étaient par la conception (erronée) de la monnaie comme attribut régalien.

Un tel euro pourrait même se placer par sa qualité au cœur du monde, non pas pour retrouver les oripeaux impérialistes de l'Europe d'antan, mais comme l'instrument et le gage du libre échange entre les peuples. Alors, le désastreux Vingtième Siècle sera enfin clôturé et dépassé.

Appendix C: Original French Questions from Epilogue (Philippe Simonnot)

QUESTION 1:

Au moment (20 mars 2020) de mettre sous presse notre dialogue, l'économie planétaire est tout soudain ravagée par la pandémie du coronavirus. La dernière grande pandémie mondiale (la dite "grippe espagnole") s'est soldée par des millions de morts. En effet, ses effets délétères ont été aggravés du fait que les premières populations attaquées par le virus avaient été affaiblies par quatre ans d'une guerre qui avait battu tous les records d'atrocités. Ne peut-on craindre que les conséquences économiques et financières de la présente pandémie ne soient accrues du fait que nos gouvernants ont battu ces dernières années des records de mauvaise gestion de la monnaie comme nous le montrons dans cet essai?

QUESTION 2:

Le 12 mars 2020, Christine Lagarde, présidente de la BCE, lors d'une conférence de presse, a eu cette phrase, que l'on a jugée immédiatement dangereuse: "La BCE n'est pas là pour resserrer le « spread »" (écart entre les taux des

---

[8] Ludwig von Mises, *L'Action humaine, Traité d'économie*, traduit de l'américain par Raoul Audouin, Pressezs Universitaires de France, 11,985, p. 490.

obligations allemandes, jugées les plus sûres, et ceux des autres pays). Le spread italien s'était tendu, passant en quelques jours de 1,6% à 2,6%. Mme Lagarde semblait prendre le contrepied de son prédécesseur, Sr. Draghi. Affolement sur les marchés, où l'on entrevoyait déjà une dislocation de la zone euro Mme Lagarde a dû corriger ses propos. Deux jours plus tard, elle lançait un plan record de rachat de titres pour 750 milliards d'euros. Les traités fondateurs de l'euro ne sont-ils pas violés sans que personne ne proteste? Et où va nous mener cette fuite en avant?

QUESTION 3

Dans la nuit du 24 au 25 mars, aux Etats-Unis, les leaders démocrates et républicains se sont mis d'accord sur un plan de relance de 2000 milliards de dollars. Ce plan qui est un record historique (Roosevelt dépassé) prévoit notamment que le Trésor américain versera 500 milliards de dollars directement aux particuliers. Helicopter money a décollé pour de bon…Pouvait-on faire autrement dans les circonstances actuelles? Et quel sera le résultat?

QUESTION 4

Depuis le déclenchement de la crise sanitaire, la zone euro est plus divisée que jamais, notamment sur l'émission éventuelle de *coronabonds*.

a) que penser de cette nouvelle tentative de mutualisation des des dettes?
b) Pour le "coup d'état monétaire" franco-allemand que nous préconisons, cette division aggravée n'est-elle pas une opportunité?
c) Si oui, comment la saisir?

Dans ces conditions, l'"hégémonie du dollar du dollar" que nous avons décrite dans ce livre ne risque-t-elle pas d'être prolongée et même re^{nforcée}?

Index

A

Anchors to the monetary system, 4
Asset inflation, 3, 10, 12–15, 17, 18, 24, 34, 35, 39, 41, 44, 52, 53, 55, 56, 89–91, 98, 100, 105, 106, 118, 129, 131–133, 136, 140–142, 181, 185–188, 193, 196, 197

B

Ben Bernanke speech at 90th birthday of Milton Friedman, 51
Boom-bust in Weimar Republic, 41
Bretton Woods System, 44, 62, 63, 65

C

Carry trades, 12, 16, 34, 35, 44, 89, 90, 98, 100
Churchill and Sterling's "return to gold," 36, 38

D

Deflation phobia, 24, 25, 103
Deposit insurance, 6, 70, 72, 73, 88, 123, 124, 157, 159, 163
Deutsche mark as hard money, 79, 109
Dollar hegemony, 3, 33–48, 200, 201
Draghi Mario, his "do whatever it takes" boast, 111

E

ECB adopts 2 per cent inflation standard, 136
Euro debt crisis 2010–12, 131

F

Friedman, Milton, 3–5, 9–13, 51–54, 56, 66, 69–75, 149, 153, 157, 162, 205–209, 221
Friedman's views on Great Depression, 51

G

Global credit crisis of 1931, 132
Gold during Second World War, v59, 62
Gold euro, 148, 150, 151, 153–156, 163, 169
Gold exchange standard, 29, 33–35, 39–41, 61–63, 179, 181, 204, 207, 224, 226
Gold inflows to US during First World War, 38
Gold standard, 3, 4, 10–12, 24, 25, 27–30, 33, 38–43, 47, 54, 59, 61–64, 70, 73, 75, 79, 99, 148, 150, 151, 153–160, 162, 163, 165, 169, 179, 181, 182, 192–194, 199, 203–204
Gold standard collapse in First World War, 3, 42

I

Inflation camouflaged in goods and services markets, 52
Inflation standard, 8, 14–15, 23, 70, 89, 103–107, 138, 140, 201, 214–215
Inflation tax, 7, 17, 18, 59, 128, 140, 141, 146, 182, 194, 198, 200

K

Keynes, John Maynard, 27, 36, 38, 39, 42, 51, 57, 61, 69, 181, 182, 203, 205, 206, 226–228

L

Large denomination banknotes, the case for, 159

M

Malinvestment, 5, 10, 14–18, 24, 38, 98–102, 132, 133, 141, 162, 164, 168, 186–188, 193, 196
Monetarism, 5–8, 10, 66, 69–71, 84
Monetary base control, 85
Monetary hegemony, 40, 41, 43, 45–48, 205
Monetary repression tax (MRT), 7, 14–15, 17, 140, 141, 146, 171, 194
Monopoly capitalism, 102
Moral hazard, 92, 93

N

Nazi past and the euro, 80, 81
Neutral interest rates, 104
Nixon-Burns inflation, 46

P

Paul Volcker ends US monetarist experiment, 168

Q

Quantitative easing (QE), 6, 8, 55, 113, 125, 127, 131–133, 138, 151, 172, 180, 194, 200, 225

R

Reserve requirements, 6, 55, 70–72, 84–86, 115, 158, 162
Roosevelt Recession 1937–38, 55

S

Schacht, Hjalmar, 36, 59, 60
Shale oil and gas mal-investment, 100, 101
Sound money, 4–10, 14, 18, 24, 28, 34, 35, 37–41, 45, 46, 48, 53, 63, 66, 70, 72, 75, 78, 80, 91, 102, 112, 115, 135, 136, 138–142, 145–147, 153–160, 162–164, 167, 171–173, 188, 189, 192–194, 200, 201, 219
Sub-prime crisis, 88, 89

U

Unsound money tyranny, 3–18, 28, 137

GPSR Compliance

The European Union's (EU) General Product Safety Regulation (GPSR) is a set of rules that requires consumer products to be safe and our obligations to ensure this.

If you have any concerns about our products, you can contact us on

ProductSafety@springernature.com

In case Publisher is established outside the EU, the EU authorized representative is:

Springer Nature Customer Service Center GmbH
Europaplatz 3
69115 Heidelberg, Germany

www.ingramcontent.com/pod-product-compliance
Lightning Source LLC
LaVergne TN
LVHW010339260326
834688LV00036B/790